Richie & Nina,

I hope this book
helps others to better
understand thes
which affect al
Thanks for you

Karen Thompson

Why Can't
Sharon
Kowalski
Come Home?

Why Can't Sharon Kowalski Come Home?

By Karen Thompson and Julie Andrzejewski

spinsters / *aunt lute*

SAN FRANCISCO

First Edition
10-9-8-7-6-5-4-3-2-1

Spinsters/Aunt Lute Book Company
P.O. Box 410687
San Francisco, CA 94141

Cover and Text Design: Pam Wilson Design Studio
Cover Illustration: Pauline Phung
Typesetting: Comp-Type, Inc., Fort Bragg, CA
Production: Brenda Cummings   Jeanette Hsu
            Martha Davis   Cindy Lamb
            Debra DeBondt   Kathleen Wilkinson
            Lorraine Grassano

Publication of this book was made possible in part through grants from the Chicago Resource Center and the GGBA Foundation.

Spinsters/Aunt Lute is an educational project of the Capp Street Foundation.

Appendix B: Creating your own Durable Power of Attorney forms from *A Legal Guide for Lesbian and Gay Couples* by Hayden Curry and Denis Clifford, 1986 © NOLO Press, 950 Parker St., Berkeley, CA 94710.

Printed in the U.S.A.

Library of Congress Cataloging-in-Publication Data
Thompson, Karen.
    Why can't Sharon Kowalski come home? / Karen Thompson, Julie Andrzejewski.
First edition
        p. cm.
    ISBN: 0-933216-56-4
    ISBN: 0-933216-46-7 (pbk.)
    1. Handicapped—Legal status, laws, etc.—Minnesota. 2. Handicapped—Civil rights—Minnesota. 3. Kowalski, Sharon. 4. Guardian and ward—Minnesota. 5. Visitation rights (Domestic relations)—Minnesota. 6. Lesbians—Legal status, laws, etc.—Minnesota. I. Andrzejewski, Julie, 1945-   . II. Title.
KFM5491.H3T48 1988
346.7301'3—dc19
[347.30613]   88-18502
                                                                     CIP

DEDICATION

We dedicate this book to Sharon Kowalski and other disabled people who have not been allowed to speak for themselves in determining their own lives or to fight for the rights they have been denied.

◆◆

ACKNOWLEDGEMENTS

We want to thank the many individuals and organizations who have given of their hearts, time, energy or money to help sustain the struggle to obtain the human rights which have been so systematically violated in this case. Karen would not have been able to cope without the emotional support of her family and many friends—too many to name. We would like to thank especially Elizabeth Baraga, Karen Bjorkman, Mary Anne Daniel, Lisa Everts, Jann Hillenbrand, Julie Miller, Judy Polipnick, Paul Reichert, and Mary Wild.

We want to express our appreciation to Sue Wilson and Toni Pomerene, Karen's attorneys, for daring to take on a complicated case at the appellate level.

The case could never have been actively pursued without the organizational efforts of people across the United States who have shared information about the case with others, sponsored Karen in speaking engagements or coordinated fund-raising events. We especially want to thank the many people involved in the Free Sharon Kowalski or Bring Sharon Home groups in various states, and the Boston Self-Help Center for taking donations. We wish we could personally thank all of the individuals who sent donations to help with the legal expenses and all of the people who have welcomed Karen into their homes when she was visiting their communities.

A number of individuals have been actively involved with the case for a long time. We want to thank Jacky Abromitis, Sheila Barry, Rose Boden, Suzanne Born, Peg Cammack-Chemberlin, Karen Clark, Tacie Dejanikus, Judy Fjell, Caroline Foty, Emma Hixson, Margot Imdieke, Jane Jackson, Peri Jude, Polly Kellogg, Mary Ann Kirkbride, Judy Lindquist, Alison Mierzkowski, Eileen Olson, Connie Panzarino, Carol Jean Pint, Denise Rettenmaier, Nancy Sigafoos, Pamela Slycord, Kim Surkan, Cheryl Vitow, Carolyn Weathers, and Kiki Zeldes. We also want to thank Bob Jansen and others in Duluth, and the members of the Committee for the Right to Recovery and Relationships for their early help on the case.

We recognize that without the support of the alternative press, especially lesbian and gay publications, the story would never have been disseminated at all, since the mainstream press coverage was either nonexistent or biased in the extreme by sexism, handicapism and homophobia. We want to thank all of these publications and especially certain individuals who have pursued the case relentlessly: John Ritter (*Equal Times*), Emily Kahn (*Philadelphia Gay News*), Stephanie Poggi, Ann Phibbs and Marco Ticovas (*Gay Community News*), Tracy Bain (*Windy City Times*), Kathryn Stifter (*Coming Up!*), Peter Frieberg (*The Advocate*), Marge Schneider and Kathy Hagen (*Women's Braille Press*) and Susan Janecki (*Womanwise*).

Even though we found the overwhelming majority of medical, legal and press personnel either steeped in their own biases or too afraid to confront the biases of others, a small minority were brave enough to declare what was best for Sharon regardless of the pressure to remain silent. We want to thank the few medical personnel who observed Karen working with Sharon and weren't afraid to chart it in the records or testify in court.

We thank the many organizations who have helped this case in one way or another. We are grateful for the tremendous support received from the National Organization for Women. The Metropolitan Community Church has also been supportive. We especially thank Jamie Becker from Handicapped Organized Women; Janlori Goldman and Nan Hunter from the Minnesota Civil Liberties Union and the American Civil Liberties Union; Jane Hoyt from Nursing Home Action Group and United Handicapped Federation; the staff of People Too, Independent Living Center; Marilyn Saviola from Center for Independence of the Disabled in New York; Paula Ettlebrick and Abby Reubenfeld of Lambda Legal Defense and Education Fund.

Karen is grateful for support she received from St. Cloud State University. Numerous faculty, administrators and students have expressed their support. We especially want to thank Stephen Weber, Academic Vice President; the faculty, staff and students of the Center for Human Relations and Multicultural Education; and the Physical Education and Recreation Department. The Gay/Lesbian Support Group was immensely helpful at many key points in the struggle.

Numerous people have helped with the book itself. We are grateful to those who have read, edited, discussed, printed and designed components of the book. We cannot express enough how grateful we are to Joan Pinkvoss and Sherry Thomas of Spinsters/Aunt Lute for their personal support, their endless hours of editing and excellent suggestions.

Karen Thompson and Julie Andrzejewski

❖

I want to thank Karen for having the courage and fortitude to carry on this case against all odds for the benefit of all unmarried couples, disabled people and, in fact, anyone who has not designated a guardian of her/his choice. Throughout all of the outrages and agony, Karen has remained steadfast in her commitment to Sharon and in her decision to press this case and the issues it represents to the furthest possible conclusion, regardless of the personal consequences.

Julie Andrzejewski

❖

I want to thank Julie on two levels. First, I appreciate her professional skills and knowledge of oppression, human rights issues and social change which she brought to bear on this case. She wrote and disseminated the first press releases and organized the first fund-raising. She acted as my personal mentor and tutor as I was painfully initiated into an understanding of systemic oppression. As important as her professional skills were, maybe even more important to me was the personal friendship that developed with Julie and Mary Anne in the hours we spent together exploring possible courses of action and writing the book. They provided a safe place where I could be myself or fall apart, and the encouragement to get up the next day and carry on.

Karen Thompson

AUTHORS' NOTE

Numerous documents, correspondence, court records and newsmedia articles were utilized in writing this book. Occasionally, where there was an obvious typographical or clerical error in the document, we have changed the word, placing it in brackets to indicate the change. We have put ellipses (. . .) to indicate where material was left out.

Major portions of Chapter 10 regarding the doctors were drawn from a document by Sue Wilson called "Summary of Doctors' Involvement." We are grateful to Sue for allowing us to use her words rather than rewrite what she had already written so clearly.

We have tried to select the most pertinent components from the documents, both positive and negative, regarding Karen Thompson, her relationship with Sharon Kowalski and the guardianship case itself. There are obviously materials and information unavailable to us (e.g., information about Sharon after Karen's access was denied, the motivations of Sharon's parents and their interactions with Sharon, etc.). We cannot speculate on how this information might have changed this book, but rather can only acknowledge that we have tried to write this book as honestly as we could, based on the information available, and acknowledge that it is from Karen's perspective. In no way do we wish to attack or discredit any person.

JA & KT

TABLE OF CONTENTS

Introduction 1
1. The Accident 3
   November and December 1983
2. Coming Out 17
   January and February 1984
3. Guardianship Struggle 33
   March to June 1984
4. Move to a Nursing Home 47
   July to September 1984
5. The Separation 65
   September and October 1984
6. Park Point Manor 79
   October 1984
7. Maneuvers in Court 93
   October and November 1984
8. Early Support 105
   October 1984 to January 1985
9. Sharon's Depression 119
   January to May 1985
10. Testimony 129
    May 3 to May 9, 1985
11. Fena's Ploys 147
    May to August 1985
12. The Appeals 165
    September 1985 to March 1986
13. From Disillusionment to Change 183
    March to September 1986

14. Speaking Out... 193
    September 1986 to March 1987
15. "The Silent Ordeal" 203
    May and June 1987
16. Becoming an Activist..................................... 209
    July and August 1987
17. Thoughts of Sharon 217
    April 1988
Epilogue 221
Appendix A
    Timeline of Significant Events
Appendix B
    Creating Your Own Durable Power of Attorney

*Why Can't
Sharon
Kowalski
Come Home?*

INTRODUCTION

This book is about the lives of Karen Thompson and Sharon Kowalski, two women who fell in love and began to share their lives together. After four years of a committed and extremely closeted relationship, Sharon was hit by a drunk driver while driving to northern Minnesota on a cold November afternoon in 1983.

Sharon's four-year-old niece, Missy, and seven-year-old nephew, Michael, were in the car with her. Missy died shortly after the accident. Michael recovered with few permanent injuries. Sharon, however, suffered a severe brain stem injury which left her with drastic and permanent damage. How drastic and how permanent is difficult to assess since it is the contention of this book that Sharon's recovery was and still is being detrimentally affected by the efforts to remove Karen Thompson from her life.

Sharon was initially in a coma and not expected to live. Karen Thompson literally spent every minute she could with Sharon, willing her to live and to recover. Later, Karen spent hours, weeks and months helping Sharon relearn basic movements and skills. When Sharon's family told Karen to discontinue visitation with Sharon, she sought advice from medical personnel and attorneys. Driven by fear of being separated from her lover, she revealed her relationship to Sharon's parents, praying that they would see that her love could make a difference in their daughter's recovery. When they reacted with anger and denial, Karen filed for guardianship, thus initiating an historic legal battle which continues to have far-reaching effects on disabled people, unmarried partners—regardless of sexual orientation—or any individual without a designated guardian of choice.

This is also the story of parochial attitudes, bigotry, and institutionalized injustice. Homophobia—the irrational fear and hatred of lesbian and gay people—permeates the institutions Karen is forced to deal with. Handicapism—the fear, embarrassment and paternalism toward disabled people—is also painfully apparent. She is confronted with powerful professionals who sympathize with her in private but hedge their statements in public and decline to confront the blatant homophobia and denial in Sharon's parents. When the case reaches the 'justice' system, power politics, conflicts of interest and greed compromise the importance of the most basic human rights: Sharon's right to the highest quality of life, the right of Karen and Sharon to associate, and eventually the right of Sharon, a disabled person, to select her own court representation or to make any other decisions she is capable of making.

And, finally, this is a story of growth and change in the person of Karen Thompson. Growing up with a naive belief in a just world, in a conventional protestant religion, and in the fairness of professionals, institutions and society, Karen developed a strong sense of commitment and principles. These characteristics eventually brought her full circle to question and challenge the very institutions which fostered them. This is the true story from the eyes of Karen Thompson.

Julie Andrzejewski
August 1988

CHAPTER 1

The Accident

"Save Monday night for me," Sharon whispered as she kissed me and ran out to the car where her niece and nephew were already buckled into their seat belts. Missy and Michael had just spent the weekend with us and Sharon was going to drive the 180 miles back to Nashwauk where her sister was living. It was a drizzly winter Minnesota afternoon. Fearing that it would become icy, she wanted to get them back before dark.

But the events of the next few hours were to make Monday night very different than either of us expected. That Sunday changed our lives irrevocably, forcing each of us to face feelings and challenges that we never anticipated. In no way was I prepared for the phone call I received late that afternoon.

I answered the phone and listened numbly as Donald Kowalski, Sharon's father, told me there had been a head-on collision involving Sharon's car, an hour and a half from St. Cloud, near Onamia. Missy had been taken to Onamia Hospital, Sharon to St. Cloud Hospital and Michael to the University of Minnesota Hospital.

Donald said, "We're going to Minneapolis to see Michael."

"Is Michael the most seriously injured?" I asked. "What's happened to Sharon and Missy?"

Don said that he knew nothing about the circumstances of the accident nor the condition of the three.

My mind was whirling. My God, in order to reach Michael, the Kowalskis will have to drive through Onamia and St. Cloud. Why wouldn't they be stopping to check on Missy and Sharon? Surely they were as concerned about their daughter and granddaughter as they were about their grandson.

We discussed my going directly to St. Cloud Hospital to find out about Sharon while they went on to Minneapolis. In a state of shock, I quickly gathered up some clothes for Sharon, thinking that she might need them, and not knowing whether she could come home or would have to stay in the hospital. It would take me about 20 minutes to reach the hospital in St. Cloud, and by the time I had been called it was already three hours since the accident had occurred.

I parked and ran into the emergency room to find out where Sharon was and how seriously she was injured. First I was told to go to the information desk; they said they could not divulge any information to non-family members and then sent me back to the emergency room. No one would give me any definite information concerning where Sharon was or how she was. Finally I was told she might be up in intensive care. By this time, I was beginning to panic and my thoughts were frantic. Where is she? Is she dead? Is she alive? What is happening to her?

When I got to the intensive care unit, I found that I'd have to use an intercom system to communicate with the staff. At the side of the intercom was a description of rules and regulations on how to use it. Clearly printed among these rules was the stipulation that only family members were allowed to visit patients in this unit. In the midst of all my fear for Sharon I wondered, Who will I say I am? How can I make them understand how important I am to Sharon without giving away our relationship?

I stuttered into the intercom, "I would like information concerning Sharon Kowalski. Is she here? . . . Can I see her? What's her condition?"

A voice responded, "What is your relationship?" After some hesitation, I said, "We live together and I'm a close friend."

"I'm sorry. We can't give out information to anyone except immediate family members," the intercom spit out.

I wanted to scream, "I *am* Sharon's family! I'm her *chosen* family!" Knowing that no one would understand that response, I made myself calmly state, "But her parents are on the way. They want me to find out what the situation is here while they check on the others who were in the accident." I was almost beside myself. By this time I had been at the hospital over an hour and still had no idea what was happening to the person I loved more than anyone else in the world.

As I was struggling with the intercom, a priest overheard the panic in my voice and asked if there was any way he could help. "My very close friend, Sharon Kowalski, has been in a car accident. Her family won't be here for hours and no one will tell me anything about her because I'm not 'family,'" I explained.

He was sympathetic. "I'll check on her condition and either get back to you or see that someone talks with you."

I waited for what seemed like an eternity. He returned and said, "Sharon is here. She's alive. They're still working on her and as soon as the doctor is available, he will talk with you." I sat immobilized in the waiting room.

Although I still knew nothing about Sharon's injuries, at least I knew she was alive. Never in my life had time passed so slowly. There was nothing I could do but wait. Waiting was to become a way of life for me.

Two hours after I arrived at the hospital, the doctor came into the waiting room. He informed me matter-of-factly about the extent of Sharon's injuries. "She has suffered a severe head injury and is in a coma. She also has a compound fracture of her left femur which at some point in time, if she lives, will involve major surgery. For now, it has been placed in traction. Both knee caps have been split open and she has multiple lacerations and abrasions."

"What do you mean? Isn't Sharon going to live?"

"I don't know whether she will live through the night. But the longer she does live, the greater her chances of survival will become. The longer she stays in a coma, however, the more severe her head injuries probably will be and the more negative the prognosis. It's a waiting game. It will take time to see how much the brain will swell, and as the edema recedes, how much permanent damage to the brain cells there will be."

I was sick to my stomach. I could hardly breathe or swallow. "If she does live, what will her condition be? How long will she be in the hospital?"

"If she does live, we're looking at a long, long time for recovery. Even if she lives, she has been drastically changed and may never be as you knew her before."

Two weeks later, bending over Sharon, he actually said, "Well, it appears she might live but you may live to regret it."

But that night, not understanding the extent of her head injuries at all, I thought about what an athlete Sharon had always been. Will she still be able to play basketball, ski? Will she be able to walk normally? The possibility that she might not be able to walk at all still hadn't entered my mind. I couldn't begin to take in the larger issues—whether she would be able to think, to communicate, or to make decisions concerning her own life.

The doctor said I could go in and see her. I didn't know what to expect. Will she remember me? I wondered. Will she remember our relationship? She might wake up any minute and ask for me. How will that look? Will people guess about our relationship? Still not comprehending the full extent of Sharon's injuries, I feared for our secrecy as much as I feared for her life.

As I approached the room, nothing prepared me for the shock of actually seeing Sharon. I had never thought of Sharon as being vulnerable or helpless, but that was my first reaction seeing her lying there in the hospital bed. Her leg was in traction. As I came closer I saw her face. Blood was seeping through the pores on her chin and the left side of her face. The tremendous impact of the crash had brought blood to the surface of her skin. Though both eyes were closed, her left eye was badly swollen. There was not a single cut on her head so it was hard to imagine the extent of the possible brain damage the doctor was talking about. It all felt very unreal to me. Can this really be happening? Is this the Sharon who left our house just eight hours ago? I stared at her in disbelief remembering how we had laughed with the kids that morning.

I sat down by the edge of the bed with thoughts whirling through my mind. You can't die. I'm not going to let you die. I love you. I need you. You've got to keep fighting, Sharon. You can win. Don't give up. We can make it through this. Oh, Lord, give us a chance.

As I sat there, I had an overpowering feeling of just how important she really *was* to me. I had never consciously admitted to myself that I could really *need* someone else. Sharon had taught me how to laugh, how to live. And yet, here she was, possibly dying. All of a sudden I knew that without Sharon a part of me would die. I willed her to live with all the strength in my being.

I found myself breathing with Sharon, *for* Sharon. As I heard her labored breathing, I got closer to her, breathing deeply and slowly to keep her going. I hadn't known we could be so close, that I could physically feel the pain in her body as I sat there with her.

I was allowed to see Sharon for only five minutes and then for only five minutes each subsequent hour. Back in the waiting room, I grappled with what to pray for. Is it okay to pray for Sharon to live? Should I pray for God's will to be done? Is it selfish of me to want her to live so badly? Maybe that wasn't God's plan . . . . I struggled, but I prayed anyway, prayed that she would live, that she would be all right. After several hours, the staff allowed me to have longer visits.

Each time I saw her, I wondered if that would be the last time I would see her alive. Suddenly, my future was completely shaken. The dreams we had shared, which had seemed so important to me just a few hours before, became insignificant in relation to the gravity of what was happening now. Our excitement about the house we had just purchased together and being able to ski in the park behind our new home was no longer important.

Later that night, I drove to my sister Linda's house in St. Cloud and told her about the accident. She immediately offered her home as a place for the Kowalskis and me to stay or leave messages. The next time I got a chance to call Linda from the hospital, she told me hesitantly, "Sharon's brother Mark called. Missy has died. They didn't expect that to happen." I couldn't speak. I sensed her desire to reach out and help me through this crisis even though as yet she had no idea of its magnitude.

Immediately, I pictured Sharon putting on Missy's coat earlier that afternoon and the kids both shouting, "I get to sit next to you on the way home." They had flipped a coin to settle the issue. Could a coin toss have decided who lived and who died? As I sat waiting endlessly, I agonized over how Sharon would ever accept Missy's death. Will she blame herself? She had loved those kids so much and had spent a lot of time with them.

At the scene of the accident Missy had appeared to be the least seriously injured. Yet when the Kowalskis stopped at Onamia Hospital to drop off Debbie, Missy's mother, they were informed that Missy had died. Evidently, the shocking news of Missy's death had changed the Kowalskis' plans to go straight on to Minneapolis. Instead, they came to St. Cloud after calling and finding that Sharon's prognosis was more serious than Michael's. It was nearly 2:00 a.m. before they arrived. By that time, they had driven for four hours in bad weather and had dealt with the formalities of Missy's death. They were numb and exhausted. Together we waited, through that long night, taking turns visiting Sharon. There was no change in her condition.

"Should we get a second opinion?" I asked Don and Della. I tried to present my case logically. Right on my Blue Cross card it states, "Second opinions are mandatory before any major surgery." Needing to do something to help, I had made phone calls earlier that evening to get information about head injuries. I knew there were procedures to relieve brain pressure, and that time might be critical in this case.

Donald said, "The doctor knows what he's doing." He gave me the impression that the doctor should never be questioned.

"But what harm would there be in getting a second opinion?" I asked him. "Maybe a second doctor would say the same thing—that we just have to wait. But maybe there is a way to relieve some of the pressure on the brain." I tried to reason with him without giving away the desperation I was feeling.

"We'll just do what the doctor says," Donald said firmly.

Hours faded into days of waiting. I stayed at the hospital almost day and night. The Kowalskis were in and out—they made funeral arrangements for Missy, visited Michael, and handled business related to the accident. Since it was finals week at St. Cloud State University, where I taught in the Physical Education Department, I was able to spend the majority of my time at the hospital. I could grade exams and attend to other duties while waiting to see Sharon.

Within a couple of days, the blood disappeared from Sharon's face and only the black eye was visible. When I entered her room, she looked like she was sleeping normally and for a moment I expected her to wake up, just as she had always been. During this time, her broken leg was still in traction and hadn't been permanently set. Sometimes it would spasm and slip out of place, but Sharon showed no signs of pain.

Several times during those early days, I tried to broach the subject of a second opinion again. I asked a friend of the family if she would talk to the Kowalskis about it. She responded, "You've got to give them time. You have to understand . . . their granddaughter has just died . . . their daughter and grandson are still in critical condition."

"But Sharon may not have time," I argued with her. "She may need decisions made now that will affect her forever." In my mind, I continued to argue with myself. If they aren't capable of addressing these issues *now*, maybe somebody else should take over. I only have Sharon's best interests on my mind. I knew I had access to information and resources that could help her, but my fear that people would guess how much I loved Sharon prevented me from pushing harder. As a result, I would always wonder whether Sharon's condition would have improved if the pressure on her brain could have been relieved.

When the Kowalskis were at the hospital, I walked on eggs. I asked for permission to visit Sharon even though I felt it was my right to visit her. I acted as a host to the family, still trying not to let them guess the extent of my love for their daughter. They showered at my sister's house; I ordered food for them; we played cards and passed the time as best we could.

On November 22, just a week after the accident, surgery was performed on Sharon's femur, putting in a rod to avoid a cast. But still there was no response from Sharon. By November 25, her condition had stabilized enough to move her from intensive care to the rehabilitation floor. This meant that Sharon was no longer in a life-threatening situation. Though still in a coma, she actually looked more 'normal' than many others in the new unit.

My vacation break after finals was spent at the hospital. During the days that followed, I asked medical personnel what I could do for Sharon. Following their instructions, I continued talking to her, reading the Bible out loud, playing music for her, and massaging her fingers and wrists. Like most coma victims, she had a tendency to curl into a tight fetal position, so I would massage and straighten her head and shoulders to prevent her muscles from permanently pulling her head down to one side.

I felt I was living in uncertainty. Sharon was precariously hanging on to life. The questions about whether she would live or die were still present on a daily basis, making it difficult for me to ever leave the hospital for fear that something would change before I returned. If she does live, what will happen to our lives? Will she be in a coma the rest of her life? If she regains consciousness, what will she be like? What will she remember? I worried and wondered constantly. Death would have been clear and I would have dealt with it somehow. But not knowing kept me in a constant state of limbo. I wasn't even sure what I could grieve for since I didn't know yet what was gone. This feeling was to become all too familiar in the years to come.

At the beginning of December, Don asked me how much money Sharon owed me for rent, phone and electricity. I was caught by surprise. I had just assumed it was my responsibility to cover Sharon's bills. At this point, we all still held an expectation that Sharon might be able to go home again when she came out of the coma. Evidently, Don wanted to insure that she could return to the house if she was able to and that I wouldn't rent to someone else.

How could I even begin to explain the situation to Don since he thought we were just good friends? We had put the house in my name at Sharon's insistence. Because she could not afford half of the expenses, her pride would not allow her to have her name on the deed yet. But we definitely considered the house as *ours*. Sharon was not just renting. If anything, it was a house in a location that she had chosen and loved even more than I did. She would always be able to come back.

I discussed Don's offer with two lesbian friends who also knew Sharon's parents well. They felt I should take the money so the parents could feel supportive of Sharon. After all, Don would not be able to comprehend why I wouldn't take the money. In addition, I was told the money would come out of Sharon's insurance and wouldn't really be paid by Sharon or her parents. So, I gave Don a breakdown of what he might expect Sharon's expenses to be. Because we weren't open about my financial support for Sharon, I had to make the division seem simple and straightforward. But still, I wasn't willing to just call it rent. When I took the money, I clearly explained to Don, "Sharon was planning to buy half the house for a tax break. I'll put this money towards her half so she won't get further behind."

Against my better judgment, I took money for two months. This was a grave error which would serve to undermine the evidence establishing our actual relationship in a court of law. Indeed, this would later be used as an example of my desire to profit from the accident.

❖

December 17 was our fourth anniversary. I celebrated it with Sharon in the only way I could . . . by her bed. If I were a friend, I could have hugged Sharon without worrying what people thought, but because we were lovers, I continually feared discovery with each hug, each touch of the hand.

I brought her a gift—a gold necklace—and a card. I sat by her bed and read her what I had written:

❖ The past five weeks have taught me many things, Sharon. The most important is the depth of my need for you in my life. You represent my happiness and so much more. As I pondered what to get you, I saw this delicate gold necklace and it said it all. You are more precious to me than all the gold in the world. And as I have watched and waited these past five weeks, I have realized just how delicate and precious the human body really is. I want a rain check, Sharon, to celebrate this day with you somewhere down the line. I will wait however long it takes. I pledge you my love for a lifetime and pray for the opportunity to share my life with you. I love you, Babe, with all my heart!

As I was sitting there with her, not knowing if she was understanding or even hearing, I thought back to the time I met Sharon and the events that led to our decision to make a lifelong commitment to each other, pledging our love and exchanging rings.

I first met Sharon when she was a student at St. Cloud State University. She was older than most of my students, having been in and out of different colleges with several jobs in between. In 1976 she took two classes of mine, "Competitive Sports for Women" and "Basketball Officiating." She was the type of student who sat in the back of the class, attentive but not vocal. She was just one of many students to me. She never spoke to me outside of class, and I had to relearn her name when she took the second class. I had no idea we would become such close friends in the following year.

Sharon had grown up in northern Minnesota, in an area known as the Iron Range. Women there are expected to marry young and raise children. Sharon had always rebelled against these parochial attitudes which her family also held. In childhood, she could always get excused from doing the dishes so she could go out hunting and fishing with her grandfather. As a teenager, she played basketball, softball and volleyball, and held the state record for the most freethrows in the girls' state basketball tournament. She took up riding a motorcycle and would go out cross-country skiing in the beautiful north woods outside Hibbing. She was the first person in her family to go to college, and had worked part time in the iron mines to put herself through. Sharon used to tell me that her family's lack of financial support for college hurt her much less than their lack of emotional support.

A year after taking my classes, Sharon walked into my office one day and asked, "Do you need any help with the track team? I'd like to learn more in case I ever have to coach it."

As the head women's coach, I always needed help. After some discussion as to what kind of a time commitment she wanted to make, I made her an assistant coach. There was no pay involved, but I made it clear to her that she would be given certain responsibilities that I expected to be carried out. It wasn't unusual for me to have a student assistant, but Sharon turned out to be more responsible and mature than most. We met regularly to plan practices and discuss problem areas. As I got to know her better, I delegated more responsibilities. I knew I could count on her. Two hours a day were spent in actual practice. Sharon came at least a half hour early for preparation and was the last to leave, so for most of an academic year, we worked together at least three hours a day.

Sharon accompanied the team on all of its trips to in-state and out-of-state meets. Little by little our friendship grew that year. We shared many long hours talking about our lives, our frustrations, our religious convictions, everything that was important to us. We became best friends.

Many of our discussions were about spirituality. Church life was a central part of my life then. Along with regular church attendance, I was in an evangelism program, Bible study and two choirs. Sharon felt that I had a spiritual base that she didn't have and yearned for. We began Bible study together, and she asked many questions about my evangelism teaching.

Towards the end of that academic year, it became clear that I was going to have to begin work on my Ph.D. if I ever wanted to get a tenure position. I was granted a year's leave of absence and prepared to leave for summer school at Ohio State University.

Sharon and I were playing tennis one of the last days before I left. She told me how afraid she was that I would make other friends in Ohio and forget about her. The nine years age difference between us, and my status as a professor, made Sharon insecure about our friendship.

I assured her, "You know, just because I'm leaving doesn't mean we won't be friends." Before I left, I gave her a Bible to encourage her continued growth in her faith and also to reassure her that I had no intention of abandoning our friendship.

Less than a month later, Sharon called me at Ohio State and asked, "Can I come out and visit? I'm going East on a trip and thought I would stop in Ohio to see you."

She arrived there on her motorcycle within a week. And in the midst of papers due and classes to attend, we went for long walks together, talking constantly. Sharon would grab my hand spontaneously, asking me if I had seen a certain flower or bird, and after a while it seemed natural to hold hands.

At that time, I was living with my aunt and uncle, spending weekends at my parents' house. Sharon visited both places during that week, then left for Michigan. A couple of days later she called. "We didn't have enough time together. Would it seem stupid or create a problem for you if I came back? Would your parents think it was weird?"

I was surprised but excited. It gave me a lift just to hear her voice. "Well, sure. You're always welcome." The next day flew by as I looked forward to seeing her again. We spent the next few days constantly together. After Sharon left, we practically supported the telephone company by talking every other day. It was amazing how many ideas and situations I just had to share with her.

It wasn't until Thanksgiving break that I was able to return to St. Cloud. I spent every spare minute with Sharon. On this visit, she made constant efforts to make physical contact with me, and I found myself responding. I was beginning to be scared by my feelings for her, the rush of warmth and the heightened sense of awareness whenever I was with her. Touching seemed almost out of our control. Everywhere I was, she was. I couldn't open the refrigerator without contact with Sharon. One day she tackled me and we wound up wrestling on the floor. Finally when I had her pinned, I had an impulse to lean down and kiss her. I quickly released her and stood up.

Sharon didn't understand. "What's the matter? Is something wrong?"

"Just don't ask. I can't explain what I'm feeling. It's better left unsaid."

She wouldn't leave it alone. "Why?" She picked up a sock and mimicked a Kermit the Frog puppet. "Kermit wants to know what you're thinking and feeling."

"I never want to say anything that will hurt our friendship." I headed toward the door.

But Kermit persisted. And I told her how much I wanted to be close to her, to touch her. I confessed my impulse to kiss her. I was frightened by the depth of my feelings for her, and told her that, too. She made me say it all without giving me any indication of how she felt. But she kept asking question after question. Then she reached out to hold me. Sparks were flying.

"I really feel that I should go," I insisted, not knowing what was happening or where we were headed. She let me go, provided we would meet the next day. I didn't sleep a wink.

Against my better judgment, I stopped at her apartment the next day. We spent the whole afternoon just being close to each other. We couldn't talk about it yet. Finally, she admitted, "I feel the same way you do. I need to be close to you, too. I've been awake all night just thinking about you and us." We kissed for the first time.

Immediately after that first kiss, Sharon told me, "I knew I wanted to be close but I never intended to kiss you. I didn't think I could ever kiss another woman but it's nice."

Sharon told me she had tried to do anything to be close to me. And we laughingly remembered all the motorcycle rides which had necessitated close body contact. Although I was terrified of motorcycles, Sharon's desire to share her world with me was contagious. Sharon would say, "Why don't you just relax and put your arms around me?" It made me wonder if everyone got that excited on a motorcycle!

I returned to Ohio in a confused state, not really knowing what all this meant or what our relationship was. Now we talked on the phone every day. I flew back to St. Cloud within a couple of weeks. She picked me up at the airport. No one else knew I was in town.

By this time I had decided that I loved Sharon. I brought a ring back with me. I didn't know if I would give it to her, but I brought it. It was clear to me that if I was going to be with Sharon, I wanted a committed relationship in our eyes and the eyes of God. What I didn't know was that Sharon had a ring, too.

Riding in the car, we searched for a private place to talk. We pulled off the road into a tractor lane by a field. We held each other tightly, stumbling around for words to express our feelings. Not knowing what to say, we decided to give each other our 'gifts' and laughed that they were the same. We exchanged rings and, in a more serious mood, vowed to love each other for a lifetime.

The first night we spent together was traumatic. I planned just to sleep close to her and give her time. I didn't know what either of us could handle. If there was to be a physical relationship, I thought it would develop gradually. Sharon had other ideas. She cuddled around me and soon we were passionately making love. All night long.

This visit also began a pattern of hiding that was to continue throughout our relationship. I set up an elaborate phone relay so my parents would think I was in the library at Ohio State. I felt like I was hiding out in St. Cloud, hoping no one I knew would see me or recognize me. Our lies were mostly those of omission, but in covering up our relationship, we began something that would cost us dearly later on.

Sharon and I knew we loved each other. We simply didn't address the issue of our sexual identity. At this time we weren't ready to think or talk about any of the ramifications of two women loving each other. I felt that it was Sharon, the *individual,* I had fallen in love with, regardless of whether she was a woman or a man.

In the midst of that busy year, we flew back and forth to snatch weekends and vacations with each other. We laughed and played and loved. The year was intense apart and intense together. I learned to function on three to four hours of sleep, studying and writing frantically to keep up with my work and still be able to visit Sharon. I took my preliminary exams for my doctoral candidacy in April and passed. I still don't know how. Sharon, on the other hand, was in her last year of college and preparing for graduation with a double major in Health and Physical Education. By spring, she was student teaching.

I returned to St. Cloud in June, though I wouldn't be teaching again until September. Sharon and I immediately moved in together. It was wonderful to be able to share every day. Still, everything was not easy. Sharon was trying to find work. She wasn't contributing equally to our living expenses, and it worried her. Finally, under the CETA program, she was employed at Sherburne Wildlife Refuge. She enjoyed the work there, teaching visitors about wild edible plants and doing waterfowl counts. But she was also frustrated at not being able to teach P.E. or to use her hard-earned coaching skills.

We lived together in an apartment for a year, then in 1981 moved in with my sister Linda for another year. Linda was recently divorced and I wanted to help her through a hard time. That year was especially difficult for Sharon since we were not open with Linda. We constantly had to hide our relationship, and even came up with reasons why we needed a dead bolt between the first floor and our basement rooms!

In August, Sharon got a teaching position with Big Lake School District and taught there two years. She was an exciting and dedicated teacher and coach. Because of how she jumped wholeheartedly into everything, she got very close to her students and athletes. I would have to bite my tongue to keep from telling her the lessons—about the need for clear-cut boundaries—that I had learned from years of coaching. Hardly a day went by without a student calling or stopping by. It was causing problems between us because neither of us wanted these intrusions in our lives. Eventually, Sharon had to admit it had gotten out of hand. We got an unlisted phone number and made plans to move.

Like any couple, we had our problems. We had disagreements over teaching and coaching, partially because of our differences in age and experience. When we did have arguments, we gradually learned the importance of communicating and working through our feelings as soon as possible. The longer we were together, the more solid our relationship became.

Once we decided to move, Sharon wanted to live out in the country, near water. So we spent a few months looking for a house to buy; then in March we found what we were looking for and moved into the new house in May. It was located near Briggs Lake in a park-like setting. We could canoe or go cross-country skiing close to our house.

When Big Lake cut back on teaching positions in June, 1983, Sharon was one of the casualties. Loving her work and the students, she fervently hoped she would be recalled. Despite the trauma of losing her job, that spring and summer were among our happiest times. We had our house. We canoed, fished, and played all summer. We had been together three and a half years and were still madly in love.

Sharon was a free spirit who lived her life as she pleased. She wouldn't wear a watch, and tried to talk me out of wearing one as well. She ate when she felt like it, not according to any schedule. If we were out running, she'd stop in her tracks to look closely at a flower or watch a bird in flight. Fishing with Sharon was always an experience—she was more interested in me, the sunlight on the water, a bug swimming by, than in the business of baiting a hook. Sharon could be completely happy doing nothing at all.

I sometimes felt as though Sharon were two people at once. To her friends and students, she was very outgoing and always laughing. She liked to party, play poker and drink beer. People were naturally drawn to her. But the part of Sharon that I fell in love with was a very warm and sensitive woman who always had a unique view of the world. She hadn't lost her sense of wonder and she didn't take things for granted. Gradually, as time went on, I learned to love the more outgoing parts of Sharon just as much. She taught me how to laugh and how to live, but neither of us would ever have guessed that I would be the partner to go out into the world.

My thoughts came back to the present, sitting by Sharon in the hospital. I wondered if things would ever be the way they used to be. As I looked around the room, I saw all the barriers to the easy equality we had worked so hard to achieve. Sharon was lying in a bed with sidebars, separated by a curtain from the room's other occupant. Standing, I towered over her; sitting, I was too low. I knew that I needed Sharon every bit as much as she seemed to need me. Yet I didn't know if she'd heard anything I'd said or if she even knew I was there. I had no way to know what our next anniversary would be like, or what the future held for us.

CHAPTER 2

Coming Out

One winter night a few weeks after our anniversary, I tried to stay at our house but anxiety overwhelmed me. In spite of heavy fog and icy roads, I decided to return to the hospital in the wee hours of the morning. On one curve, my car shot into a ditch. Severely shaken, I checked to see if I was still in one piece before my thoughts shifted to the car. It was badly damaged. With no boots on, I slogged through heavy snow to the nearest house and called for towing and a friend to come and get me. Being without a car did give me an excuse to stay in town. Now, I wouldn't have to make up phony explanations to be near Sharon.

Meanwhile, I invited the Kowalskis to stay at our house whenever they came to visit. Though it had been many weeks since the accident, Sharon still remained in a coma. The Kowalskis came for a few days every other week, and stayed at our house several times.

It was during one of those stays that the Kowlaskis must have found something that indicated the true nature of Sharon's and my relationship. They moved out of the house without telling me. That evening at the hospital, Donald Kowalski asked me to leave the room and talk with him in the hall. He stated that no one could love Sharon like family could love Sharon. He said that the family could meet all of her needs; that friends weren't supposed to visit as often as I was visiting and if I didn't stop visiting so often, he would see to it I couldn't visit at all.

I just stood there thinking, Oh my God, he *knows!* What should I say? How can I respond to him? At the same time I was thinking thoughts like, but if I were her legal spouse, they wouldn't be questioning my involvement or the time I spent with her. It would be assumed that we would all be working together trying to help each other through this difficult time.

"Sharon might want me here . . . I might be important to Sharon." I begged him to think of what she would want.

He said something that implied that the time I was spending with Sharon wasn't proper or normal.

I responded, "Don't make me tell you more than you want to know."

He informed me that they were planning to move Sharon to Hibbing as soon as she was able to be moved. He didn't give me a chance to say much more. He just indicated that I was to leave.

I began to live in fear. Would I be allowed to see Sharon again? For the next few months, each time I approached Sharon's room on the rehabilitation unit, I was terrified that this would be the time that I would be refused entrance or that there would be an ugly scene. I began visiting at times when I was pretty sure I wouldn't run into her parents. I felt like a criminal, sneaking in to visit Sharon surreptitiously. Each time I entered the room without interference, relief washed over me, but the panic returned whenever someone else appeared.

Whenever I could, I became involved in Sharon's daily care. I would wash her, dress her, go to physical therapy with her. Her eyelids were open but she was still deep in a coma. Her eyes couldn't focus or follow movement. There was still no way for me to tell if she could hear me or if she even knew I was there. Many days, I would get there at 6:00 or 7:00 in the morning, go to work, then return and stay until 11:00 or 12:00 at night.

One night, I couldn't bring myself to leave. I felt compelled to stay. Sharon was running a high fever and I was afraid something might happen. I just sat beside her, watching her breathe, scared to death. The nurse checked on Sharon every hour. About ten minutes after the 2:00 a.m. check, Sharon stopped breathing. In spite of my panic, CPR training helped me to act calmly. I rang for the nurse. Sharon by then had gagged and was struggling to breathe on her own. They had to aspirate her quickly to remove fluids from her lungs. If she had been alone, she could have died before the 3:00 a.m. check. I was grateful that I had listened to my feelings and to the special communication that was between us, even now when she couldn't talk to me.

A couple of months after the accident, I noticed some movement in Sharon's right index finger and I asked her to move her finger if she could hear me. She moved her finger microscopically. I was ecstatic. She heard me! She was in there! I began to ask her questions immediately.

"This is Karen, Sharon. Do you know who I am? Move your finger if you do." She moved her finger. They say that people in a coma forget things closest to the accident, and I had been wondering how much she would remember. So I asked, "Do you remember our relationship, Sharon?"

She moved her finger again.

"Do you still love me?" Most important to me was to find out what she could remember and what she was thinking. I was petrified that she might have forgotten about our relationship or even who I was.

I told everyone about Sharon's finger movements, that I was sure she understood what I was saying. One of Sharon's doctors was skeptical and told me patronizingly that sometimes a person sees what she wants to see. "Karen, Sharon's prognosis is very poor. Even if she was moving her finger, it doesn't mean there is much hope. It may be months or years and Sharon still won't regain everything. Sharon's parents will always be her parents. They have to deal with this, but you don't. Maybe you should go back to living your own life."

I couldn't believe what he was telling me. Would he have said the same thing to the spouse of a patient? I didn't think so. No one would expect a spouse to walk away or just forget about their loved one. Indeed, most people would be offended with a spouse who did walk away. Yet I could not bring myself to confront him with the truth of our relationship. I said nothing and just continued to spend all my spare time with Sharon, anywhere from eight to ten hours each day.

Sharon displayed symptoms which indicated she still remained in a coma. For instance, when medical personnel would ask Sharon questions, she didn't respond. When she was sleeping, she couldn't be awakened and she didn't respond to pain. Through this experience, I learned that 'comas' were not always as severe or as obvious as lay people assume. Comatose states have many levels and stages, and Sharon was diagnosed as comatose even after she could communicate. In fact, she was never officially diagnosed as being out of the coma.

I continued working with Sharon as if she would fully recover. Even though the times Sharon was alert were few and far between, I didn't give up. I continued talking to Sharon for hours as if she understood what I was saying. I talked about every topic I could think of, from flowers and birds to our relationship. In the beginning, her only response was her finger movement. I always had to state things in yes and no format so that she could respond with a single movement. Little by little, she gained more control over her right hand. I started to ask her to tap individual fingers or to curl them. Now nurses and nurse's aides saw Sharon's movements as well. Weeks passed; it was more than three months since the accident.

I worked with her incessantly. "Sharon, touch my hand. Sharon, touch my hand." I raised my hand one quarter inch each time until three months later she finally touched her chin. Success breeds success. Each time Sharon succeeded, she was willing to try a little more. She seemed to trust that I wouldn't ask her to do things she couldn't do, so she was willing to try and to keep trying for me. Every change was the result of hours and hours of hard work.

I was changing profoundly during this time. I had never thought of myself as a patient person. When, as an undergraduate, I had taken a course in physical therapy, I found it a frustrating experience. I just couldn't get excited about such small increments of success. I had always preferred working with athletes and individuals who demonstrated high levels of skills. Now, I was thrilled to see the person I loved make small but incredible improvements. I never got frustrated working with Sharon, even after hours spent working on minute movements. Each new skill was a triumph.

Along with my newfound patience, I discovered that I was able to give back to Sharon some of what she'd given me. The wonder with which she would point out a particular blossom came back to me as I marveled at a particular movement of hers.

Though I had never expected to put it to such a use, my knowledge of the psychology of sport was really helpful when working with Sharon. I knew from my students that having an audience present can make it more difficult to learn new skills. In Sharon's case, I could see this clearly. In the beginning when others were present, she simply didn't react. Once she learned a skill, *then* she was willing to demonstrate it in front of others. I tried to increase tasks by tiny steps so that she would experience success after success. But when the occupational therapist at the hospital tried to have her work with blocks, Sharon was completely disinterested.

I asked, "Does it have to be blocks? Could we use balls, since Sharon was an athlete?"

I brought in balls. She was much more stimulated to work with balls than she had been with blocks. The therapist appreciated the suggestions, since I knew Sharon better. I asked the therapist what motions she was working on and if it would help if I worked on them later in Sharon's room. She encouraged me to proceed as long as Sharon responded positively and wasn't frustrated.

Sometimes the occupational therapist worked to help Sharon distinguish differences in textures. So I brought in different balls: a ping-pong ball, a tennis ball, a racquetball. This gave Sharon different sizes as well as textures to feel. Sharon showed very little facial expression during this period, but her eyes communicated her liveliness.

As she developed finger coordination, I put a pencil in Sharon's hand and helped her form letters. Finger tapping is an extremely inaccurate form of communication, since the person often taps involuntarily when they hear the instruction to tap. So, I was hoping Sharon could regain the ability to write. We practiced a few days in a row. Then one night, without instruction, she wrote her first two words, "Love you." Then she wrote my name. I threw my arms around her and hugged her. I was filled with joy and tenderness.

I was continually amazed at the things Sharon learned to do. So was the therapist. The self-fulfilling prophecy had worked. When I believed in Sharon and expected her to be able to perform certain tasks, she accomplished them. Many others expected Sharon to do little or nothing, and that's exactly what she did. But, given a chance, Sharon would make astounding leaps, writing whole words when no one else even believed she could form letters.

It had been four months since the accident. Despite the progress Sharon was making, she was still technically diagnosed as being in a coma, because her level of alertness varied and she did not respond to pain. The prognosis continued to be poor. At first, she was conscious perhaps five minutes a day. Now, Sharon's periods of alertness were becoming more frequent, and were lasting longer. She might be alert anywhere from five minutes to a half hour at a time, from once a day to five times a day. Sharon had made a beginning on the road to recovery. I had no concept of how long that road would be. The important thing was that Sharon was responding and had begun to make slow but continuous progress.

❖

During the time Sharon was beginning to show signs of recovery, I was tormented by the deterioration of my relationship with her parents. Even though there were no further confrontations with Donald Kowalski regarding the amount of time I was spending with Sharon, I became increasingly anxious. I lived in constant fear of being excluded from Sharon's life. Finally, I went to see Charles Chmielewski, a psychologist at St. Cloud Hospital.

Even though it was really hard for me, I came out to him, explaining Sharon's and my relationship. I told him about the conversation with

Sharon's father in the hospital corridor. We discussed whether her parents might already have guessed our relationship but were in a stage of denial. I talked to him about what to do if that was the case. Should I tell them the truth? Should they be confronted, and if so, how?

It was his recommendation that I write them a letter explaining the true nature of Sharon's and my relationship and send it to them to be opened in the privacy of their own home. I hoped that sending a letter would give Sharon's parents some time alone to work through any pain, anger or guilt. It's so easy to say terrible things in anger which could stand in the way of our being able to communicate later or work together for Sharon's benefit. Furthermore, Dr. Chmielewski thought that if I were to tell them face to face they would not stay in my presence to hear the whole story. He thought sending a letter would give them a chance to read it, reread it and work through it.

How does a person who has not even accepted her own sexuality come out to her lover's parents? I wanted it to be as gentle as possible. I didn't want to hurt them. I wanted them to see our relationship through Sharon's eyes, not their own. I wanted them to see Sharon as a 27-year-old woman who had made decisions regarding her own life.

It took me a week to compose the letter, going over each word, each paragraph. I was coming out to myself at the same time, putting things into words that I had not put into words before, either to myself or Sharon.

Just one week before the accident, Sharon had looked at me and for the first time said, "Karen, I'm gay. When are you going to acknowledge your sexuality?" We had never said the words. We were just two human beings who happened to fall in love because of certain qualities. Even when Sharon was able to say she was gay, I still resisted any labels.

As I sat there with the paper in front of me, struggling for words, the weekend prior to the accident flashed through my mind. We had driven to Minneapolis to a concert by Meg Christian and Cris Williamson, two lesbian musicians. Sharon had been wanting to do things like that for some time, but I had resisted. She was ecstatic at the concert, feeling support that had been missing for so long. She felt like she belonged for the first time, like she was part of a family. She wanted to talk about it, to admit who we were, to go out afterwards to socialize with other gay people.

The concert was traumatic for me. I don't like crowds to begin with. I was uncomfortable with the whole atmosphere. All the women seemed to know each other or to be looking at anyone they didn't know. I felt on display, or labeled in some way. As soon as I walked in the door of the concert, I recognized two of the athletes I coached at St. Cloud State and wished the floor would swallow me up.

There we were. For the first time in our lives, we could have touched each other in public, held hands, hugged each other or exchanged glances without worrying about how someone else would interpret them. But I sat as far away from Sharon as possible. How can I describe the burning sensation I had all evening from the time I walked in the door? Three or four of my former students came up to talk to us during the breaks. I could have died. I just wanted to survive the evening and get back to the motel. Sharon wasn't surprised at my reaction, but I think she was hopeful that things were going to start changing. Even she couldn't have guessed how fast I was going to change.

These images were crystal clear as I worded and reworded the most important letter of my life. In January I finally sent the following letter to Sharon's parents at their home in Nashwauk.

    Don and Della,

For Sharon's health and future happiness, I pray that you'll read this letter and try to understand. You love Sharon. As Sharon's parents your love and care are extremely important to Sharon. You can reach her on a level no one else can. Please realize however that others can reach Sharon on a different level and fill needs that you cannot. This is a time when everyone who loves Sharon and who Sharon loves must put aside personal feelings and desires. We must work together to see that all of Sharon's needs are met. We all want the same thing, Sharon's physical well-being and future happiness.

A few years ago when Sharon was somewhat bitter and frustrated with what she felt was a lack of understanding and support from you, her parents, I highly encouraged her to work out her feelings. Knowing my mother's precarious health situation, I tried to make her understand how life is too short not to make every attempt at communication. We as children must accept and respect our parents where they are, as human beings. We cannot change them.

Sharon has learned to love you where you are, realizing that she cannot change you. Now you must try to accept and respect, even if you cannot immediately understand, the woman Sharon has become. You do not know your daughter, who she is, what is important to her, and who is important in her life.

Don, you say no one can love Sharon as you, her parents do. No, I do not love her as you do, but I do love her. My love is for an adult, a beautiful, sensitive person who has become my whole world. For over four years we have gotten up to each other, eaten together, played together, shared vacations, and gone to bed to each other every night. We have shared every thought, hope, and dream. We have laughed together and cried together. We share a very special love, friendship, and ability to communicate. We have become as close as any two human beings can come. Whether you understand our love is not the issue. Sharon's health and happiness is. We want and need each other. I just cannot believe that you would deliberately hurt your daughter or go against her wishes.

Sharon has been unfairly punished by a drunk driver. She has had time taken away and the use of her mind and body. Please do not punish her further by thinking of taking her away from our home where *she* wanted to be. *She* chose to live there. This is where *she* wanted to live unless we decided to move out west. *She* chose to live with me. We made a commitment to each other over four years ago. I am the single most important person in Sharon's life. Do not try to take away the happiness we share. Allow us the time to try to put our lives back together again. Let it be our decision as to whether or not we can make it.

If you do not believe me as to Sharon's feelings towards me, then ask some of her friends. Sharon believed that to be close to anyone she had to tell them about us. It almost ruined her friendship with Fran because Fran didn't want to accept our relationship. Ask Pat Larsen. Sharon told her when she worked at Sherburne in order that they could better understand each other. Ask [any of Sharon's friends].

You and I have something very special in common, our love for Sharon. It would be nice if you could understand our relationship and we could all try to help each other through this very difficult time. I want very much to be able to communicate with you. But regardless, for Sharon and her chance of future happiness, you need to honor her wishes.

When she is able to leave here, she should be assured that she will be able to return to our home, where she wanted to be. I want Sharon with me at whatever level she comes back to. I want to take care of her. I have the right to take care of her. This is what she would have wanted. If the house needs to be remodeled in any way to be accessible to Sharon, that can be done. If someone needs to be hired to help take care of her when I can't, that too can be done.

You would be welcome whenever you wanted to visit or to stay for extended times. Sharon loves you and needs you too. But she has not chosen to live her life with you, just as you have not chosen at this point in time to live with her. Don, if anything had ever happened to Della, would you have assumed her parents should make all the decisions and take her home to live with them? Well, for Sharon and I the situation is similar to a marriage. We have exchanged rings. I have a right to be involved in any decisions concerning Sharon.

We have $50,000 life insurance policies on each other so in case anything ever happened, the house would belong free and clear to the other. We would have spelled out our wishes for a situation like this had we ever dreamed it could occur. Please honor Sharon's wishes. Let her go back to the place she loved and wanted to live her life in when she is able to be released from here. Let her watch the birds and the squirrels playing [in] the trees. Let her be with all our familiar things she loved around her.

Before Sharon left that Sunday, she said we were so lucky. We shared more love, happiness, friendship, and communication than anyone in either of our families. Then she asked me to save Monday night for her. Monday night never came. However long I have to wait, I want that Monday night she promised me. I believe in Sharon. I believe that our love is strong enough that we can work through this and refind our happiness together. Please do not make this any more difficult than it already is.

You can deny Sharon's and my relationship to yourselves. You can pretend that I don't exist. But you cannot alter the facts. Sharon and I love each other. We *are* each other's happiness. I am going to be around as long as Sharon's rehabilitation takes. I will never quit on her. I will be here when she needs me and will not let her down. I have a right to be here.

However, Sharon needs your love and support as well as mine. For Sharon's best interests, can we not try to work together? I would be very happy to sit down and talk with you any time.
Love in Christ,
Karen

The Kowalskis responded to the letter almost as soon as they received it. Deb, Sharon's sister, called me at the request of her parents. As I remember it, she told me, "You are a sick, crazy person who has made up this whole story. There is no way Sharon is a lesbian. You have written a bunch of trash. My parents never want to set eyes on you again!"

I wasn't given a chance for much response. I tried to reason with her, but she wouldn't listen. After her phone call, I was terribly shaken. I wondered what I should do next. Who should I talk with? At this point, none of my own family knew about my relationship with Sharon. I was still trying to pretend to them that Sharon and I were just close friends. The bad dream that had begun when Donald had confronted me outside of Sharon's room was turning into a nightmare. I spent the weekend in agony. I didn't know who I could possibly talk to, so I bottled everything up inside. The only relief I could find was in running. I ran for miles and miles, past the point of exhaustion.

I racked my mind for someone who might know of an attorney who wasn't blatantly against lesbian and gay relationships. In trying to think of someone with whom it was safe to discuss this topic, I remembered a professor on campus who had a reputation as a feminist and activist, Julie Andrzejewski. Over the years I had avoided her like the plague. It wasn't that I personally disliked her; I had never even met her, but she represented the type of person who fought for issues that I didn't even think were problems.

Julie was intensely involved in a class action suit against the university which was filed by another professor. Three years earlier, I had been asked by their attorneys to join the suit. I personally felt I had never been a victim of discrimination, even though a decision had been made in my department to promote a male instructor with similar credentials to mine while not offering me a promotion as well. I thought perhaps the university had made a mistake in judgment but I certainly didn't believe it was sex discrimination.

Several times throughout the first couple of months following Sharon's accident, friends suggested that Julie might be able to understand what I was going through and could possibly help me. Even though I still found her terribly threatening, I finally decided to talk with her. My fear of associating with someone like Julie was less than my need for information. But that still didn't make me comfortable on the day I went to her office.

She closed the door and I sobbed through my story. I wanted her advice and the name of an attorney.

Trying to reassure me, Julie said, "Karen, I am also a lesbian and I have already heard what happened to you. I was hoping you would come to see me since I'd like to help any way I can."

"I don't know what to do," I said, not quite comprehending that she had just come out to me. I still didn't use the term lesbian for myself. "I don't know what my rights are or even if I have any. But I need answers from someone qualified in legal matters. Who is safe to talk to? Do you know anyone in town?"

"It's a good idea to seek legal advice, for sure. Let me consult with some people about an attorney and get back to you right away. But, how are *you* doing? This must be a terrible strain. Do you have someone to talk to? Have you seen a counselor for some support?" From the very beginning, Julie was concerned about my own support system, which was the furthest thing from my mind.

I kept trying to get her back to the main problem—Sharon. "My first priority is to find an attorney to give me legal advice," I said firmly. "But, I know I have lots of questions I have to deal with on a personal level too. For instance, it's scary to think of coming out as being gay when I'm not even sure I am gay. I don't know what I am. I just know I love Sharon. Whatever that makes me, I guess that's what I am. I hate labels and stereotypes. Why do I have to label myself anything?"

As I said these things to Julie, I suddenly realized how much they had been on my mind lately. Questions like these were a major part of the reason I hadn't slept a whole night for months. Nights were the enemy. I dreaded the evenings—which turned into nights. Knowing that Sharon seemed scared at night made them even worse. For that reason, I would stay with her until she went to sleep. The nurses commented that Sharon seemed to sleep more peacefully when I stayed with her.

But eventually I had to go home. Alone there, I often had anxiety attacks and severe headaches. I worried about Sharon, about our relationship, about our legal rights and about the possibility of publicity. What if someone made this into a gay rights issue? What if I *was* gay? What if I was really *not* gay? Either way the consequences were devastating. I didn't know who I was, only that I loved Sharon. I never questioned my love. I worried that it might be a sin, but I never, never questioned my love or my commitment. These thoughts whirled through my head but I wasn't ready to express them to Julie or anyone.

"If I am gay," I continued out loud, "the question that haunts me is, can you be Christian and gay? Do I have to choose? The Presbyterian church doctrine implies being gay is like an illness from which you need to be cured. I find it difficult to walk into church feeling like a fake, like they wouldn't accept me if they knew I was in this relationship. Yet, my personal relationship with God is extremely important to me. It's important to both Sharon and me. We've struggled with this and then we just put it on hold because we were afraid to find the answers. We were afraid to look too deeply for fear we would have to give each other up or give up God."

"I know of some religious counselors who have done a lot of work concerning gay and lesbian issues," Julie offered. "Would you like some names? I have been especially impressed with Reverend Peg Chemberlin, who is with the United Ministries in Higher Education here. Do you think you could feel comfortable talking with her?"

Julie called me later that night with the name of an attorney in town, Peter Donohue. She said he would be supportive but she couldn't speak to his expertise in guardianship law. At least it was a place to start.

I called Peter at his home that same night so I wouldn't chicken out, and I met with him the next day. Peter made me feel as comfortable as anyone could have at that point in time. However, I discovered that I had no rights whatsoever. The Kowalskis could shut me out completely unless I filed for guardianship. This was the only way I could assure their communication with me and the protection of Sharon's right to choose. We discussed whether filing for guardianship would make our relationship public since probate court is open to reporters and the public.

I would not have even considered filing for guardianship if I hadn't felt forced to by the Kowalskis' reactions, but I wanted to ensure that Sharon would receive the best possible medical care, that she would be able to live where she wanted to live and see whomever she wanted to see. I didn't care about being appointed guardian if these rights could be protected some other way, even though I was sure Sharon would have wanted me appointed guardian. I had access to resources, information, and a belief in the possibilities of rehabilitation which just weren't available to Sharon's parents. A battle over guardianship was the last thing in the world I wanted, but I was feeling desperate about what would happen to Sharon if the family had its way.

While I was pursuing advice from Julie and Peter, I continued to spend as much time as possible with Sharon at the hospital. This wasn't difficult when her parents were out of town. They were usually at the hospital for a few days every other week or so. On these occasions they rarely visited before ll:00 a.m. so I could get there by 7:00 in the morning and spend several hours with Sharon without risking a confrontation with them. When they left for lunch or supper, I could slip in and see Sharon for another hour. They seldom stayed in the evening, so I came back after they left and stayed late into the night. Constantly fearing discovery, I wanted to avoid the possibility that they would leave orders that I was not to visit Sharon.

One evening, I had just wheeled Sharon into the lounge when the Kowalskis arrived. Immediately, I searched for an excuse to leave, fearing another confrontation. As I was leaving, they asked to see me privately in Sharon's room. Don asked me if I would be willing to claim that Sharon's permanent address was in Nashwauk. He explained that if Sharon had been living at home, the car insurance policies could be stacked. This meant that when Sharon's policy limits were reached, one of the other policies at the same address would kick in. By claiming Sharon's address to be Nashwauk, she could receive an extra $100,000. (I found out later that the Kowalskis' lawyer had approached my attorney with the same request.)

Shocked, I said, "But Sharon hasn't lived at home for over six years. There's no way that the insurance company would accept that as her address when she has had full-time jobs in the St. Cloud area and has voted here."

As I remember, Don angrily accused me of costing Sharon $100,000. "You claim to love Sharon. If you really cared, you would help her get as much money as she could."

I'll never forget Della's tone of voice, and how it scared me, when she added, "We'll get even with you. Someday, we'll get even with you!"

With that, they stalked out to rejoin Sharon in the lounge. I sat there looking at my shaking hands, wondering what they meant by that.

Following that incident, I was even more careful to avoid the Kowalskis when they were in town. I worked even harder to make sure I knew what Sharon's actual wishes were. At this point, Sharon was alert more often, though there were many times when I was unable to rouse her or to connect with her at all. She had very little motor control and had to be strapped into a wheelchair. I had continued to work with Sharon, using flash cards and an erasable tablet. I would write various possible answers to questions and she was able to point to the one she wanted. Each time Sharon was responsive and alert, I always asked, "Sharon, do you want me to be here with you now or would you rather be alone? Move your finger if you want me to be here." Or I would ask, "Do you want me to come back after class?" I wanted to make sure that Sharon had a choice. I wanted to give Sharon as much control as I could.

To make sure I was following Sharon's wishes, I would often discuss decisions with her that would eventually need to be made. I wanted to know, "Sharon, where do you want to live? Who do you want to live with? Whatever *you* want is okay with me. Do you want to live with your parents? Do you want to live with me? I need to know what you want, Sharon." I held up a tablet with a list of choices. I always checked for consistency and accuracy of her responses by asking the same question in several ways. Sharon was often inconsistent with her responses to questions like "What day is this?" or "Do you know why you are here?" Her short-term memory was practically nonexistent. Yet, Sharon's long-term memory seemed relatively intact and she consistently indicated that she loved me, she wanted to live with me, she wanted me with her as much as I could be there.

It was ironic that my dissertation for Ohio State, which I was working on when the accident happened, was on the psychology of control—how a sense of control over one's environment impacts one's level of motivation and need to achieve. Working with Sharon put all these theories and ideas immediately into daily practice. It was obvious that Sharon had virtually no control over her environment, therefore I tried to involve her in as many decisions as I could so that she could experience herself in control.

Sharon and I were learning to communicate with each other in new ways. We developed something very special, based on the relationship we had before, but different. We were now two changed people. I fell in love with Sharon all over again, a new Sharon. She would watch me with her eyes—she never took them off of me when I was in the room. They were so expressive. She told me with her eyes that she loved me. We communicated with looks and signals that we had to learn together. She learned to sign "I love you" with her fingers. I talked love with Sharon. I told her over and over how much I loved her and would always love her. It was as though the intimacy had increased because of the tragic situation we were in.

In this way I discovered that Sharon and I still could have an intimate relationship. But would the outside world let us? I had no concept of what kind of a relationship we were going to have as she recovered. Seeing her there, I didn't know if we would ever again have a sexual relationship and I thought we could deal with that. But I wanted to develop our relationship to the fullest, whatever that would be, physically, emotionally and mentally.

Other than to hold her hand, hug her or kiss her goodnight, I never considered making any kind of sexual invitation to her, but Sharon had other ideas. Once when I was reaching around Sharon and tying her nightgown in the back, she reached up and touched my breast. It took me by such surprise that it brought tears to my eyes.

Thoughts raced through my mind. What did she mean by that? Did she understand what she was doing? What was she asking for? If she was capable of thinking of and wanting a sexual relationship, what did it mean? I understood that sometimes people with brain injuries may demonstrate inappropriate sexual behavior as a result of the injury. How could I make sure she understood fully what she was doing?

"Did you deliberately put your hand there, Sharon? Squeeze my hand if you did," I asked. Sharon squeezed my hand. I asked her in many different ways to see if she answered consistently. I wanted to make sure that she didn't squeeze my hand just because I told her to. I also said, "Squeeze my hand if you didn't mean anything by it." She did nothing. "Open your hand if you wanted to touch me intimately or make a fist if it was accidental." She opened her hand. I purposely turned questions around to avoid a 'response set'—so that a question she would answer one way the first time, she would have to answer another way the next time to be consistent.

By this time, Sharon was rather frustrated with me! Later on, we would actually laugh together about these tiresome, stilted conversations, but at the moment I had to know for sure what she wanted. So she took my hand and placed it on her breast. Still hesitant, I had to ask again, "Do you want me to touch you, Sharon? What are you asking for?" She could not yet nod her head so I had to phrase it again so she could respond within the limitations of her abilities on that particular day.

Why *couldn't* Sharon have a special intimate relationship with another human being? Should she be denied that just because she was disabled? If I were her legal spouse, would that make a difference? I knew I was on shaky ground, yet I didn't want Sharon to think that I wasn't sexually attracted to her because of her disabilities. And, if that was what she wanted, I wanted to reassure her that I still wanted her in every way.

It was an impossible situation. No one even knew that we were in a relationship and there was no way I could tell anyone about us. If we were in a traditional relationship, I could talk to medical personnel about sexual issues and get advice, but that simply wasn't an option for me, for us. I felt that I had to get some answers for myself before I risked coming out to more people. I called Peg Chemberlin to make an appointment.

I walked into Peg's office intending only to deal with the issue of Christianity and homosexuality and wanting to approach it as a theoretical problem unconnected to me. Peg probed much deeper until I found myself splattering all over the walls. In my emotional state, it took a lot of patience for Peg to get the whole story. In the beginning, I found Peg as threatening as I had found Julie. She talked about "God, *She . . .*" and since I was still very traditional, I certainly wasn't ready to question God's gender. I felt I had enough to address.

Even though this was a time of turmoil, I gradually found a sense of peace in Peg's office. Here I could explore, honestly and openly, the piercing questions which had plagued me throughout the course of my entire relationship with Sharon.

The fact that she was both a minister and heterosexual was extremely important to me. I knew how my own minister perceived homosexuality. I figured I also knew how a gay minister would approach it. I wanted what I perceived to be an unbiased opinion. Over the next few weeks, I met with Peg regularly to discuss reading materials she gave me. She wanted me to reach my own decision about whether homosexuality was right or wrong for me. After studying for the first time the theological arguments supporting the validity of same-sex relationships, I arrived at the conclusion that God would never condemn my relationship with Sharon. I could be both Christian and gay. This realization brought me overwhelming relief.

I had discussed my interpretation of sin with Peg many times. Sin was anything that stands between you and God, anything that blocks communication. It was clear to me that my relationship with Sharon had blocked my communication with God, so I was scared that it was a sin. Peg explained that maybe unnecessary guilt, fostered by a homophobic society, was the block. If we removed this guilt, my communication with God might be restored.

I'll never forget the day she asked if she could finally give me her opinion. "There's nothing in the Bible that condemns love, a loving, committed relationship between two people. You have nothing to feel guilty about, Karen. The love you have for Sharon is beautiful. I'm offended that society has made you question and feel guilty about your love." She hugged me, and I felt good about myself for maybe the first time in my life.

Certain at last that my relationship with Sharon was morally right and that I didn't have to give her up based on my religious beliefs, I was ready to take the next step. I filed for guardianship, now willing to risk that our relationship might become public.

CHAPTER 3

The Guardianship Struggle

With a sigh of relief, I filed for guardianship at the beginning of March. I had finally taken action. I had finally made the decision—one that I thought was most right for Sharon and most true to the life we had chosen together. Donald Kowalski immediately counterfiled, asking the court that he be named Sharon's sole guardian.

But now I wrestled with a whole new set of fears and worries. On one hand, the weeks until the hearing stretched endlessly before me. What would happen at the hearing? How would I live with the uncertainty until then? At other times the hearing seemed to loom perilously close. First we had faced the possibility of separation due to death or coma. Now, when Sharon was making progress and we were developing our new relationship, we had to face another dreadful possibility. What if the courts separated me from Sharon? I was outraged by the injustice of the situation. If we had been legally married, we wouldn't have had to go through this additional strain.

And then, too, I worried about the repercussions of our relationship becoming public. What if St. Cloud State University found out? Would I lose my job? How could I take care of Sharon if I didn't have an income? My own family didn't know anything about our relationship. What would their reaction be? I wanted to be the one to tell them. What if they found out from a reporter or from reading the paper? Everywhere I turned I was hit with a new anxiety.

I decided I needed to come out to my sister, Linda, since she was living in St. Cloud and might be immediately affected. It was not going to be easy for me. All she knew for sure was that I cared about Sharon. One day I asked her to sit down with me on her living room couch. First I explained that the reason I was filing for guardianship was to protect Sharon's rights. That seemed logical to her. She knew that Sharon's parents wanted to move her to Hibbing.

"Karen, I know Sharon would never want to live in Hibbing, right in the middle of the Iron Range," Linda reflected. "Remember that year you and Sharon lived at my house? All those walks we took when Sharon talked about her feelings? She seemed so bitter about the way women were treated. They were supposed to get married, have kids and jump when the man said 'jump' . . . and her brother rolling his car in the ditch and their parents helping him get another one . . . yet they wouldn't pay one cent for her college education . . . ."

"Yes, I know, I know, I've heard Sharon make those statements a hundred times, but I never really understood how deep her feelings went until now." After an awkward moment, I blurted out, "Linda, there's something else I need to talk with you about. I don't know if you understand how much I care about Sharon. I love her." Knowing that this statement could be interpreted many ways, I quickly added, "I've written a letter to her parents explaining our relationship and I want to share it with you before we go into court," and handed her a copy of the letter I had sent to the Kowalskis.

After she finished reading the letter, Linda folded it and quietly handed it back to me. During those brief seconds I waited anxiously for her response. Finally, she looked at me and said, "Karen, I'm not surprised. I wondered how Sharon could be sleeping in her bed when it was always piled high with clothes, softball gloves and other things. It's something I never wanted to think too much about, but whatever your relationship is, I want you to know that I'll support you in any way I can."

"I'm afraid our relationship might become public when the guardianship case gets to court. Are you sure you want to come with me to the hearing?"

"I will be there with you," she said firmly.

Though I had expected her support, I felt released from a very heavy burden. My face burned from talking about something that was so hard for me. In my family we weren't openly demonstrative. I had never learned how to express my love for my sister, so I couldn't tell her now how much it meant to me to have her support. But I felt very close to her at that moment. And proud. (Of the multitudes of hearings, Linda and Theo, the man she married shortly after the accident, attended the majority, sitting beside me and listening to some of the most outrageous things I'm sure they've ever heard.)

After Linda's response, I consulted her about my coming out to our parents. "Do you think I should talk with Mom and Dad? I'm afraid it will affect Mom's health." My mother's kidneys had failed many years before and she was living only with the aid of dialysis. Depression is common among people with her condition. At first, doctors had told us she had less than a year to live. She had already proven them wrong but I didn't want my actions to endanger her health any further.

"This may not come out at all. I don't think we should say anything to them unless it's absolutely necessary," Linda was quick to respond.

I was relieved to hear her answer because I didn't know how to approach my parents, especially since they were living in Ohio—almost a thousand miles away. I wondered, at the time, if it was right to burden them with my problems just because I needed their love and support. I had not yet learned the lesson of how crucial it was to be honest with parents about intimate relationships.

"Can I tell Theo?" Linda asked.

Theo taught Health at St. Cloud State University. His office was only three doors down the hallway from mine. It was scary to think of him knowing, but I trusted him. Besides, it wouldn't be fair to ask Linda not to share this critical information with him. She would probably need to have support too. "Of course." My voice was calmer than I felt.

❖❖

I still wanted to avoid the hearing if it was at all possible. I searched for any manner of communication with Don and Della. I had noticed that they seemed to talk a lot with the mother of another brain-injured woman. Clutching at straws, I thought maybe she might be able to get through to the Kowalskis. One day she approached me while I was with Sharon in therapy.

As she was pointing out the advantages of a new type of Pampers for adults, I nervously interrupted, "Angie, can I talk with you sometime?"

"Sure, when's best?" she responded, and we proceeded to set up a time.

We met in the coffee shop a few days later. I tried to explain the difficulties I was having communicating with Don and Della. In desperation, I decided to be totally frank with her and let her read the letter I had sent. "Now maybe you can understand that when Sharon is able to leave here, Angie, I want to bring her back home," I said. "I'm sure you know that disability advocates recommend people be allowed to return to their homes as soon as possible . . . that research shows this really aids recovery. I want Sharon to have the best chance of recovery possible."

"But Karen, do you understand the responsibility you're planning to take on?" She told me that, one by one, her daughter's friends had disappeared. Indeed, she and her other daughters were dedicating almost all of their waking hours to taking care of her disabled daughter.

"I'm aware of the responsibility and commitment involved and that it won't be easy. But I've always been able to do what I set my mind to, and I want to do this in the very best way I can," I assured her. "Certainly, I plan to take advantage of whatever services are available in St. Cloud to help us. Of course, no one can guarantee the future. If I found that I couldn't take care of Sharon at the house, I'd have to consider an institution again. But what harm would it do to give us a chance to try? I'm just afraid if I have to fight for this in court, someone will try to turn the guardianship case into a gay rights battle. That's not what I want. Do you think there's any possibility you could reason with Don and Della?"

She seemed to understand and indicated that she would talk with them. I never knew whether she did until months later when I read the affidavit she had filed on behalf of the Kowalskis. In that document she stated that I wanted "to deprive Sharon's parents of their love and care," and that I "intended to make a 'gay rights issue' out of the matter." She added that I would try it out for a period of time and if I couldn't handle it, then I "would let the parents have her." She concluded, "Even assuming that Karen Thompson is sincere in her desires, it is my absolute opinion that she would never be able to last in the job of caring for Sharon Kowalski."

A few weeks before the hearing was scheduled, completely frustrated, I wrote another letter directly to Don and Della, making one last appeal for them to sit down and talk with me. I didn't consult with my attorneys before sending it because I felt they wouldn't approve. It was not the most tactful letter.

❖   Don and Della:
        For Sharon's sake, I am making one last appeal to you to look at things through Sharon's eyes instead of your own . . . to consider what Sharon would want instead of what you want. Somehow I'd like to make you understand why I feel compelled to take legal action to protect Sharon's rights. It is not what I wanted to do. But you won't even make an attempt at communication . . . .

In the next pages I tried to reinforce how Sharon perceived our relationship and the importance of loved ones in the recovery process. I stressed that it might even be detrimental to her if I were prevented from visitation. Another objective of the letter was to help them to see me as a human being and to see the agony I was experiencing. I was blunt. I was probably too blunt to accomplish my purpose. But these were the people who had played poker and foosball in the rec room of Sharon's and my house. These were the people who, just a few months before the accident, Sharon and I had visited for a weekend to help them build a garage. I felt I almost needed to shake them into remembering that they had once treated me and Sharon like human beings.

❖   . . . I can't even begin to express how childish and selfish I feel it is for people to refuse to talk with someone and at least be decent for Sharon's sake. I have never failed to say hello, goodbye, or ask how things are going. I've offered you meals, a house to stay in, to do laundry for you, etc. In return I have been treated as if I have the plague or am a second-class citizen. I haven't deserved this . . . . I am a human being with feelings.

I have been totally devastated by the injury to the person I love most in this world. I have been forced to practically sneak in and out of Sharon's room, live in constant fear of an open confrontation, and live in anxiety that you will pack her up and take her away.

I have never and would never want to keep you from Sharon. It isn't my great desire to bring everything out in the open for all to see, but I will do whatever is necessary to protect Sharon's physical and psychological well-being. I am still more than willing to sit down and try to talk through things for Sharon's best interest. As I said before, we have something very special in common, our love for Sharon. Aren't you even willing to attempt to work things out?
Love in Christ,
Karen

FIRST HEARING OVER THE
GUARDIANSHIP OF SHARON KOWALSKI

There was no response. Attempts to communicate with Sharon's parents out of court clearly had failed. On March 23, 1984, the day of the hearing finally arrived. My lawyer, Peter Donohue and his partner, Beth Ristvedt, were both present in district court. The attorneys were asked to meet with Judge Bruce Douglas in closed chambers, so Linda and I sat in the waiting room while they met in an office down the hallway. During this meeting the judge decided to appoint a neutral third-party guardian for a month until the case could be investigated. At the same time he appointed Tom Hayes as an attorney for Sharon Kowalski, who was now considered a ward of the court. Then my attorneys asked the court to order counseling between the Kowalskis and me. It was my hope that these sessions would help us to reach a solution together that would be better for Sharon. According to Beth and Peter, the judge's response was to order one session, saying something to the effect of, "You can lead a horse to water, but you can't make him drink."

He set up separate and equal visitation times with Sharon for me and for Don and Della. All times which weren't assigned were open times during which either party could visit. Probably because the Kowalskis were so adverse to seeing me, they seldom were there during open times. It seemed to me this segregation perpetuated the lack of communication which began when Don suggested I stop visiting so often. The longer this went on, the worse the communication became. Instead of being forced to deal with each other and work through our feelings, we were kept apart, and the mistrust and bitterness were allowed to grow.

The Kowalskis' animosity was apparent during the times our paths did cross. A week after the hearing I was washing Sharon's hair at a sink in a room down the hall. Della Kowalski stormed into the room and demanded, "Just what are you doing?"

"Washing Sharon's hair," was my startled reply. "The nurses know we're here."

She stood and glared at me while I finished. I chattered to Sharon to cover my nervousness. When we were finished, I wheeled Sharon back toward her room. In order to ease the tension, I asked Sharon, "Would you like your mom to dry your hair?" I thought I would leave then and Sharon would not be exposed to the hostility.

"I assure you I can do it just fine," Della retorted, even though I hadn't implied she couldn't.

"I'm sure you can, Della," I stated evenly. I left after saying goodbye to Sharon.

The next week, another incident occurred. A nurse and I were washing Sharon before bedtime when Della entered the room. I was immediately worried that there would be a scene in front of Sharon and the nurse. While we continued, Della attempted to place a sheepskin on Sharon's foot to prevent bedsores. Observing her difficulty, I offered a suggestion, "The flap part goes on the top."

"I'm sure you know how to do everything!" Della hollered.

Embarrassed, I responded, "Hey, I just thought you wanted to fix it."

"Well, you just better cool it!" she snapped.

"I'm not the one who's upset," I stated quietly.

For the next month things continued as they had been. I was visiting as often as I could. The Kowalskis were in town every couple of weeks for only a few days at a time. Knowing that I had been given equal visitation, the medical staff began including me in consultations and I was even invited to attend staffings on Sharon's progress. I was able to quit watching Sharon's therapy and become an active participant. Therapists encouraged me to assist and started to give me positive feedback. "Sharon's just more responsive when you're here, Karen."

Tom Hayes came to visit Sharon while I was in the room, so I introduced him to her. Sharon and I had communicated about the hearing and the fact that he would be coming to visit. I wanted Sharon to understand as much as she could and to be prepared. I always approached her with the attitude that she had a right to know what was occurring and what she didn't understand or couldn't take in at the time, she just wouldn't.

I had started to observe that people talked with sick or disabled people differently from able-bodied people. Sharon couldn't speak so they assumed she couldn't hear, and would raise their voices when speaking to her. Others would change their entire tone of voice and speak down to her just like some adults treat children. Once, when a doctor had just talked to me at length over Sharon's bed as though she weren't there, I asked her how she felt about it. She wrote on her slate, "Shitty." I was becoming painfully aware that sick, disabled or elderly people are stripped of their dignity and I didn't want to see this happen to Sharon.

"Sharon, will you show Tom some of the skills you're working on?" She indicated with her finger that she would. We showed Tom several finger dexterity exercises and hand and arm movements.

Tom watched us together. When I walked him out of the room, he told me, "Sharon never took her eyes off of you. She only acknowledged my presence when you introduced me. Even when the telephone rang, she followed you with her eyes the entire time."

I was relieved and hopeful that Tom had seen the closeness of our relationship and seemed to realize how important I was to Sharon. I prayed that he would be a strong advocate for Sharon's rights.

The second hearing took place about a month later, at the end of April. Again, it was in closed chambers with the attorneys and Judge Douglas. I waited in a conference room with the witnesses who were there on my behalf. As the hours passed, the tension mounted. My whole future was being decided and I couldn't even be there!

Beth and Peter emerged from the judge's chambers to consult with me. "We feel that you should settle out of court. We may get a lot less if you insist on a full public hearing." With no legal background and no experience in the courts at all, I agreed to a settlement which included the following:

♦ The Court recognizes that Karen Thompson and Donald and Della Kowalski each have a significant relationship with the ward, Sharon Kowalski, and finds each to be a suitable and qualified person to discharge the trust. However, in light of the difficulties existing between them the Court is unwilling to appoint joint guardians. Therefore, the Petitioner, Karen Thompson, agrees to the appointment of Donald Kowalski as guardian with no recognition that he is the most suitable and best qualified among those available and willing to discharge the trust, but is willing to accept the Court's appointment of Donald Kowalski under certain conditions and restrictions in order to avoid a contested hearing in the matter, which might not be in Sharon's best interest and in order to make every effort to resolve the difficulties existing between them.

The restrictions, cited in the settlement, gave the Kowalskis and me equal access to Sharon's medical and financial information and equal access to Sharon with visitation continuing as previously scheduled. Finally, it guaranteed that 'the ward' could not be moved from St. Cloud unless by mutual agreement or by court order.

This agreement, on the surface, seemed to protect everything I wanted. However, once guardianship is granted, that person is in a position of power that was not reflected in this settlement. A guardian can bring in any doctors or attorneys for the case and have them paid for out of the insurance and available aid. The guardian can hire the attorney for the personal injury suit to represent the injured person. While initially this didn't seem threatening, the attorney they chose would become deeply embroiled in helping Don Kowalski's guardianship case in order, as far as I could see, to protect his interest in the personal injury suit. In addition, it is extremely difficult to remove a guardian once he or she is appointed.

I soon realized that I should never have settled this hearing out of court. It was a grave error, in my opinion, not to obtain, through court testimonies, important information that could be used later in the case. It was my first lesson that attorneys do not always make settlements that are beneficial in the eyes of their clients.

But, at the time, I experienced a great sense of hope and relief. It was over. Sharon and I had rights after all. Nothing had become public. Now we could get back to the important issue of Sharon's recovery. I didn't have to feel like a criminal, sneaking in and out of her room to see the person I loved more than anyone. I had a right to be there.

The following day, during my visitation time, I was in the physical therapy room with Sharon and her physical therapist, along with other patients and therapists. We were continuing the range of motion exercises. In walked Don and Della. "What are you doing here?" Don asked.

"What do you mean? This is my visitation time," was my surprised response.

"We want you to leave. There aren't visitation times anymore."

At this point, the therapist asked us to continue our conversation out in the hall. Not wanting to disrupt Sharon's therapy, I hurried toward the door.

As soon as we were outside, I said, "Oh yes there *are* visitation times. They're the same as they were before." I looked at him incredulously. Weren't we at the same hearing? Had something new happened? What was going on?

"I'm the guardian now and I don't want you here," he retorted.

Realizing I couldn't reason with him, I left to avoid a scene. But on the way out I said, "I think you had better contact your attorney to find out what the facts really are. You are the guardian but there are visitation times still in effect. You don't seem to understand the settlement."

They must have conferred with their attorney because they weren't there during my visitation time that evening. So, we settled into a pattern once again.

Sharon continued to improve. She hadn't been able to show much facial expression since the accident. Only her eyes showed her alertness and some of the personality of the old Sharon. One day, she looked at me and smiled. It had been such a long time! I was so excited by that smile, it seemed that the whole world would be okay.

The smile brought to mind a day before Sharon was moved to the rehabilitation ward. I had taken a walk through the ward, knowing Sharon would soon be placed there. What would this move be like for her? It tore me up to see the people there, in various stages of recovery. I sought information about the brain-injured patients on the ward.

One young man had already been there for nine months. He was sitting slumped over in a wheelchair, head hanging and mouth drooling. Everyone was excited about the progress he was making. I was shaken. Nine months after the accident and he was still in this condition? As I asked questions, it became clear that he was not even as seriously injured as Sharon. I wanted to scream, Sharon will never be like this! My denial of Sharon's real condition forced me to begin to face my own fear and prejudice about disabled people. Sharon, lying in a coma, had looked perfectly normal. I hadn't wanted to face the reality of Sharon's physical condition when she came out of the coma.

Now, looking at Sharon's smiling face, I realized how much I had already changed. The first time I had to wipe off her mouth or change her pants, I had cringed. Now I didn't think about it, except to keep challenging Sharon to do what she could for herself. I had passed through the stage of realizing that Sharon would be unable, for the present, to take care of even her most basic physical needs, including washing, dressing or eating. I began to see Sharon as a real person again, regardless of her physical limitations. Sharon was a vitally alive human being with many capabilities. We just had to explore and discover them.

As Sharon gained strength, she spent more time in a wheelchair. Even when she was in intensive care and in a deep coma, she was put in an upright position for a period of time each day to avoid pneumonia. Now, she was in her wheelchair at least three times a day, sometimes for two to three hours at a time. We could do a greater variety of activities when she was up than when she was in bed. Being up didn't guarantee that Sharon would be alert or responsive, but the periods of responsiveness were increasing in number and in length.

As a result of tests conducted to determine Sharon's ability to swallow, Sharon was allowed to begin having jello and soft foods. Liquids were more difficult since they can go down into the lungs before the person has a chance to swallow. One night the hospital staff made homemade strawberry ice cream. After feeding Sharon a couple of spoonfuls, I asked her if she wanted to try feeding herself. She dipped the spoon into the cup and brought it to her mouth. Again and again. She had ice cream all over her but she was doing it! I was so proud. I caught myself . . . I had almost not asked her if she wanted to do it on her own.

From that time on, I continually reminded myself to give Sharon a chance to help herself. Part of the fun we had was to be teaching each other. Sharon wasn't the only one learning.

On one of our early excursions outside the hospital, I had brought Sharon's softball cap and laid the bill in her hand. I was wheeling the chair out the door when the sun hit her eyes. The next thing I knew, Sharon had flipped the cap onto her head and looked up at me with a cocky smile. We enjoyed that moment together. Much of what we did was plain hard work but we learned to get excited about small things and make them special. We would look for things to celebrate.

On another outing, we saw a flower. I asked Sharon, "Do you know what kind of flower this is?"

Sharon responded "yes" with her finger.

When we got back inside, I handed her an alphabet board which I had made several weeks earlier. I had wanted her to be able to start communicating in more than finger signing, so we could begin to have real conversations. It was simply a big white poster board with all the letters of the alphabet on it. I chose red for the letters because I knew Sharon would like bright colors. "Can you spell out the type of flower you saw, Sharon?"

She pointed to each letter until she had spelled out "bluebell."

"Are you trying to pull the wool over my eyes? I wouldn't know if that was a bluebell or not."

She grinned and pointed to the "y" (which she had started to use as shorthand for "yes") to indicate that it was, indeed, a bluebell.

Later I brought in a flower book and we looked it up. Of course Sharon was 100 percent correct. I hadn't looked up the flower because I doubted Sharon; I wanted to make a point, to show her that I knew she knew things. Not only did I want to reinforce Sharon's relearning process but I also wanted her to realize that she could still teach me, that it wasn't just a one-way street.

Meanwhile, Sharon's insurance had run out and she was on medical assistance. Under new medical assistance regulations, Sharon wasn't making fast enough progress for them to continue to support her in the hospital. She would have to be transferred to a nursing home. Only a month and a half after the hearing, I was faced with the fear of losing Sharon again. Her parents wanted to move her to a nursing home in Hibbing, three hours away. I was totally opposed to such a move. St. Cloud had some of the best handicapped services and programs in the country; Sharon, as an adult, had chosen St. Cloud as her home; and if she were moved, there was no way I could spend the hours working with

Sharon that I was spending now, thus reducing her rate of recovery.

I began talking with medical personnel to see if they would be willing to take a stand on Sharon's behalf. They were afraid to get involved, let alone 'take sides.' They were willing to admit that it was beneficial for loved ones to be involved in a patient's care and treatment. They would attest to my "eagerness and willingness to assist in Sharon's care and treatment and in fact . . . has assisted her in therapy sessions." They would also admit that they had "observed positive responses from Sharon in response to Karen." And some of the braver would say, "it could be very detrimental to Sharon's continued progress to be deprived of Karen's continued involvement."

Won't anyone get really involved on Sharon's behalf and defend what's best for *her?* I silently pleaded.

One evening I thought my prayers were answered. Dr. Keith Larson came up to me to tell me that he had made a decision. "I've been struggling with this situation and have decided that someone needs to speak out on Sharon's behalf. I want you to know that I do not want to be called as one of your witnesses but I will be there as a friend of the court." He didn't tell me what he was going to say but I sensed that he had Sharon's real interests at heart.

I didn't want Sharon in a nursing home. To me that implied a step down—that they had given up, that they believed she was never going to recover enough to leave. I thought of nursing homes as long-term. But, if it had to happen, I wanted to find the best. I visited all the nursing homes in the St. Cloud-Sartell-Sauk Rapids area. The personnel all wanted to know, "Who are you? Who are you to the patient?" I was always uncomfortable, on guard not to give away our relationship. Then, as I'd walk through the halls, some of the residents would grab at me, trying to get me to stop and talk with them. I wasn't the kind of person who could reach out to them. I just felt hopeless and lonely.

On my tour of Country Manor Nursing Home in Sartell, I became more hopeful. I was really impressed with the social worker and the way she related to the residents. The physical therapy facility seemed much better than the others I had seen. The ratio of staff to patients was more than the minimum that I'd seen elsewhere. The occupational and physical therapists were better qualified and seemed to genuinely care about their patients. I decided to recommend Country Manor to the court. The Kowalskis recommended Leisure Hills Nursing Home in Hibbing.

The matter came to court on June 26, 1984. On the way into the courtroom, I overheard the Kowalskis speaking to Dr. Larson. Don admonished the doctor that if he was there to recommend keeping Sharon in the St. Cloud area, it was the same as killing her. Without responding, the doctor went on into the judge's chambers where the attorneys were waiting for him.

The testimony took place in closed chambers without the Kowalskis or me present. Tom Hayes, Sharon's attorney, called Dr. Larson as a witness and he gave the following testimony:

❖   The reason I'm here today is as a friend of the court and to deliver an observation that I have agonized over, and thought a great deal about, and prayed a little bit, and I must say to the Court that you are being asked for an intensely Solomonly decision and it certainly is not my intent, by stating what I have observed, to imply that I feel that the love of other individuals is any less, but I cannot help but say that Sharon's friend, Karen, can get out of Sharon physical actions, attempts at vocalization, and longer periods of alertness and attention than can really any of our professional therapists.

    The reasons for this may be varied, and I don't think it is my place to speculate upon them, but I am here mostly to convey the impression that this friend also seems to function, from my point of view, as a medical doctor [and] an effective therapist for this patient.

    Therefore, I guess it would be my thought that if that contact can [in any way] be enhanced, or at least not removed entirely, I think it would be [to] this patient's benefit.

Despite several attempts by Kowalski's attorney, Keith Spellacy, to discredit or dilute the doctor's opinion, Dr. Larson remained firm. Beth Ristvedt, my attorney, finally asked, "So Karen is able—what you are telling the Court is, Karen is able to get responses that up to date no other person has been able to?"
He agreed, "On any sort of reliable basis."

Three days later, Judge Douglas concluded that "[t]he best interests of Sharon Kowalski will be served at the present time through her transfer from the St. Cloud Hospital to the Country Manor Health Care

Center." Once again, I felt an overwhelming sense of relief. Sharon would be able to stay in the St. Cloud area, close to her own home, and we would be able to continue working together toward recovery, toward the growth of our new relationship, and toward the day when Sharon could permanently return to our house near Briggs Lake.

CHAPTER 4

Move To A Nursing Home

Though times would be difficult, the fact that Sharon would definitely remain in the St. Cloud area meant we could settle down into a manageable routine. Maybe now, given time, I could forge a new relationship with Don and Della. We would just have to learn to work together—for Sharon's sake. But within two weeks, the Kowalskis were planning a new motion to have Sharon moved to Duluth for retesting.

Don and Della left town right after the hearing. Since the court had ordered Sharon's immediate transfer to Country Manor Nursing Home in Sartell, near St. Cloud, the St. Cloud Hospital planned to move her as soon as possible. I began talking to Sharon about the move. From reading and talking with various specialists in brain injury, I knew that changes could be very frightening to Sharon and might mean losses in her recovery process.

Of course, I was upset that Sharon would be going to a nursing home at all, but I wanted to help make the move as positive for her as possible. I explained that there would be more flexibility in her daily schedule and we would be able to do more activities together. I described the scenery and the wildlife. Ducks congregated at a pond on the property and a wheelchair path wove around the perimeter of the buildings. Still, Sharon seemed afraid.

Louise Muggli, a social worker, was charged with the responsibility for Sharon's release. I asked her how Sharon would be moved and if her parents were riding with her. If not, I said, I'd like to go with her. Louise didn't know. The Kowalskis had not come back to town. Finally, she was able to reach Don by phone. He informed her that since he was Sharon's guardian, the hospital could not release her without his signature. He then said that he would not be coming to sign the release. Given this circumstance, Louise had to make a number of phone calls and wait for authorization from the district court to allow the discharge to proceed. Since the Kowalskis clearly were making no arrangements for her move, I packed Sharon's personal belongings, took her posters off the walls, and stayed with her to reassure her.

In July of 1984, seven and a half months after the accident, Sharon took her first ride in a vehicle. I rode with her in the Transit Special Service bus to Country Manor. She gripped my hand tightly the entire way. Kathy Sims, the social worker, met us outside and showed us to Sharon's new room. She had a bed by the window looking out on the grounds.

Sharon loved ducks. When she worked at Sherburne National Wildlife Refuge, the waterfowl count was one of her favorite activities. As soon as we could, I wheeled Sharon outside to see the duck pond which was filled with ducklings. Her eyes lit up with pleasure. "Sharon, what is the mother duck called?"

She spelled out on the alphabet board, "Hen." Thus, our new life at Country Manor began with promise.

Day by day, my attitude toward nursing homes went through a radical change. The staff really seemed to care about the patients' well-being. I started to feel that God did have a plan for us. Initially Sharon was moved there because she wasn't making enough progress, and I had worried that she would not be receiving the intensive professional therapy sessions that were prescribed for her at the hospital. Instead, the relaxed atmosphere seemed conducive to Sharon's progress. She was much more alert and began to make major strides—or what seemed like major strides to us. The very first day she was given fluids. Sharon learned to drink through a straw. She was shown how to use the call light and pushed it successfully right away.

When I tried to participate in Sharon's care the first day, I was informed that Don had called in orders to cancel my rights to help with Sharon's care and treatment. He also indicated that he wanted to change doctors. Kathy had to check with Tom Hayes as to what kind of involvement I could have in Sharon's care. Although I never knew exactly what transpired, I was allowed to continue with my care and Dr. Larson remained involved.

Another major stride for Sharon was the improvement of her writing skills. One day we had stopped to talk with the head nurse in the hall and I asked Sharon, "Would you like to show her how well you can write now?" On a piece of paper, using a pencil, Sharon wrote her name and several other words.

When Kathy Sims heard from the head nurse about Sharon's accomplishment, she thought her parents would be excited to hear about it. She called Don and told him about Sharon's writing. Don's response was, "I suppose Karen showed you something Sharon supposedly wrote."

Kathy replied, "No, my head nurse observed it and told me."

Although I hardly knew Kathy, the conversation must have been on her mind because when she next talked to me she said, "I thought they would be excited. It was almost as if they didn't want to hear it."

I hadn't dared put it into words but a thought kept recurring: could it be that they don't *want* Sharon to recover or to communicate? Are they afraid they will have to deal with her as a gay person?

One day I walked into Sharon's room after the Kowalskis had been there. I noticed that Sharon looked disturbed. I asked her, "Is there something you want to talk about?" She responded "yes," there was. I asked her dozens of questions to find out what was on her mind. I obviously didn't ask her the right ones because she still indicated she wanted to talk and was very frustrated with me for not hitting on the subject. This went on for three days. In passing, I mentioned to Kathy that Sharon seemed to be upset about something and I couldn't figure out what it was.

Kathy responded, "Did you know that Sharon's mother and sister told her about Missy's death?"

I was astounded. "Why? What earthly reason did they have for doing that? And why now . . . and then they just left town?" Kathy nodded. "How is Sharon supposed to work through her feelings and grief without them here? She's just starting to make progress. Why risk setting her back?" (Earlier, when I had asked the doctor when to tell Sharon about the details of the accident or about Missy's death, he had replied, "When Sharon wants to know, she'll ask. Then answer her questions honestly.")

Kathy and I went to Sharon's room and I asked, "Sharon, have you been wanting to talk with me about Missy's death?"

Sharon got tears in her eyes and indicated "yes." We talked about the weekend Missy and Michael spent with us, the accident and Missy's death. Sharon was relieved that we were finally able to communicate about what had been bothering her for three days. She was so sad. Even though brain-injured patients are likely to have short-term memory problems, Sharon seemed to be able to remember some things. She had certainly held onto her feelings about Missy's death for three days.

Finally, we were cleared for our first day pass, our first opportunity to actually leave the grounds. I arrived early to bathe Sharon, dress her and feed her breakfast. This whole process took us over an hour. Then we signed out.

Two close friends of ours were visiting from Ohio, so it felt like a festive occasion. We borrowed my sister's van so we could wheel Sharon's chair into the back. We gave Sharon a choice whether she wanted to sit in her chair or be transferred to one of the seats. With no hesitation she indicated with her hand that she preferred the seat. The seat belt held her into the seat very well. I could tell Sharon felt uneasy but excited. I wondered how she would feel when we drove up to our house. Would she remember it?

As we approached the house, I could sense a change in Sharon. "Do you need a little time just to sit here before we go in?" I asked, aware that she seemed to be experiencing emotions she couldn't express. Her eyes filled with tears.

Not yet having a good communication system, I kept asking questions to see if I could help her put her feelings into words. If possible, I wanted to share this hard moment with her. "Are you okay?" I asked. "Are you glad to be here?"

She indicated "yes" to all, but by her expression I could tell there was something further she wanted to tell me.

Suddenly I knew what she was thinking. "You never thought you would see our house again. Is that it, Sharon?"

Immediately, she touched my hand with relief and gratitude. That was it!

When Sharon indicated she was ready, we went on into the house. This was not an easy process since I didn't yet have a ramp. As able-bodied people, we simply are not aware of all the barriers that exist for disabled people until 'easy' tasks become exceedingly difficult. At first Sharon just wanted to sit and look around the living room. Then she wanted to touch things. She indicated she was tired, so I asked her where she wanted to lie down. She had a definite preference—the waterbed.

By then I needed to change Sharon's diapers and wash her. Since this procedure was necessary many times during the day, I had done it often. This time was a little different, though, because I wanted to see if I could do it on my own—to see if it would be possible to take care of Sharon at home one day.

After I changed her, I put her through her passive range of motion exercises, as I always did every couple of hours. Ideally, she needed to be stretched that often, but nursing home personnel usually don't have that kind of time, so I had assigned myself the task.

She was all ready to rest for awhile. Yet, there was something else Sharon wanted. I wasn't sure what it was. She reached up, took my hand and pulled me towards her. "Do you want me to lie down next to you?" I asked.

Leaving no doubt, she hung on to me fiercely to show me she wanted me there. I lay down next to her and held her. That physical connection was the most wonderful thing that had happened to us since the accident—an intimacy that brought peace and certainty to our relationship. She snuggled against me, finally content. She slept soundly. And for the first time since the day Sharon had been taken to the hospital, I, too, slept soundly.

What a wonderful feeling to wake up together! It was like turning a new page in our old life. I just knew it wouldn't be long before we would be home to stay. I changed, washed and dressed her again. I almost broke my back trying to find the best way to get her up on the rail of the waterbed. From there we did our standard one person standing pivot transfer with the transfer belt, meaning I wrapped the belt around her and assisted her to a standing position. We congratulated ourselves on how good we were getting to be. Sharon's feet stayed flat on the floor because her tendons were stretched out enough and, therefore, she was able to bear weight with my help. We had had lots of practice the last few months. And the accomplishment of this maneuver meant I could help Sharon get around at home without assistance from a third person.

Back in the living room, we tried playing Pac-Man and other games on the Atari with our friends. I brought her a Mr. Freeze, Sharon's favorite popsicle. She held it herself and licked until she was tired of it. Already, it was time to go back. It had been a wonderful day that we didn't want to end. Even though we both were tired, the process of getting ready to leave was tackled with spirit.

I was concerned that Sharon would be extra tired on the day after our pass, but I was wrong. Kathy also noticed. "I expected Sharon to be tired and less responsive today. Instead, she seems much more alert and motivated." Later she said that Sharon's progress really began with her first day pass. The energy from that day renewed both of our spirits, pushing us to work even harder on Sharon's recovery.

A couple of days later was my birthday. My friends, after consulting with Sharon, brought me a cake. We invited Kathy to the party in the day room. We were chatting when we all noticed at the same time that Sharon was busy with the cake. She was dipping her finger into the frosting and making numerous trips to her mouth. We asked her if she approved of the cake and she grinned with a mouth full of frosting.

Our next pass was shortened at the last minute when we were informed that Sharon's parents would be visiting at 1:00 in the afternoon. Regardless, our friends accompanied us to the house again for an enjoyable morning.

Back well before the designated time, we stood around Sharon's chair talking while I was combing her hair. Suddenly, Don and Della rushed into the room and Della demanded loudly, "Get out! How dare you take her out when you knew we were coming!" Right in front of Sharon, with our friends watching, Della grabbed my arms and shoved me. She grabbed me two more times attempting to shove me against the wall. Don just stood by the door watching.

"Hey, the pass was approved and I had her back by the time I was supposed to," I said, shocked. I held my arms up to protect myself but made no effort to fight back. I couldn't believe they would make such a scene in front of everyone. A nurse, hearing the commotion, hurried into the room to ask all of us to come out into the hall. We all left the room, except the Kowalskis, who stayed and slammed the door shut. I worried about Sharon until my next visitation time that evening.

As I arrived, I met the Kowalskis with their new attorney, Jack Fena, leaving the room. Don had stopped using the previous attorneys on the personal injury suit case for reasons we were never told. (Spellacy, at this point, continued as their lawyer for the guardianship case.) This was my first encounter with Mr. Fena, who was now in charge of the personal injury suit. He patronizingly tried to reassure me, "I understand there was a minor confrontation earlier and I want to assure you that nothing like that will happen again."

"I hope not. I have already discussed this with my attorney." His whole demeanor changed from friendly to furious as he stalked away down the hall. Following him, Della shook her fist at me as she walked by.

My friends and I went into Sharon's room. Sharon appeared upset and bothered about something. One of them noticed that the ring Sharon had been wearing earlier that day was missing. It was the ring we had exchanged more than four years earlier. Our friends questioned Sharon about the ring until she made it clear that her mother had removed it. She clearly indicated that she wanted it back. She tried to keep the ringless hand out of my sight.

I reassured her as best I could. "I'll try to get it back for you, Sharon." I personally didn't think we would ever see it again. Later, Kathy questioned Sharon and, getting the same information, called the Kowalskis' attorney to request the return of the ring. Fena suggested, through Kathy, that I consent to having Sharon moved to Duluth for retesting in exchange for returning the ring. I told Kathy to forget it. I'd buy Sharon a new ring if that was the price.

Visitation times became another source of contention. Although the courts had required that notification be made if one party did not plan to use the assigned visitation time, the Kowalskis seldom complied. Therefore, I was required to leave the room even if they were not intending to visit during their scheduled time. The nursing home realized this was a problem and left a note in Sharon's room stating that if either party wasn't there after a half hour, the time would become open.

Sometimes even this short interruption would result in unnecessary disruption of Sharon's routine. For instance, if I was feeding her and she wasn't finished by the end of my visitation time, I would have to leave for a half hour while the nursing staff finished feeding her. Since Sharon didn't eat as well for anyone else and was upset when I had to leave abruptly, she ended up paying the price.

After Sharon had been at the nursing home about a month, Tom Hayes once again came to check up on her condition at Country Manor. Sharon, again, went through her regained skills, which were even more extensive than when he had visited at St. Cloud Hospital. She demonstrated a standing one person pivot transfer, finger dexterity skills, bilateral stretching, drinking, writing, word association, toothbrushing, hair combing, playing checkers, and more. He was extremely impressed.

After an hour or so, Tom needed to leave. I walked with him to the outside door. "You should be recommended for sainthood!" he exclaimed. "I can't believe you can continue working on all these things when you're under so much pressure from her parents and the continued legal battles." I was grateful to him for understanding, and felt reassured that he would continue to support what was best for Sharon.

As time went on, I took Sharon out on evening passes as well as on weekends. Once, we went to my sister Linda's house. Sharon looked at pictures of Linda's trip to Greece and laughed out loud at a joke. It had only been a couple of weeks since Sharon had begun to actually laugh. It was great to share laughter again. It doubled my belief that, though we had a different future ahead of us than we had expected months before, it still held wonderful possibilities for us.

Linda played a piece on the piano. "Sharon, what's the name of that song?"

Sharon wrote on a piece of paper, "You Light Up My Life."

Linda played another piece and asked the name again.

Sharon wrote something that was too squiggly to make out, so Linda asked her to write out the first letters of each word. Sharon wrote, "H S B." The piece was the theme from *Hill Street Blues*.

Each time Sharon was able to demonstrate complex cognitive functions, I was overjoyed. The impression I continued to get from the medical professionals was that Sharon would probably be incapable of such skills. I *knew* that Sharon's mental capacity was still unexplored, and she continued to surprise even me, the most stalwart supporter of her capabilities.

I wanted to make a videotape of Sharon so she would be able to see what she could do. I wasn't sure she was really aware of how much she had accomplished. My intent was to tape her again later for purposes of comparison. I also had a secondary motive. Sharon still demonstrated more skills for me than for anyone else. I hated to ask her continually to demonstrate them for others. Yet I wanted to be sure that medical personnel and her attorney knew what Sharon was capable of doing. Later, this tape was to provide invaluable documentation.

I asked her permission. "Is it okay for me to videotape one of our work sessions, Sharon?" She gave me one of her microscopic nods. We had been working on head movements.

So I hauled the equipment in from the car and videotaped her doing all the things we had shown Tom Hayes. Sharon was very cooperative and patient when I asked her to repeat the numerous types of activities she had learned over the last few months.

One hot day in August, Sharon and I were laughing together in the hall of Country Manor when a former colleague of Sharon's from Big Lake High School appeared, with her two children in tow. Sharon was very alert during their entire visit. She played with the children, shooting balls across her lap tray for them to catch. When they tired of that game, she turned on the television with the remote control and showed them how to change channels. (The occupational therapist had suggested that the visual and auditory effects of a television would stimulate Sharon's brain, and that color television stimulates more cells than black and white. So that same afternoon, I had gone out and bought Sharon a new TV with the money Don had given me for her 'rent.' I had also bought a remote control so Sharon would be able to choose her own stations or to turn the TV off and on when she wanted to.)

Sharon continued to improve. One Saturday, when we were spending time with two of our closest friends, Sharon wanted to play chess and impressed us all by knowing where the chess pieces were placed and how they moved. This was a good day for Sharon. She drank water and fed herself. She showed them her finger dexterity and stretching exercises.

After working together for months on vowel sounds like "ah" and "oo," Sharon had finally been willing to vocalize sounds in front of other people. Tonight was to be special. At one point, Sharon just looked at us and whispered quite clearly, "Turn me." I thought I was hearing things. I looked at the others for verification that I hadn't imagined what she had said. We all had heard the same thing. I hurried to turn her onto her other side.

"Are you comfortable now?" I asked, hoping she would talk some more.

Instead she just nodded in the affirmative. But later she again astounded everyone—I think even herself—by whispering, "I'm cold." I rushed to cover her with a blanket. I was so excited. She could talk! I had felt all along that Sharon could talk and just hadn't. Now I started to imagine endless conversations with her.

The next morning the four of us went to church together. Sharon had indicated she wanted to go to Newman Center, the church she had attended before her accident. Sharon listened intently to the guitar. When the priest instructed the congregation to pray, Sharon bowed her head and closed her eyes. I had to remind myself to include Sharon in every part of the service. During the responsive readings, I made sure that Sharon could see the pages. She impressed me by following the words across the page with her eyes. Her active participation in the service was such a significant experience for me . . . for us. And I had been very close to overlooking this possibility. Every day Sharon made me more aware of how I, as an able-bodied person, must provide opportunities for disabled people to participate in all aspects of life.

One of the activities Sharon and I shared, even while she was still unresponsive, was reading the Bible. I had begun reading to her, hoping she would hear and understand. Now, we regularly spent time reading and discussing Bible verses and praying together. Sharon indicated that she was angry with God. I felt inadequate to address whatever questions and feelings she was experiencing. I asked her, "Do you want to meet a really neat woman? She's the person who helped me work through my questions about being Christian and gay. She's such a loving, caring person, I think you'd enjoy meeting her, Sharon. And I think she could help you work through some of your feelings."

Sharon seemed fascinated. She wanted to meet this woman.

A few days later, Peg arrived at Sharon's room. I introduced her to Sharon and the three of us talked for about fifteen minutes until Sharon appeared comfortable with Peg. Then I left to give them a chance to talk alone.

Reverend Peg Chemberlin later testified in court regarding her impression of Sharon's ability to understand and communicate. During that first meeting, she had asked Sharon to indicate what she wanted to do. "Do you want me to leave and let you go to sleep? Do you want to ask more questions? Do you want me to read some more biblical passages? Do you want to pray?" Sharon indicated by a finger movement that she wanted to pray together.

Peg testified that she went through a list of things to pray for, "including [Sharon's] improvement, her understanding of why these things happen, for her family, and for Karen. Sharon's responses were immediate and clear." It was Peg's impression that Sharon comprehended what she was discussing and that she knew what she was responding to. Sharon indicated to her that the discussion was helpful and that she would like Peg to return.

Throughout Sharon's entire stay at Country Manor, I was constantly plagued by the fear that Sharon would be moved to Duluth, as requested by her parents. They had actually filed the motion to move her on August 16 and the hearing was scheduled for September 13. Jack Fena now seemed to be working with Spellacy, the attorney that the Kowalskis originally hired for the guardianship case, even though an official affidavit associating him wasn't filed until later. Eventually Spellacy withdrew from the case, leaving Fena as the Kowalskis' sole attorney on both the personal injury suit and the guardianship case.

One of the requests made by the Kowalskis, preceding the hearing, was that Judge Bruce Douglas be removed for prejudice and bias against Donald Kowalski. They moved that Sharon be re-evaluated at Polinsky Memorial Rehabilitation Center at the Miller-Dwan Hospital in Duluth. This would effectively remove her from St. Cloud and make it harder for me to visit—two goals of the Kowalskis.

Tom Hayes contended that the motion to remove the judge was untimely. He asked for Sharon's re-evaluation to be conducted at Country Manor by Sister Kenny Institute from Minneapolis, based on his observation that Sharon had made progress since her admission to Country Manor. In addition, he asked to be reimbursed for services rendered on Sharon's behalf. Hayes' motion stated, "Donald Kowalski has asserted an unfounded position solely to delay the ordinary course of the proceedings or to harass and otherwise acted in bad faith by informing the undersigned [Tom Hayes] of his intentions to contest payment of fees . . . ."

In response to the Kowalskis' motion to move Sharon to Duluth, my attorneys filed a countermotion to remove Donald Kowalski as guardian on the basis that he had consistently failed to abide by the orders of the court and to act in Sharon's best interests. This was demonstrated by his refusal to sign the discharge papers from St. Cloud Hospital, his efforts to block day passes and to block my participation in Sharon's care and treatment.

In addition, we contended that Kowalski's actions had jeopardized Sharon's continued residence at Country Manor. We made it clear that I had no objection to a proper evaluation of Sharon, provided it did not interfere with her continued day-to-day progress. If a re-evaluation was warranted, we supported Tom Hayes' recommendation of Sister Kenny Institute.

I felt that since Sharon was making progress, it could be risky to move her. I agreed with Hayes' contention that Sharon should be evaluated within the environment of Country Manor since it seemed to be beneficial to Sharon. He suggested that Sister Kenny Institute provide an on-site evaluation prior to any inpatient evaluation.

COURT HEARING ON ARRANGING
AN EVALUATION FOR SHARON

The dreaded day arrived and I found myself in court once again. The judge declined to remove himself from the proceedings. Donald Kowalski was the first witness. He testified that Sister Kenny would be extremely costly and inconvenient for them. (In truth, if the court had decided and ordered the testing of Sharon, Medical Assistance would have had to pay for it.)

Although Don testified that Sharon could use an alphabet board, when asked by Beth Ristvedt, my attorney, "Do you accept the fact that Sharon has made progress?" he replied, "Some—very little."

Beth asked Don about day passes. "When the question of day passes came up . . . did you have any objection to Sharon going out on a day pass?"

Kowalski answered, "Yes."

"Were you informed by Kathy Sims of the nursing home that day passes had been checked out with Sharon's doctors and with the nursing home staff and they felt that it was appropriate?"

"Yes."

"Even after you had that information, you still objected to the day passes?"

"Yes."

"You know that Karen has been taking Sharon out on day passes for the last couple months, don't you?"

"Yes, I do."

"Is there any reason that you haven't done so?"

"Well, in our opinion we didn't feel that Sharon was that good to be handled like that and for us to drive that far, where would we go with Sharon?"

"Did it ever occur to you to take Sharon to the local shopping center?"

"Yes, it did."

"Was the reason that you didn't want to take her then . . . that you didn't feel you could handle taking Sharon out?"

"No, it isn't that. I didn't feel that way. I didn't feel that we wanted to put Sharon on display in a shopping center in her condition."

"Did it occur to you to take Sharon to a church service?"

"No, that would be putting her back on display again amongst the public."

"So is it your opinion that you would not want her anywhere out in public?"

"No, I wouldn't," he stated adamantly.

"Have you discussed day passes with Kathy Sims regarding the progress and Sharon's attitude toward day passes?"

"Just at the beginning, a little bit," he said. ". . . she told me that she thought Sharon responded better in some way or in that way, I guess, to be going out. I don't know just now how to explain it."

"You were informed by Kathy that Sharon was getting a positive benefit from the day passes?"

"That is the way I took it from Kathy."

"Did you believe what Kathy was telling you?"

"I don't know. I never seen Sharon so I had to take her word, yes."

"In any event you haven't made any effort to take Sharon out?"

"No, I haven't."

"If Sharon is in Duluth, do you think that is going to change your willingness to take her out?"

"When she is fit and we think she should be taken out."

Beth later questioned Donald about Sharon's response to me. "Mr. Kowalski, are you aware that Sharon's doctors and other medical personnel have stated that Sharon gives more consistent responses and a greater degree of response to Karen than to other persons?"

"Yes."

Beth went on to explore Don's refusal to sign Sharon's release from the hospital and the problems with visitation.

When Beth finished her cross-examination of Donald Kowalski, Fena continued presenting evidence in support of their motion to move Sharon to Duluth, closer to her parents' home. Fena submitted a letter from Dr. William Wilson from Hibbing to show the advantage of such a move to the family.

 Dear Mr. Fena:

I am writing you concerning a patient of mine, Della Kowalski, who I am seeing for depression and anxiety.

For the past several months, she has been experiencing symptoms of moderately severe depression, including sleeplessness, weight loss, lack of energy and chronic anxiety. Her response to medications and counseling has been less than adequate.

The onset of her symptoms coincides with her daughter's placement in a nursing home in St. Cloud and her inability to spend much time with her daughter. I am very concerned about Mrs. Kowalski's mental and physical health and I do feel that the lack of ability to visit her daughter frequently because of the distance involved is directly contributing to her medical problems.

I understand that consideration has been given to moving her daughter to either Polinsky Institute in Duluth or the Sister Kenny Institute in the Twin Cities. I feel that both of these institutes are very acceptable in terms of long-term care for her daughter, but I feel that moving her to Duluth would definitely benefit Mrs. Kowalski and would certainly benefit her daughter. I do not anticipate an improvement in Mrs. Kowalski's condition until the above matter is resolved.

Witnesses in support of Hayes' motions on Sharon's behalf and my motions focused their reports on what was best for Sharon. When Kathy Sims, the Country Manor social worker, took the stand, Beth asked, "[H]ave you made any observations regarding the level of responses and the consistency of responses between Sharon and Karen versus Sharon and other persons?"

"Yes," Kathy answered.

"And can you tell the Court what observations those are?"

". . . I have observed times when she has been unresponsive with myself and with numerous other persons. I have not, to my recollection, been a witness to a time when she has not been responsive to Karen."

"Have you also observed instances when Sharon would be present with her parents and her parents were unable to elicit a response?"

"Yes, I have."

"Have you observed anything in Karen's manner and her dealings with Sharon that you would not consider to be a benefit to your patient?"

"I have seen nothing."

In regard to Sharon's wishes, Kathy Sims testified that "she has consistently responded to wanting to remain in the St. Cloud area."

Beth pursued this. "Has Sharon appeared to understand what is going on or what she is discussing with you?"

"Yes."

Further evidence by Sims, in affidavit form, affirmed Sharon's social and psychological progress. "Following a day's pass, Sharon would respond that she had a good time and wanted to go again." Sims observed that Sharon could write "one to three word clusters, would say 'hi,' play checkers, could respond consistently if Sharon wanted to and could move her right hand. For example, an 'okay' sign, the 'I love you' sign, the 'thumbs up' sign. Sharon could voluntarily wave goodbye, wipe her mouth, smile and interact with people . . . . [O]n one occasion when Karen Thompson was present, I heard Karen ask Sharon what was on her mind, Sharon wrote the words 'I love you.' I observed this and recognized the words clearly."

Sims' testimony was followed by that of Stephen McCaffrey, the physical therapist, whose observations corroborated Sharon's responsiveness to me. "I would say she responds more consistently when Karen Thompson is present in the PT sessions . . . . She does consistently better. She responds quicker . . . . There are times when I've worked with her when she has not responded at all and she consistently responded when Karen is there."

On another topic, Beth inquired, "And for the most part, do you believe her communication is to be reliable?"

"Yes, I do."

He further verified Sharon's desire to remain in the St. Cloud area. "Sharon responded in front of me that she would rather remain in St. Cloud rather than go to Duluth. She did this by being asked a question in the alternative. Such as . . . 'If you want to go to Duluth, put out your little finger.' She indicated St. Cloud. Sharon was also asked to point on a piece of paper to either the word 'Duluth' or the word 'St. Cloud,' when asked where she would like to be. She pointed to 'St. Cloud.' It is my opinion that Sharon understood what she was being asked and made a conscious choice between the two."

McCaffrey submitted another important observation about Sharon's improvement. He testified that she "had improved head control . . . more consistency of responses . . . greater tolerance of therapy sessions. I observed Sharon to independently wipe off her mouth on repeated occasions."

Vicki Lundeen, the other physical therapist at Country Manor, confirmed McCaffrey's observations and added, "I found carry-over from one session to the next and even carry-over over the weekend. I could ask Sharon to put her weight down on her open right palm and Sharon would do so. Sharon was able to sit unsupported one time on the mat . . . . She also independently shifted her weight to the right . . . ."

Each witness from the staff of Country Manor who spent hours with Sharon on a daily and weekly basis verified Sharon's improvement while she was there. The occupational therapist, Joan Thralow, testified that Sharon "was able to remain alert for 30- to 45-minute sessions and generally actively participated in therapy sessions, performed fine motor tasks with her right hand, such as matching pictures, word cards, wiping her mouth independently and scratching her head."

Thralow had tested Sharon's reading comprehension and found that "Sharon was reading a paragraph consisting of five sentences and 42 words and taking a comprehension test consisting of five multiple choice questions the last time she was tested and had 100 percent accuracy. Sharon was able to add and subtract one digit numbers—i.e., 7+2, 9-5, writing down the answers."

Dr. Keith Larson, the neurologist in charge of the case and also the head of the Rehabilitation Center at the St. Cloud Hospital, submitted the following medical testimony: "She has [made] extremely slow progress and has not retrogressed at any phase." In a later report, he stated, "It is clear the patient is making some strides . . . . At this juncture it is my judgment that she has not improved to the level of reliability as of yet to consider more intensive rehabilitation, but the present, rather moderate rehabilitation effort in physical therapy and occupational therapy with the documented gains would appear to be appropriate and adequate."

Even though Dr. Larson's testimony was somewhat weaker, the rest of our professional witnesses testified clearly to Sharon's improvement. That, coupled with Hayes' strong recommendation for Sister Kenny Institute, made me almost certain that Sharon would be able to remain at Country Manor and would not have to risk a setback as a result of a move. Even though I hadn't wanted Sharon to be in a nursing home, it was clear that, for whatever reasons, she began making significiant progress there. I felt that was where we were meant to be for the present.

But the hearing took a turn toward the end which was to provide a slim rationale for the decision of the court. First of all, Spellacy and Fena had submitted medical testimony from Dr. Terence Pladson, a doctor in Internal Medicine specializing in diseases of the chest, who treated Sharon when she had pneumonia in the hospital. According to the testimony, Dr. Pladson visited Sharon on one occasion, at Country Manor on September 9, 1984. Based on this visit and with no indication of reviewing any of the nursing, physical therapy or occupational therapy notes, he gave his 'expert' opinion. "It is my overall impression that Sharon has shown little progress since discharge from the hospital in spite of daily physical therapy . . . . [S]ince the present method is not apparently successful, I feel a trial of therapy at a rehabilitation center might be in order . . . ." This opinion was in direct contrast to those of Dr. Larson and *all* of the other medical professionals at Country Manor.

I was confused by the Kowalskis' case. In order to move Sharon from a nursing home to an inpatient rehabilitation center like the one in Duluth, they would want to demonstrate that she'd made enough improvement to warrant a rehabilitation center. Yet they were arguing that Sharon should be moved for evaluation *because* she "wasn't making progress." In addition, I questioned the validity of testimony which concerned rehabilitation but came from an internal medicine specialist, especially when it conflicted with testimony from therapists who worked with Sharon every day and with the rehabilitation specialist as well.

As I was pondering this, Tom Hayes appeared to change his mind about his own motion. All of a sudden he appeared to be siding with Fena. Hayes wavered, "I recommended, Your Honor, Sister Kenny Institute, but I think there are some factors that the Court has to keep in mind . . . . Number one, Mr. Fena indicated that there is a bed available tomorrow . . . . I cannot indicate to the Court speed with the same degree of swiftness that Mr. Fena can . . . . Mr. Fena . . . indicated to me many times, somewhat of a strategy in terms of civil litigation. There is no question the civil litigation is important to the issue here today because that is where we will be looking at for paying for some of these services."

"Mr. Fena," Hayes continued, "indicated that he wished to use Dr. Pollard and Mr. Kowalski testified that Sharon indicated that she wished to go back to see Dr. Pollard . . . . I think it is important that Dr. Pollard be involved in this . . . . [M]y checking indicates that he has been a courtroom doctor who is a very formidable witness."

The civil litigation referred to by Hayes was a personal injury suit against the drunk driver and against the establishment that served him to the point of inebriation, which was liable under the Dram Shop Law in Minnesota. It was likely that the personal injury suit would result in a substantial monetary settlement. Fena had used Pollard in other cases.

Sharon indeed had seen Dr. Pollard for a previous injury. However, Dr. Pollard was a neurosurgeon, not a neurologist, as Hayes himself pointed out. Sharon did not need a neurosurgeon at this point but a neurologist to be in charge of her rehabilitation program. Ironically, although the case was made for moving Sharon to Duluth in order to involve Dr. Pollard, he never became involved in Sharon's treatment in any way whatsoever after her move.

So the major arguments by the Kowalskis and Fena were: Della's mental condition, Pladson's absurd report of no improvement, the immediate availability of a bed in Duluth and the importance of involving Pollard. Hayes' equivocation at the end of the hearing served their case against his own motion. It was also interesting that after Hayes changed his position, Fena asked the court to authorize payment of the fees to Hayes which the Kowalskis had contested.

Although I was confused by Hayes' about-face, it was my impression that the preponderance of his evidence and testimony supported Sharon's improvement at Country Manor and focused on what *her* needs were as opposed to her mother's needs or the pending civil litigation. In addition, after the hearing was formally brought to a conclusion, Judge Douglas, and anyone who wanted to stay, viewed two videotapes—the one I had made and one submitted by the Kowalskis showing Sharon generally unresponsive. I thought my videotape documenting Sharon's improvement would be a deciding factor if one was needed.

Therefore, I was stunned when the court order was issued the very next morning, September 14, 1984.

❖   Sharon Kowalski shall be immediately transferred to the Nat G. Polinsky Memorial Rehabilitation Center . . . Duluth, Minnesota for evaluation to see whether it is appropriate that she enter a course of inpatient rehabilitation, and if so, to evaluate where said rehabilitation should occur . . . .

All previous orders of the Court in this matter remain in effect . . . including visitation provisions . . . .

CHAPTER 5

Separation

I was visiting Sharon the Friday morning the court order came out. The Director of Nursing at Country Manor came in to tell me. "I'm really sorry, Karen, but the court has ordered that Sharon be moved to Duluth for an evaluation. Her parents will be coming to get her within the hour."

I was utterly devastated. It took every ounce of concentration and control I'd ever learned not to cry in front of Sharon. Since I had to be at class in half an hour, I hurriedly tried to explain to Sharon what would be happening. "Sharon, your parents will be coming very soon to move you to Duluth for an evaluation. I have to go to classes now, but I will drive to Duluth as soon as I'm done, to see that you're settled."

In the middle of our discussion, Sharon's parents arrived with Fena. They started packing Sharon's things and removing pictures from the walls. I was sitting close to her by the edge of the bed. I continued to reassure Sharon, "Just because you're going to Duluth doesn't mean we're going to be separated. I'll come and see you there. If necessary, I'll take some time off to be with you." We touched hands with the "I love you" sign and I left the room.

In the hallway, I couldn't hold back the tears. Jack Fena had followed me out into the hall. "Don't come to Duluth. It will be better for Sharon if you don't come. Give her a few days to get settled in."

"I don't want to talk to you. Leave me alone." It was an emotional time for me and I wanted to have a few minutes to myself. I couldn't believe he had followed me out into a public hallway to give me orders. But he continued to talk to me, even though my attorneys had told him earlier to leave me alone. I'd been told that it wasn't ethical for him to give me 'advice' when I'm represented by my own attorneys.

Completely frustrated, I said, "I'll do everything I can to get you off this case." I was remembering how he had asked my attorney to lie about Sharon's place of residence so they could stack insurance policies and get an extra $100,000. "I don't think you're the type of person Sharon would want representing her. By fighting dirty you might wind up hurting Sharon's case."

He retorted that I was the one hurting Sharon's case by insisting that Sharon had lived with me. He continued to insist that I should let Sharon be evaluated "in peace," and told me, over and over again, in spite of my protests, not to come to Duluth.

Fena's behavior was making me really angry. "You don't really care about Sharon. All you care about is your $200,000 out of the injury suit. You don't deserve a cent. You're not interested in the money for Sharon— she'll get the same care regardless of how it's paid for. By the time your share and all the expenses are taken out, there won't be any money for Sharon anyway." I was shaken and turned to go. "Just leave me alone. I'm going to be late for class."

I struggled through my classes with my emotions on a see-saw, then rushed home to pack my suitcase for the weekend. I drove to Duluth sobbing the whole way. I knew it wasn't the best way to drive, but I couldn't hold it in any longer.

The Kowalskis were gone by the time I arrived so I was able to see Sharon immediately. Friday was my regular visitation day—all day—as assigned by the court. I took all my papers with me to make sure I would have no problem with visitation. Fortunately, everyone was courteous and provided me with information.

Right away, I noticed that Sharon was not in the proper kind of wheelchair, nor was she properly positioned. The back was not high enough, the leg supports were separate and Sharon's feet could not rest flat on them. As a result of Sharon's spastic movements, her feet would get in between the supports and bang up against them. At St. Cloud she had a padded foot board, with a back, to prevent accidental foot and leg injuries. Proper foot placement allowed Sharon to bear weight on her feet which helped to minimize her spastic movements.

The Kowalskis had not taken her lap board from Country Manor, Kathy Sims told me later. It provided a resting place for her elbows and enabled Sharon to sit properly in the wheelchair. Without the lap board, her arms hung down, which caused a separation at the shoulder. The sock that Sharon usually wore on her right foot to keep the skin from rubbing against her other foot and the padded railing for the bed were missing too.

These seemingly small details were actually of extreme importance to Sharon's comfort and well-being. I couldn't stand Sharon suffering any more pain than she had to, and that first weekend I saw too many problems. Sharon had already been charged at Country Manor for an eggshell mattress which helps to prevent bedsores and should have been brought with her. It was not there. The splint for positioning Sharon's left arm and hand was nowhere to be found. And many of Sharon's personal belongings were missing—the Bible I had given her, pictures of our home, and the balls we exercised with were conspicuous in their absence.

I spent most of that weekend with Sharon, trying to reassure her and to help her adjust to her new environment. Regardless of my efforts, Sharon appeared scared and withdrawn throughout that weekend and most of the five weeks she was at Miller-Dwan. Sharon's whole level of alertness changed. At St. Cloud she'd been alert most of the time she was awake. Now there were very few periods of alertness.

When she would respond, she indicated in front of nurses, therapists and friends that she was upset at being in Duluth and wanted to return to St. Cloud. In fact, she held *me* responsible for her being moved to Duluth. Sharon had informed me many times that she wanted to stay in St. Cloud, and I had not been able to accomplish that. Now she seemed fearful that I would leave her and never come back.

The next week, I drove to Duluth every evening after class. I would start from St. Cloud at 2:30 in the afternoon and arrive at the hospital by 5:30, spend the evening with Sharon and leave around 9:30 or 10:00 to get home at about 1:00 a.m. Because I was unable to get there before the day staff left, no one could give me information regarding the testing process or how Sharon was doing. That Friday, a week after Sharon's move, I arranged to be there for the whole day so I could talk with the therapists and check on Sharon's progress.

I was able to speak to and attend sessions with the physical, occupational and speech therapists. They all seemed to appreciate information regarding Sharon's previous therapy and were surprised that no therapy notes had accompanied Sharon from Country Manor. They said they usually reviewed all notes before testing. I was astonished. "You mean you haven't seen any reports on Sharon from Country Manor? I'll check on where they are and why they've been delayed."

When I got back to St. Cloud, I called Kathy Sims at Country Manor and discovered that the reports were never requested. When she had tried to send them with Sharon's parents, she was told that nothing was wanted from Country Manor. I decided to pick them up from Kathy and deliver them myself.

However, something happened between Friday, when I had spoken with the therapists, and the next Wednesday, when I brought the reports to them. The same therapists who had welcomed me to Sharon's therapy sessions now discouraged me from coming. They reluctantly took the reports and no longer expressed interest in their contents. Further— and this caused me some concern—they told me that Sharon was making little or no progress. They felt that progress couldn't be expected on a day-to-day basis, but that maybe on a month-to-month basis we would see something.

I didn't really know anyone in Duluth that I would be able to stay with for any length of time, and I knew I could not afford to pay for motels on a regular basis—especially since the cost of gasoline for my car was likely to be astronomical. So I established a pattern. When I visited during the week, I would drive home the same evening. On Thursdays, I would drive up, visit Sharon as long as I could, and find a place to park my car where I thought it would be safe to sleep. I had a station wagon so I put my sleeping bag in the back. Because I was afraid for my safety or that it might be illegal to spend nights in a car, I parked in a different place each time.

Friday mornings I would put my toothbrush and washcloth in my pocket and would wash in the restroom of a local fast-food restaurant before I went to the hospital. Friday nights I rented a cheap hotel room for $6.00 a night so I could take a shower. Saturday nights I stayed in my car again.

After three weeks, one of the nurse's aides at the hospital, possibly noticing I looked a little crumpled on occasion, asked, "Where are you staying when you spend the night in Duluth?"

I asked her if she really wanted to know, because I felt a little sheepish about sleeping in the car. But when she said, "Sure," I described my routine to her. That same day she arranged for me to meet with a friend who could put me up. I was nervous. I wasn't used to coming out to strangers, but she would need to know my situation. When I told her that I loved Sharon, that we were in a relationship, and that I didn't want it to create problems for her, she assured me that it was no problem. I was grateful and relieved. No more sleeping in the car. An actual room to come home to on weekends!

A few weeks after Sharon's arrival, a psychiatrist with a part-time practice, George Cowan, visited her to make an evaluation. He was not on the staff of Miller-Dwan Hospital's Polinsky Institute and was not asked by their staff to make the evaluation. Indeed, he had no special training in evaluating multiply handicapped patients. Jack Fena, who had worked with Cowan before on personal injury suits, specifically requested this visit. Cowan wrote the following letter to Fena regarding his evaluation:

 Dear Mr. Fena:

Please be advised that at your request I interviewed Sharon Kowalski at Miller-Dwan Hospital on October 4, 1984. Prior to my examination, I reviewed the chart.

Sharon was lying quietly in bed, appearing to be completely helpless. When I came into her room, the nurse was putting on her night clothes.

I attempted to interview Sharon but she was unable to speak. I was informed that she could answer questions by blinking once for a yes answer and two for a no answer. I proceeded therefore to determine if she was well-oriented, etc. but when she did respond her answers were inconsistent. At one time she would blink once and when the same question was repeated she would blink twice.

Apparently Ms. Kowalski will require a fairly prolonged period of nursing home care along with some intensive physiotherapy and possibly psychotherapy if her condition improves to the point where she is amenable to such therapy. However at this point and in the immediate future she will require a great deal of tender loving care and parental love which is unconditional.
Sincerely,
George M. Cowan, M.D.

Although Cowan later testified that a nurse told him Sharon used the eyeblink method of communication, there was no documentation that she had ever used it. No therapists had ever used this method of communicating with her. In my observations, Sharon was not able to control her blinking.

It was also my experience that Sharon was less likely to be alert after she had been up for a period of time and was being prepared for bed. Yet on the basis of this one very brief visit, utilizing an unreliable method of communication, Cowan concluded that Sharon would "require a fairly prolonged period of nursing home care." This letter seemed to significantly influence the outcome of the next hearing.

And though I disagreed with Cowan's evaluation about the length of nursing home care, it was clear that Sharon was not functioning at the level she had attained in St. Cloud. Thus, I thought that if any weight were put on Cowan's 'medical evidence,' it would only support my contention that she was not in an environment conducive to her well-being. In fact, I was beginning to believe that Sharon's lack of alertness might be caused by depression.

Three other visitors to Miller-Dwan documented Sharon's regression. My sister, Linda, noted in her deposition:

❖   I visited Sharon in Duluth on Monday, October 15, and was shocked at her appearance. Her sitting posture and head control was very poor and much worse than it had been at Country Manor when I visited her there. Sharon appeared resigned and like she had no hope. Her whole attitude and demeanor was totally different than at Country Manor and at my home. She never moved her head, her eyes did not seem to focus, she had no facial expressions, and made either no response or inconsistent responses to questions. Sharon's right hand and arm movement were very limited when compared to what it was while in St. Cloud.

Another friend, Linda Weisbrich, expressed similar concerns about Sharon. She added in her affidavit that, "The husband of the other patient in Sharon's room commented to me that Sharon seems to respond more to Karen than anyone else he'd seen her with, and that Sharon is more willing to do things with Karen than others. As Sharon lifted her head to look at Karen, he looked shocked and stated that he had never seen her do that before." When asked later to sign an affidavit regarding these observations, the husband refused because he didn't want to get involved.

I was to find that many important witnesses chose that same stance themselves or were 'advised' not to voluntarily testify by attorneys protecting the various institutions involved. However, when informed that they might be subpoenaed, the witnesses were allowed to submit very cautious affidavits that had gone through reviews and changes under the advice of the institutions' attorneys. In retrospect, I realize that affidavits do not carry the same weight as actual court testimony. Courtroom questioning can elicit additional, and more detailed, information, and preserve that information in court documents. For instance, certain observations supportive of my contentions could simply be eliminated from the affidavits. In court testimony these same supportive observations could be highlighted. My attorney, Beth Ristvedt, however, had advised me that the court would rather be presented with affidavits than court testimony. Knowing what I know now, I would argue for court appearances.

So, watered-down affidavits were finally obtained from several nurses at Miller-Dwan. Even then, all five said that they had observed me with Sharon and were impressed with how well we worked together. They had all observed a special relationship and rapport between Sharon and me. One went on to say that "soon after Sharon's transfer to Miller-Dwan Hospital I observed how good Karen was with Sharon and I felt it important that the head nurse and her doctor know this. Unsolicited and without having discussed this with Karen Thompson or anyone else I informed both of these persons of my observations."

Several of the nurses stated that Sharon responded that she was depressed about being in Duluth and wanted to return to St. Cloud. They also observed that she was afraid that I would not come back and observed her indicating that she was mad that I was not there as much as I used to be. They observed that Sharon responded more to me than she did to other persons, including other nurses, family or friends.

During times when I did find Sharon alert, I continued, as I had all along, to establish what she was feeling and what her wishes were. I began to express my concern to her that we would need to have support from more people or groups who might be able to act on her behalf. On several occasions, I discussed with her the pros and cons of coming out. I checked with her in different ways to make sure her responses were consistent. "Sharon, in order for a group to understand the whole story and why it is so important for you to live in the St. Cloud area close to me and our home, we may need to explain our relationship. How would you feel about that?"

Sharon consistently indicated agreement.

"Do you understand, Sharon, that if I do come out, I'm probably bringing you out with me?" I asked.

She laughed and nodded her head, "Yes."

Weeks later I would tease her, "Can you imagine me being the one to come out? Aren't I just the most likely person you can imagine to stand up for gay rights?"

She snickered and typed, "Least likely."

❖

No arrangements had been made by the court as to what would happen with Sharon following the testing by the Polinsky Institute at Miller-Dwan, which was only supposed to take a week to ten days. Sharon, therefore, had to remain at Miller-Dwan Hospital until motions could be filed, a court date determined, and a judge's decision made as to where Sharon should be 'placed,' based on the testing. My attorneys' motion asked that Sharon be returned to Country Manor Nursing Home where she had been making progress or to the St. Cloud Hospital Rehabilitation Unit, depending on the results of the evaluation. The Kowalskis opposed this motion.

In the meantime, Sharon was scheduled for a daily routine of intensive rehabilitation therapy sessions. I attended the few sessions which took place on Fridays when I could be present during the day. It was very difficult to get Sharon to demonstrate the skills she had relearned in St. Cloud.

The contrast with St. Cloud was very frustrating. There I had been able to attend daily therapy sessions or receive information about Sharon's day which had served as the basis for our evening conversations and recreation. I would try to find a creative way to reinforce the skills she had worked on during the day while making them fun. Now it was not unusual that I would arrive and spend the evening watching her sleep.

When I was able to be in Duluth, I was still involved with Sharon's daily care: washing, dressing, getting her up, repositioning her, and so on. I no longer fed Sharon because the medical personnel had determined that she couldn't swallow and therefore had put her exclusively on tube feedings. A tube was surgically inserted into Sharon's stomach, replacing the naso-gastrointestinal tube she had been using since the accident. This meant that Sharon was deprived of the stimulation of taste and thus one more chance to activate brain cells. For almost four months before she was transferred to Duluth, she had been able to eat some of each meal, which was then supplemented by tube feedings.

About a week before the next hearing, I received the Miller-Dwan/Polinsky Institute evaluation results. I didn't think they were surprising, but I also didn't think they were an accurate reflection of Sharon's capabilities. I'd thought all along that Sharon might not do as well if she were moved. The evaluation clearly indicated that she was not performing at the same level that she had been previously. As with Cowan's statement, I thought the report would support returning Sharon to St. Cloud. But the hearing would interpret the evaluations in a completely different way.

Shortly before the hearing, we were handed a depressing piece of news. My attorney Beth Ristvedt was informed by the attorney from Country Manor Nursing Home that they were unwilling to take Sharon back under the present conditions. If either I or a third party were appointed sole guardian with the ability to make decisions *alone*, then Country Manor would consider taking Sharon back.

This decision—that Sharon couldn't go back to Country Manor as long as Donald Kowalski was the guardian—took away the possibility of recommending to the court that she be returned there, to an environment where she had clearly been happy and had made progress. Now I would once again have to investigate other nursing homes in the St. Cloud area. And I wouldn't even be able to say that the new recommendation was the best since I really felt that Country Manor was the best in the area. I half-heartedly made the rounds of nursing homes. Of the institutions that had openings, I felt Good Shepherd Lutheran Home was the best choice.

I also visited with Kathy Wingen, Director of Handicap Services in St. Cloud, to investigate the types of services and programs available to Sharon and to discuss how she and I could progress to a home-living situation using whatever programs were available. She informed me that St. Cloud was one of the top 25 cities in the country known for its handicapped services. We discussed the benefits of returning the disabled person to his or her home. She confirmed my earlier information that disabled people show increased motivation and more rapid and greater levels of improvement in familiar living situations. She seemed to believe, from what I'd told her, that Sharon could be cared for at home.

Kathy explained to me that the testing results from Miller-Dwan were invalid, regardless of their findings, since they had violated Sharon's rights under Section 504 of the Rehabilitation Act of 1973. Under Section 504, a disabled person is guaranteed the right to have a personal advocate present during testing so they have the best possible chance to do well on the test.

When I discussed with Beth the possibility of bringing Sharon home versus placing her in another institution, she discouraged me from pursuing that course for the time being. She felt we had a better chance to get her back into an institution in St. Cloud, especially since one of the recommendations of the test results was to place Sharon in a nursing home.

The Polinsky Institute was charged with the task of evaluating whether or not Sharon was ready to be in a rehabilitation center, but they went a step further. Steven Goff, the doctor in charge of the case, wrote:

❖ In summary, we feel that Sharon is incapable of handling her own affairs and making decisions at this time. She is severely to profoundly affected in her cognitive and motor functions. For the immediate future, estimated to be over the next three to nine months, I feel the best facility available to handle Sharon's needs would be a nursing care facility with a special head injury unit.

Such a unit is available in the Young Adult Rehabilitation section at Park Point Manor, Duluth, which would fill Sharon's needs.

Based on this recommendation, I decided to visit Park Point. I knew immediately that Sharon would not be happy there. There was a lot of loud, aggressive and sometimes violent behavior in the young adult ward. Since Sharon became scared and startled easily, this behavior could only be detrimental to her well-being. Also, the ward was predominantly male, and most of the patients were ambulatory and wandered in and out of each others' rooms, which would further her discomfort. I filed an affidavit to provide this information to the court.

HEARING TO DETERMINE SHARON'S
PLACEMENT IN A NURSING HOME

The hearing took place on October 18, 1984. Most of the evidence was submitted in medical report or affidavit form with final arguments. Among the findings of fact (that is, what the court determines to be the factual and relevant information for the case, given the testimony it hears) were

❖ the conclusions of Dr. S. K. Goff . . . that the ward's communication responses are inconsistent and variable . . . that the ward's cognitive capabilities are quite limited and that she is presently functioning below a six or seven year age level, that she suffers from upper extremity paresis, visual dysfunction, that she suffers from many other physical dysfunctions, and that her overall condition indicates a severe level of impairment, from significant brain stem and cerebral dysfunction.

Goff has recommended that the ward, Sharon Kowalski, not be placed in a prolonged inpatient hospital rehabilitation unit because of her severe impairment, slow rate of recovery and limitations of potential. He does, however, recommend that the ward, Sharon Kowalski, have the benefit of an ongoing rehab program including daily physical therapy, occupational therapy, speech therapy which is to be closely monitored and evaluated, along with contributions from psychologists and cognitive retraining.

The court appeared to accept at face value the judgments of Goff and Cowan. Nowhere in the findings of fact or court order was there an indication that a comparison was made between Sharon's progress and achievements at Country Manor and the evaluation of her 'capabilities' by the Polinsky Institute. In spite of all the evidence to the contrary—provided by staff at St. Cloud Hospital, Country Manor and the videotape—the Polinsky Institute evaluation report concluded that Sharon was incapable of the very skills she had previously demonstrated. For instance, they found that Sharon "demonstrated no spontaneous communication or behaviors . . . did not seem to demonstrate any affects such as sadness or happiness through expression of facial features or through behavior . . . was able to inconsistently read and comprehend at the single word level . . . Unable to comprehend paragraph length material . . . ."

Sharon had not responded to several tests conducted at Miller-Dwan. I can only speculate on why she did not or could not demonstrate the skills she had already mastered. Even though the report acknowledged that her "ability to respond is likely to be somewhat confounded due to her poor upper extremity motor coordination," it went on to state: "Estimates of her degree of cognitive functioning based on her color preference would place her below a six or seven year age level." In court from this point on, her level of functioning seemed to be based on just this one test, the color preference test.

Contrary to overwhelming earlier evidence that demonstrated Sharon's ability to communicate, the testing psychologist stated that though she "at times seems quite alert and seems to be able to make responses which suggest a higher level of functioning than she is actually able to demonstrate at this time," it was nevertheless "likely that her judgment or her ability to make decisions for herself is also severely impaired. This is predominantly due to her difficulty in establishing a reliable means of communication . . . ."

Another strategy pursued at the hearing was to mount a personal attack on me, the object of which seemed to be to discredit my importance to Sharon. As it became clear how much time and energy Fena was putting into bringing forth witnesses for this purpose, I began to worry. And justifiably. It was an attack that would be intensified through the course of the hearings with the goal of removing my visitation rights entirely. The main points of the attack, as represented in affidavits introduced by Fena, were that, before the accident, I had been controlling and had harassed Sharon a lot about money; that Sharon really didn't want to be living with me and had talked about moving to Colorado; and that I used a condescending approach with Sharon in the hospital.

The accusations about money and my attempts to control Sharon were baffling, especially in light of the fact that Sharon was always telling me how guilty she felt about not paying half of our expenses. I would reassure her that it didn't matter, but how could I prove that in court?

The idea that Sharon wanted to move to Colorado without me could, in the vulnerable position I was in, have made me wonder if she had been hiding something from me all this time. But in actuality Sharon and I had discussed moving to Colorado together. It was very hard on her not to have work and I had agreed that if she had not found a teaching position within the next year, I'd consider looking for jobs in another state. Colorado was our first choice because there were a large number of teaching positions there and a large number of the outdoor sports we loved. The irony, of course, was that as a closeted lesbian Sharon was not able to talk to her family about moving with *me*—someone they mostly thought of as Sharon's landlady. Besides, I had a lot of evidence to support my own certainty that we were happier than we'd ever been. Nine days before the accident, on November 4, 1983, she had accepted a position as Women's Golf Coach at St. Cloud State University. One of my vivid memories of Sharon's smiling face was when she walked into my office that day to tell me she had gotten the job. (Later, the SCSU Women's Athletic Director submitted an affidavit substantiating Sharon's acceptance of the position.)

One of the affidavits used against me was from Karen Tomberlin, a coach who knew Sharon from her sophomore year in high school. She came to visit one day while I was in the room and I asked Sharon if she wanted to demonstrate some of her skills, hoping Karen Tomberlin would take the information back to the Kowalskis. Instead she interpreted my actions to the court as a "condescending type of approach."

She went on to say,

❖   She had Sharon opening her fingers, wiggling her fingers and things like that. She had Sharon moving some balls toward her chin and moving a ping-pong ball to a different colored ball and things of that sort. Karen Thompson then said to me now I would see the best thing that Sharon had learned to do. Karen Thompson turned to Sharon and said write the word "Karen". . . . She then put a marking pen in Sharon's hand and Sharon started to write. She wrote the word "help." Karen Thompson became very agitated and upset over this. She took the notebook paper and looked at it and said, "Sharon! You're writing the word 'help'! I am very upset about this! Obviously, if you need help, something is bothering you. Wiggle your little finger if your legs hurt."

There was no response to Karen Thompson's request of Sharon that she wiggle her little finger. She then went through other things asking Sharon to wiggle her little finger if she was saying the word "help" because of any of those reasons. There was no response. I had seen Sharon wiggle her little finger in response to questions, so I knew that she could do it. However, she was not respondent to Karen Thompson's explanation or attempted explanation of the writing of the word "help."

I felt that Karen Thompson was trying to cover something up. I was very uneasy and upset about this . . . . As a friend of Sharon's, I myself am very concerned. I fear for her safety and her well-being.

Indeed, Sharon wrote "help" many times for various reasons. Sometimes she wanted to be repositioned because she was uncomfortable, sometimes she was in pain, sometimes she was tired and wanted to go to bed, sometimes she wanted to go home to our house, and so on. It was my practice to identify what she wanted through asking a series of questions until I came to the right one. Occasionally, I was never able to discover the reason.

But the fact that this incident could be interpreted to the court by one person, on the basis of one visit, to suggest that I was a reason to "fear for Sharon's safety" was unbelievable!

My attorney assured me that the judge would place no value on affidavits such as these. She thought the affidavits from professionals describing my visits with Sharon, her level of response to me, and my role in her rehabilitation would carry more weight. In fact, they carried very little. Even the Polinsky Institute's report carried little weight in the final analysis.

THE COURT ORDER TO
KEEP SHARON IN DULUTH

Though the evaluation report gave a guarded prognosis for Sharon, it concluded that, "The disposition of this patient is uncertain for reasons stated in this report. *It is felt that eventually she could be cared for in a home situation.*" (Author's emphasis.) This conclusion was ignored by the court; the judge ordered that Sharon would "require long-term confinement at a nursing home . . . ." Based on this 'finding of fact,' the judge found that Park Point Manor Nursing Home in Duluth (one of three such units in the state that has a young adult rehabilitation ward) was more closely suited to Sharon's needs than the facilities recommended by me. All other provisions of the previous orders were the same with the stipulation that all parties would obey the rules, regulations and directives of Park Point Manor Nursing Home. This ruling supposedly maintained my equal visiting rights, but the new stipulation, along with the power Fena and the Kowalskis gained by having Sharon in Duluth, would eventually undermine even that.

CHAPTER 6

Park Point Manor

On October 22, 1984, just four days after the court order, Sharon was moved to Park Point Manor in Duluth indefinitely. I didn't think it would be possible to feel more devastated than I already was. But now I was faced with the probability that it would be some time before Sharon could come back to St. Cloud. I still was not ready to admit that Sharon might be in Duluth for months or even longer.

I knew that I could handle anything for a short period of time. That's why when Sharon was at Miller-Dwan I was able to get to Duluth 30 out of 37 days. But I was paying a price. I was physically exhausted. How much was I capable of sacrificing to see Sharon? How long could I continue to drive six hours roundtrip? And Sharon had already expressed that she was not seeing me enough. She was more and more reluctant to let me go, crying and holding onto me to keep me from leaving.

I considered the possibility of looking for jobs in Duluth. If Sharon was going to be there permanently, I wanted to be where she was. I was already separated from many of my friends because I couldn't spend time with them. I didn't have time or energy to spend on anything.

I had never experienced the kind of intensity that my present situation required. My job, which had always been a very central part of my life, took a back seat to my concern for Sharon. I concentrated my work into shorter and shorter periods of time. I expected myself to be functioning at peak level every minute I was at work, accomplishing the same duties in half the time. I tried to make my driving time count by preparing my lectures or exams on the road. I wasn't sure how long I could go on like that.

My inability to protect Sharon and my rights without public support, and the advice of several friends, including Julie, made me finally turn to the media.

There were multiple reasons for deciding to be open with the press. Whatever the cause, Sharon was going downhill and I wanted to attract the interest of disability organizations and/or civil rights groups, hoping they would advocate for Sharon. I naively believed that if people could see the blatant differences between Sharon's documented progress at Country Manor and her documented condition after five weeks at Miller-Dwan's Polinsky Institute, they would take some concerted action to protect Sharon's right to recovery.

I was tired of living in fear that the press would pick up the story. Probate court is open to the public, and newspapers often gathered information there. Every day I went to work wondering if people knew or if someone had contacted the university administration and my job would be in jeopardy. Because of the animosity expressed by the Kowalskis, and actual threats to get even with me, I feared what they might do. As long as Sharon and my relationship was invisible, the courts, the nursing homes, all the institutions could go on denying it—denying us our rights—and no one would ever know. I could be passed off as a 'friend' or whatever other euphemism was convenient for the institution. They certainly would not recognize me as 'family.'

What I didn't know was that the press is as homophobic as the medical and legal institutions. So, the coverage the case received from the mainstream media generally served to perpetuate societal fears about gay and lesbian people, and about me in particular. The very first article, which I later came to view as more objective than most, is a case in point:

 Gay Issue Clouds Fight For Custody
St. Cloud Daily Times, October 18, 1984

It has been almost a year since Sharon Kowalski was rendered a quadriplegic in an automobile accident caused by a drunken driver.

The 28-year-old Iron Range native was an unemployed teacher living on Briggs Lake south of St. Cloud at the time she suffered a crippling head injury on Nov. 13.

The two-car crash occurred about six miles south of Onamia, killing Kowalski's four-year-old niece and injuring her nephew.

Out of that tragedy has come an ugly court battle between Kowalski's parents and Karen Thompson, an assistant professor at

St. Cloud State University (SCSU) who claims to have carried on a secret lesbian relationship with Kowalski for the past four years.

The two sides have fought for the right to be Kowalski's legal guardian because doctors have judged her to be incapable of making her own decisions.

Thompson said she will set a national precedent for homosexuals if she is designated Kowalski's guardian. She said her goal is to take Kowalski home with her to Briggs Lake and provide her with the highest possible quality of life.

Kowalski presently is confined to bed or a wheelchair and she takes food intravenously, Thompson said. She is being treated at the Nat G. Polinsky Memorial Rehabilitation Center at Miller-Dwan Hospital and Medical Center in Duluth. Tenth District Judge Bruce Douglas was expected to rule today on where Kowalski will be placed next.

"In our minds, we're married and are devoted to each other for a lifetime," said Thompson, who teaches health, physical education and recreation at St. Cloud State. "I want the chance to take her home. I believe I could take care of her."

Kowalski's parents, Donald and Della Kowalski of Nashwauk, have said that no one can love their daughter as much as they can. In a telephone interview this week, Donald Kowalski said there is "no way" his daughter and Thompson have had a lesbian relationship.

Kowalski's attorney, Jack Fena, Hibbing, has written in documents filed in court that Thompson is trying to separate the Kowalskis from their daughter by seeking control of Sharon.

"(Karen Thompson) is about as sick as they come," Donald Kowalski said in a telephone interview this week. "They don't come much sicker."

Donald Kowalski said his daughter never has admitted being a lesbian. He said he and his wife are worried that Thompson will sexually abuse their daughter if Thompson is allowed to continue visiting her.

Thompson has been familiar with the Kowalskis' position ever since she mailed them a letter following the accident to describe her relationship with Sharon, she said.

"I was called and told what trash I had written and how sick I was," Thompson said. "They've told me that 'You just want to see her naked,' or 'Have you sexually abused our daughter today?'"

In a decision filed April 25, Judge Douglas chose Donald Kowalski as the legal guardian in the case. But the judge's order gives Thompson input into decisions made about Kowalski's future because of their "special relationship," said Peter Donohue, St. Cloud, one of Thompson's attorneys.

Disagreements between the two sides are expected to be settled in court, according to the judge's order.

According to court records, the latest disagreement between the two sides is over where Kowalski should be placed for further treatment.

Doctors at St. Cloud Hospital and the Polinsky Center have recommended that she undergo rehabilitation in a setting that is less demanding than what they offer, said Elizabeth Ristvedt, St. Cloud, Thompson's other attorney.

At today's court hearing, Donald and Della Kowalski were expected to argue that their daughter should remain in Duluth at a nursing home, closer to home, Ristvedt said.

Thompson said she wants Kowalski placed at a nursing home or other care facility in the St. Cloud area so she can continue to help her through recovery.

To avoid further disagreements and to achieve "peace of mind," Thompson said she probably will file an appeal to be appointed Kowalski's legal guardian.

She has been afraid to take the action in the past partly because she fears losing her job by calling attention to the case and revealing her homosexuality. Thompson said she has coached women's cross country and track at St. Cloud State for the past nine years.

"Sharon shouldn't have to worry about us because of her parents," Thompson said. "An accident should not deprive Sharon of our love."

According to Thompson, Kowalski would be better off if she were in her care. She said she is responsible for Kowalski's recovery, which at its peak included speaking in small sentences, eating and communicating consistently on a letter board.

Kowalski's parents are a detriment to her recovery, Thompson claims. The couple pamper their daughter and are condescending to her, Thompson said. They have objected to taking Kowalski out in public because they think that would be "putting her on display," Thompson said.

"They talk to her like a seven-year-old and I want her

treated as an adult," Thompson said. "She is a woman and she has a right to recovery."

Court affidavits filed by nurses, doctors and therapists have said that Thompson is a key to Kowalski's recovery.

Subliminally, the parents may be blocking their daughter's progress so she never will be able to communicate her feelings about Thompson, Donohue said.

"The whole issue is us being gay," Thompson said.

Donald Kowalski said he would have more to say on the case after today's hearing.

After the Duluth paper carried a similar account, making the story public in the Kowalskis' own territory, I talked to Ellen Rogers, a reporter for WDIO-TV in Duluth. She was very interested in the story and asked to interview me on tape and wanted to view the videotape of Sharon. Again, my hope was that people seeing the videotape would see that Sharon was a vitally alive human being with potential—not a 'vegetable.' But that story never materialized. After Rogers had called me several times, she suddenly stopped calling. Finally, I called her to see what the status of the interview was. Ellen apologized and explained that the attorney for the guardian had gone over her head, and she had no control over the outcome.

Ristvedt received a copy of a letter Fena wrote to the president and news director of WDIO as part of the proof that I should be restrained from visiting Sharon and that my motivation for seeking press coverage was questionable.

❖ Dear Messrs Befera and Skorich:

This is a follow-up to our conversation we had on Tuesday, October 30, 1984. I very much appreciate the forbearance of WDIO, at least up to this time, in not running any story on Sharon Kowalski. When I talked to Duke Skorich and Ellen Rogers of your news department, they informed me that Karen Thompson had given them a videotape of herself and Sharon Kowalski.

It was at that time that I very firmly and definitely stated to Ellen Rogers and yourselves that I considered that use of that tape to be an invasion of Sharon Kowalski's privacy and also the whole entire story involving Sharon Kowalski to be libelous, slanderous and defamatory. I realize that you are getting some pressure from Karen Thompson to run this story. I told Ellen Rogers that I refused to go on camera and I would not go on camera, and my clients, Donald and Della Kowalski and Sharon Kowalski, will not go on camera. I don't want to try this case in the press or on a television camera.

Your television transmitter on the Range is ten miles from my clients' house in Nashwauk and as I stated to you, all of these news releases and news stories disseminated by Karen Thompson have had a terrible effect upon and have caused great mental anguish to my clients, Don and Della Kowalski.

I am again setting out the Kowalskis' position and I am hopeful that WDIO will restrain themselves and not inflict this further suffering upon my clients.

The Court records are clear and unequivocal in showing that Sharon Kowalski is at the mental age of six or seven years old. She is unable to speak or communicate on any type of level that would allow her to defend herself. This condition appears permanent. She is totally helpless, totally disabled.

She is in no way a public figure and my position remains that the publication of Thompson's press releases and videotapes are libelous and slanderous and therefore damaging and destructive to Sharon Kowalski and her family.

I am asking you, not only on that basis, but on a humanitarian basis, to please not run this story that Thompson is trying to push upon you. I appreciate your cooperation in this matter and I appreciate talking to you, Duke Skorich and Ellen Rogers about this matter; and I hope this follow-up letter will serve to protect Sharon Kowalski and her family.

Very truly yours,

Jack Fena, Attorney at Law

How, I wondered, could the videotape demonstrating that Sharon was *not* "totally helpless" and "totally disabled" be defamatory? To the contrary, wasn't it libelous, slanderous and defamatory to misrepresent the Polinsky report as being "clear and unequivocal in showing that Sharon Kowalski is at the mental age of six or seven years old"? Was it not defamatory to claim that "she is unable to speak or communicate on any type of level that would allow her to defend herself" when, in fact, she could write or type words, phrases or sentences? Nowhere in the records did any medical personnel say the condition was "permanent." Even Don Kowalski, in his letter to Tom Hayes, had said that Sharon had told them the name of a doctor she wanted to see.

My goal in seeking media attention was to portray Sharon as a human being with rights, feelings and certain abilities that should not be discounted, even though her disability made her 'different' in the eyes of an able-bodied society. In fact, even if Sharon were functioning "at the mental age of six or seven," weren't six or seven year olds still significant individuals with rights? Regardless, it was important that she not be written off, viewed as subhuman, as worthless.

❖

I had to teach on the day in October when Sharon was moved to Park Point Manor. I left immediately following my classes to drive three hours to the nursing home. At approximately 5:00 p.m., not knowing what the staff there had been told, I arrived with all my relevant court orders in hand. Since the daytime staff had already left, I delivered them to the night nurse and asked that she get them to the proper authorities. Always nervous about meeting new officials, I tried to act confident.

I finally located Sharon's new room and walked in. Right away I noticed that Sharon's feeding tube into her stomach was gone. I asked the nurse what happened and was told that Sharon had pulled it out or it had fallen out earlier. I asked when they would be putting it back, knowing that the longer it was out, the harder it would be to put it back through the hole. She replied that they would put it back as soon as they had time.

By the time they tried to put it back in, the tube had been out for at least the two hours I had been there. No one seemed to know how long it had been out or who had noticed it. The tube would not go in. So, Sharon had to be transported to a nearby clinic to have a doctor reinsert it. The doctor seemed perturbed with me as though it was my negligence that had allowed the tube to be out that long. He indicated that the stomach muscles had decreased the size of the hole, making it impossible to reinsert the same size tube. He had to put in a smaller one, forcing it in while Sharon hung onto my hand. She would then have to go back in a day or two and have the larger tube reinserted.

That same evening I discovered there was no wheelchair for Sharon and was told it would be a couple of weeks until a specially ordered one would arrive. No arrangements were made for a temporary replacement chair. Ever since the accident and even while she was in intensive care, Sharon was seated in a wheelchair to prevent pneumonia and maintain trunk and head control. Were they simply planning to leave Sharon in bed in her room for two weeks?

When I followed up on the wheelchair, I was told that it might be four weeks before it would arrive. At this point I asked the nursing home if they thought it was important that Sharon have a wheelchair. If they did, perhaps they could ask the guardian if he would consent to the rental of one. He did consent, but it was unclear if anything would have been done had I not pursued the matter.

On Wednesday, October 24, I called the nursing home to say that I would be up on Thursday night and all day Friday. I wanted to meet the various staff members involved in Sharon's care and treatment. I wanted to help ensure that everything would go as smoothly as possible—that the staff members would understand all of my rights for equal visitation, equal access to medical information and involvement in Sharon's care. However, when I arrived on Friday I had difficulty getting any information.

I talked with Barb Sallard, the Program Director of the young adult rehabilitation ward. She informed me that she was unaware of any special papers regarding my role in Sharon's care but she would be glad to check and see that everything was straightened out. I especially asked about the status of day passes and was told they didn't know but would find out.

I had learned that the St. Cloud State volleyball team was playing in Duluth that week, so I had hoped, before talking to Barb Sallard, to be able to take Sharon to the game. It had been difficult to think of activities that would put some sparkle back in Sharon's eyes after the deadly six weeks since her move from St. Cloud where we had experienced so much freedom.

When I had mentioned the match to Sharon, she had immediately given me her full attention, eagerly typing out, "Great, let's go."

"I'll check it out, Babe," I had said. Now, it looked doubtful we'd be going. I felt frustrated at every turn.

That same day, Sharon was going back to the clinic to have the feeding tube replaced since it was out again. Sharon had indicated to me that she was scared about this and wanted me to go with her. Her parents were not in town so I was the only person available. When it came time to accompany Sharon to the clinic, I was informed that I could not ride with her because I was not 'family.'

I asked to use a phone at the nursing home and was told I could use one in the office behind the nursing station. I went to call my attorney. As I was making the call, my eyes happened to notice a memo on the wall which was labeled "Guidelines for Handling Karen Thompson." In spite of the fact that I had delivered all the appropriate legal papers, the memo indicated that I was to be treated as they would treat any other friend of Sharon's. It stated that I was to be given no additional information, that I would be told only how Sharon's day had gone, that I would be given no specifics and that I could not view the medical records. I was furious! It seemed clear to me that they had lied. I decided to read the memo to Beth, who was on the phone. At this point, Barb Sallard arrived to declare that the memo was private property and tried to remove it. She seemed very aware of its content. "Private!" I responded. "It's got my name all over it!"

I had been led to believe that the nursing home would have to check on my status and day passes, when they had already written a memo on the matter. Indeed, they knew that day passes had been approved by Dr. Goff, who had specified that they were up to the father's discretion. I was extremely upset at this violation of the court order for equal access. I insisted that I talk with the administrator in charge.

Sallard immediately called Joann Susens, the head administrator of Park Point. It was decided that a conference call would be arranged among myself, Susens and Ristvedt, my attorney. Sallard was present but not on the phone. Susens stated that she had not received copies of the court orders. After a long discussion, it seemed to me that the problems were resolved. Susens agreed to have their attorneys review the court orders to ensure that everyone's rights were protected.

Until further clarification, Susens stated that the nursing home would have to follow the doctor's orders that passes be at the discretion of the father. My hopes of taking Sharon out rapidly diminished because I realized it was probably fruitless to seek Donald Kowalski's approval. I asked anyway and he refused. Obviously, I did not have equal access if I couldn't take Sharon on passes.

When Beth called Goff about his order, he said that outings could be with family, friends or staff at the father's discretion. He said this was standard. He admitted that it was not a medical decision as to who should approve those passes, but that in this situation he wanted some direction from the court, or "someone with authority," as to who could approve the passes.

It was Beth's opinion, restated for the court's benefit, that the "prior Orders on this matter and the discussions in chambers are clear that the parties have equal access to the ward and day passes, if and when available, would be available to both."

But when Susens tried to have the court clarify the passes, the judge responded that he never intended to go against 'medical opinion.' So the doctor passed the buck to the court and the court passed the buck to the doctor, who had already admitted that it was *not* his medical opinion. Indeed, Ristvedt stated, "it is clear from the Affidavit of Kevin Spellacy and the testimony of Donald Kowalski at the hearing on September 13 that the parents will not take Sharon out." Thus, while I was losing my 'equal access,' Sharon continued to lose her right to recovery—

in this case, the opportunity for daytime outings which had stimulated her and had increased her motivational level.

KOWALSKIS FILE FOR
RESTRAINING ORDER AGAINST KAREN

On October 30, six days later, the Kowalskis filed an application for a temporary restraining order to stop me from visiting Sharon. Spellacy, who at that point was still working on the guardianship case for the Kowalskis, filed an affidavit stating the 'reasons.' The first reason given was

◆ that Karen Thompson was involved in a lengthy confrontation with the Park Point Manor Nursing Home personnel and particularly Joann Susens, the administrator, over a request by Thompson to remove Sharon Kowalski from the premises on the following day to attend a volleyball game or some other local event . . . . Donald Kowalski has made it clear that he does not want Sharon Kowalski removed by anyone from the facility . . . . [T]his confrontation was very upsetting to Joann Susens, as she appeared to be quite concerned and agitated during the course of [my] lengthy telephone conversation with her.

Why was my concern about the duplicity of the nursing home portrayed as a negative 'confrontation,' while Susens' agitation was justification for denying me visitation rights? Whenever I displayed any emotional involvement, I was portrayed as unstable, vindictive or demanding, yet when others were challenged for illegally denying me my rights, their emotions were valid and normal. Obviously I *was* emotionally involved— and still am—because I have a relationship with Sharon, and that relationship was in jeopardy due to the arbitrary intervention of an institution. And why did they intervene? What were they protecting besides their prejudices?

Another major 'reason' given by the Kowalskis' lawyers in order to obtain a temporary restraining order was the direct result of media pressure. It was outlined in an affidavit filed by Spellacy that expressed concern over

◆ . . . the ability of the Park Point Manor Nursing Home to screen potential visitors who might accompany Karen Thompson so that the privacy and security of Sharon Kowalski can be maintained.

Joann Susens was upset about an article about this case of today's date in the *Duluth News Tribune*. She does not want the media on the premises, as the same could impair the privacy of Sharon Kowalski, the ability of the nursing home to render optimal care for Sharon Kowalski, and the privacy of other patients. Moreover, she is concerned about misuse of Sharon Kowalski's private medical records, or dissemination of the contents of the same to the press, which might then appear in follow-up articles.

Karen Thompson went to the *St. Cloud Times* on or about October 16 and disseminated details of this case to one or more of the reporters. Since that time, articles have appeared in the *St. Cloud Daily Times* on October 18, and again on October 24. An article has appeared in the *Minneapolis Tribune* on October 25 . . . . The Kowalskis are deeply concerned that the continuing efforts on the part of Thompson to publicize this matter could impact the efforts of the Park Point Manor Nursing Home to render proper treatment for Sharon Kowalski.

As the Court well knows, it is imperative that Sharon Kowalski receive optimal care at this time if she is to stand any chance of meaningful progress. The conduct of Karen Thompson, if unrestrained, will jeopardize that care and will cause irreparable harm to Sharon Kowalski.

As I answered in my affidavit, "none of the contacts which I have had with the press have hampered the efforts of Park Point Nursing Home to render proper treatment for Sharon. And I have never done anything to jeopardize Sharon's care and treatment. My only goal has always been to insure that Sharon has the best possible chance for optimal recovery."

It was unclear to me how press coverage would affect the actual care and treatment that personnel would give Sharon unless they were admitting that they would discriminate against lesbians. If that were the case, it would seem most beneficial to address the discriminatory actions rather than simply to hide the condition.

MODIFIED RESTRAINING ORDER

On November 7, 1984, the court ordered a modified restraining order ostensibly placing limitations on both parties. However, the impact and the inferences of the order fell disproportionately upon my behavior and my relationship with Sharon and the nursing home personnel. Judge Johnson ordered:

❖   1. Neither Karen Thompson nor Donald Kowalski shall be permitted to examine the medical records of Sharon Kowalski on the premises of Park Point Manor Nursing Home. Copies of said records shall be provided to attorneys for Thompson or Kowalski upon request and compliance with Park Point's normal procedure for provision of copies. Both parties shall refrain from disseminating the contents of said records to any third parties, including the media . . . .

      2. All parties to this action shall refrain from bringing anyone else with them onto the premises of Park Point Manor unless such other persons are approved for visitation by Park Point Manor . . . .

      Until further order of this Court, no party to this action shall remove Sharon Kowalski from the premises of Park Point Manor. It is contemplated that Sharon Kowalski may participate in Park Point Manor Nursing Home-sponsored group outings when her condition warrants . . . .

      3. All parties to this action shall refrain from engaging in any disruptive conduct, confrontations or arguments with the personnel of the Park Point Manor or anyone else on its premises, either inside or outside of the building and further, shall refrain from engaging in any other conduct which could, in the judgment of the Park Point Manor administration, impair their efforts to render optimal care and treatment for Sharon Kowalski or any other patient.

The reason I had shown medical information to the media was to present the contradictory picture of Sharon's medical condition when she was in the St. Cloud area versus when she was moved to Duluth. A radically different picture of Sharon was documented in the Polinsky Institute medical information, demonstrating either that Sharon had regressed since the move to Duluth or that she wasn't properly tested. My belief was that Sharon's basic right to recovery was being denied.

The ruling by the court, which placed a restriction on the dissemination of medical records to the media, effectively limited the facts available to the public to understand the case. In addition, this restriction would limit the information that disability rights groups might be able to use in order to advocate effectively for Sharon.

The visitation limitation would affect Sharon's options for meeting new people and keep her from getting a new support group in the Duluth community that could provide stimulation for her. While it was possible to get people on the Park Point list, it was difficult for me to get them approved. Certainly, I felt I could not openly identify people from the gay and lesbian community who wished to support Sharon and expect the nursing home to 'approve' them. I was quizzed on each person I wanted to add. "What relationship does this person have with Sharon? Why do they want to see her?"

Probably the most detrimental restriction in this court order was the section 'limiting' Sharon's right to leave the premises of the nursing home with either party. Although the nursing home could have taken her out on group outings, they never did—probably because she needed more help than the other patients. I was the only one who had taken Sharon out on passes before and now there would be no possibility. So, essentially, this order didn't just *limit* Sharon's right to leave, it removed that right altogether.

Clearly the order regarding disruptive conduct applied to my challenging the abuse of my rights by the nursing home. The court essentially gave Park Point Manor the power to make any decisions they wished, while removing my right to 'confront' them. I have since learned that an institution which is engaging in questionable behavior will always identify the one who is challenging them as the disruptive party or problem.

Regardless of the court order, I was still placed in the position of acting as Sharon's patient advocate on a number of occasions over what appeared to be small issues but which were very important to her well-being. In most of these instances, changes were made as a result of my intervention but I seemed to be the only person raising the issues.

For instance, I began to notice that Sharon always smelled. I had never noticed this any place she had been before. I inquired how often Sharon was bathed and they told me she had a bath every day. I accepted this at face value until later, when another discussion made it clear that Sharon was only bathed in bed, never in a tub or shower. When I asked why, I was informed that Sharon could not sit in a shower chair to take a shower, and that they had no way to get Sharon in and out of a tub.

"You mean you don't have any handicapped tubs with hydraulic lifts?"

"No."

Was I to believe that Sharon was specially placed in this facility because it was one of three in the state with a young adult rehabilitation ward and they had no handicapped facilities for bathing?

"Do you know that Sharon has taken showers since she was in a coma at St. Cloud Hospital? She was able to sit in a shower chair then. Do you mean she can't now?"

They had just assumed that Sharon would not be able to sit in a shower chair and had never tried. At my request, the nurse's aide received permission to try, so Sharon got her first shower after weeks of bed baths. Not only was this better for hygiene purposes, but Sharon needed the stimulation of water on her skin.

On another visit, I noticed that Sharon was improperly positioned in her wheelchair because a roll had been placed behind her hips. This forced her hips several inches from the back of the chair, causing a strain on her back and resulting in poor posture. In this position she was unable to work on any of her activities. When I brought it to the attention of the nurse, I was told it had been ordered by the physical therapist.

At the first opportunity, I asked the therapist, "What's the purpose of the roll?" She appeared surprised and said that the roll had been put in the wrong place. It was to have been pushed down in the space between the seat and the back of the chair. Finally after several days, the roll was placed in the correct position.

The temporary restraining order had now placed conditions on Sharon's life which eroded her basic constitutional rights, her quality of life, and her recovery and rehabilitation. The court's action literally imprisoned Sharon in an institution whose care I was beginning to have serious concerns about.

CHAPTER 7

Maneuvers in Court

Meanwhile, new motions had been filed in court by the Kowalskis asking for several changes. They were requesting transfer of venue from Sherburne County (where Sharon and I lived prior to the accident) to Itasca County (her parents' residence) on the grounds that it was "reasonably clear that she will require treatment and care at the Park Point Nursing Home indefinitely." Donald Kowalski wanted to have full power to make all the decisions concerning the best medical treatment and care for Sharon, to eliminate my right to equal access to medical and financial information, and to have full discretion to determine access to Sharon by any party.

KOWALSKIS' MOTIONS

Affidavits to the judge from Fena and his associate attorney Spellacy outlined their 'evidence' of the need to remove me. Spellacy contended that "Karen Thompson has, for a considerable period of time, engaged in a course of conduct seriously detrimental and inimical to the best interest of Sharon Kowalski." They presented their plans for testimony. The testimony of Angie Workman (the mother of the brain-injured woman whom I had asked for help in reaching Sharon's parents) would be presented as documentation of my intentions to "make a 'gay rights' issue out of the matter and 'take it nationwide'" if I was unsuccessful in obtaining custody. Further evidence regarding my intentions would be given by Donald and Della Kowalski.

The joint counseling session ordered by the Court in response to my request for counseling had taken place in March at the St. Cloud

Hospital with Dr. Steven Vincent. The Kowalskis were to contend that I "admitted that [I] was willing to give the guardianship a try, but if it didn't work out, then [I] would throw it back to the parents." Spellacy commented that "[t]his statement is deeply troublesome for it evidences the 'throw away' nature of Thompson's commitment to Sharon Kowalski, which contrasts sharply with the permanent commitment of the parents."

Spellacy planned to argue that my decision to contact the press was "a cynical attempt . . . to influence the Court's ruling . . . ." He contended that I was responsible for the publicity given to the case, including the follow-up articles in newspapers, radio and television, most of which were unfavorable to me and to Sharon.

In an attempt to portray me as an unbalanced and psychologically disturbed individual, Spellacy referred to several events. First, he included with the affidavit an anonymous letter received by Jack Fena suggesting that "a serious backlash against Karen Thompson's 'gay rights' is developing in St. Cloud . . . and that this may spur Thompson to even more outrageous conduct." Secondly, he pointed out that I had "received a considerable course of psychological therapy from Dr. Charles Chmielewski at the St. Cloud Hospital and has been undergoing such therapy since December, 1983. Nevertheless, Thompson's conduct is becoming more irrational, as evidenced by her attempt to try this case in the press."

As further 'evidence' of my mental state, Spellacy continued:

❖ The Court is aware of the problems that Thompson caused on Friday, October 25, at the Park Point Manor Nursing Home in Duluth, where she threatened and quarreled with Joann Susens, the administrator, for several hours with her demand to remove Sharon Kowalski during the upcoming weekend. Thompson attempted to misuse the Orders of this Court and the Court was nearly required to personally intervene. Sharon Kowalski's well-being is not at all enhanced by bullying and intimidating conduct . . . .

Spellacy's last argument implied that Sharon's and my relationship could be discounted, since it had never been proven in court.

❖ [T]he parties have never litigated the type or nature of [the] relationship between Karen Thompson and Sharon Kowalski, and the Court has never had occasion to make findings of fact concerning the nature of that relationship. The parties merely stipulated that there has been a special relationship between both Karen Thompson and Sharon Kowalski and Sharon Kowalski and her parents . . . . the Court has certainly never considered evidence of any type concerning such a special relationship or whether it be a gay lesbian relationship or otherwise.

Fena's affidavit presented his version of the interaction that took place between us when Sharon was transferred from St. Cloud to Duluth. Fena said, in part:

❖ As we watched, Karen Thompson made some signs with her right hand, held her thumb out to the left and her little finger straight out, closing the two fingers in between. She then manipulated Sharon Kowalski's fingers in the same position and then got down closer to Sharon within two or three inches of her face and said, "Don't give up, I'll never let you go, I'll get you back here" and things of that sort.

As we were moving down the hall, Karen Thompson confronted me, stating "I'm going to move heaven and earth to get you off this case. You fight dirty. You have hurt Sharon's case by bringing this out." Her fist was clenched and she was very angry.

Then Karen Thompson yelled at me and said I was only in the case for the money, that I was going to get $200,000 which she said is one-third of $600,000, that I would never see that money. She went on to state that Sharon would never see that money and that she was not going to take this. Then she accused me of hurting Sharon and I simply asked her to tell me how. Karen Thompson got very flustered and did not answer.

It's amazing how different his version was from mine. He obviously didn't recognize the sign for "I love you" since he described it as manipulating fingers. Sharon always made the sign and we touched fingers in parting, as Kathy Sims had noted at Country Manor. And I wondered how it could be interpreted that I confronted *him* when *he* was chasing me down the hall. I wasn't even clear what point he was trying to make unless this was part of the technique to cloud the real issues by making me appear crazy and unstable.

KAREN'S COUNTERMOTIONS

I counterfiled in response to their motions, asking for a second evaluation of Sharon's psychological condition. I also requested a dismissal of the petition to change venue and eliminate my involvement. For the first time, I formally requested that Sharon be allowed to be present at hearings, provided there was no medical reason preventing her presence.

This was a position I had been advocating for some time. Never once had Sharon wavered on her desire to be involved in the court proceedings. I continued to check and double check how she felt.

On one occasion I might ask her directly, "Sharon, do you want to go to the hearings yourself?"

She responded affirmatively. On another occasion, I would suggest that it might be difficult for her and ask, "Do you think it will upset you?" She was adamant in her response. "I want to be there."

Since the Kowalskis' lawyers continually discredited Sharon's ability to have input, my first concern was that Sharon be re-evaluated so her wishes could be taken into consideration. As long as she was portrayed as having "less than a six-year-old mentality," no one would give her expressed wishes any credibility. Beth Ristvedt's affidavit in support of my motion stated:

❖　　It is clear that the various personnel performing the psychological examination of Sharon Kowalski did not seek to find out the best method of communicating with Sharon prior to performing their evaluation . . . . Furthermore the personnel of the Nat Polinsky Institute did not want Karen's participation or input into the evaluation despite the prior testimony that Sharon's best and most consistent responses were to Karen Thompson.

I requested that Donald Kowalski be removed as guardian and that either myself or a neutral third party be appointed. I spelled out in detail the problems I had observed visiting day after day, which had an immediate impact on Sharon's ability to function to full capacity. My affidavit said, "Donald Kowalski . . . has consistently failed to act in his ward's best interest in that he has failed to recognize instances in which his ward needs changes in her care or treatment . . . ."

I thought it was ironic that the Kowalskis used the counseling session with Vincent to support their contention that I lacked commitment to Sharon and that they used Chmielewski's therapy sessions as evidence of my increasingly irrational and outrageous conduct. I felt these were my best witnesses and their affidavits reinforced my perceptions of the events referred to by the Kowalskis and the need for a re-evaluation of Sharon.

Dr. Steven Vincent submitted the following affidavit in November, 1984:

❖   . . . I am a psychologist at the St. Cloud Hospital.

. . . I saw Karen Thompson and Donald and Della Kowalski in a joint consultation session.

. . . [I]n my opinion, Karen Thompson appeared very committed to Sharon and in maintaining her relationship with Sharon . . . . I do not interpret anything which was said . . . as evidence of a throw away nature to their relationship. There appeared to be no lack of commitment to Sharon Kowalski from Karen Thompson.

. . . [T]here was nothing that I saw or heard that left me with the impression that Karen Thompson was in need of psychological treatment.

It has been reported to me that based upon Sharon's performance on a Stanford-Binet Color Performance Form Test that she has been placed at the level of a five or six year old. It is my opinion that it may be useful to obtain a second opinion of Sharon's psychological performance. I question the appropriateness of comparing the performance on a functional intelligence level and emotional level in that it is an apples and oranges comparison and that it is risky to assign an overall age level to someone in Sharon's condition because there are differing developmental levels in different areas on different occasions.

It was a real relief to see that Vincent validated my actions and that his comments showed my strong commitment to Sharon and not some psychological impairment. I remembered clearly asking in our session with him, "How does anyone know what the future holds five or ten years from now? But what would be the harm in letting me take Sharon home? If we can't handle it in the home environment, Sharon could always be returned to a nursing home or rehabilitation center." I believed that Sharon and I could work through the obstacles that would face us at home; I certainly wanted the chance to try. I never implied that I would walk away from her even if things didn't work out.

Dr. Charles Chmielewski's affidavit from November, 1984, stated:

❖   . . . I am a Licensed Consulting Psychologist employed at the St. Cloud Hospital.

. . . I saw Karen Thompson professionally a total of ten times between February 14, 1984 and March 26, 1984. Five sessions were formally scheduled therapy appointments, and five were informal sessions which occurred during chance meetings around the Rehabilitation Department of the Hospital.

. . . [I]n regard to Karen Thompson's commitment to Sharon Kowalski, it is my opinion, based upon my contacts with Karen, that her commitment is sincere, has been there for a significant period of time and that Karen spoke of the commitment as a life-long commitment.

. . . I would characterize my contacts with Karen as crisis intervention therapy and . . . related in large part with Karen's difficulties in knowing what to do in the situation where Sharon's parents were indicating that they were going to remove Sharon to the Hibbing area and the parents did not know of the relationship between Karen and Sharon. Karen did not have any ongoing mental problems.

. . . Karen and I discussed possible resolutions of the matter and one possible approach suggested was that the parents be written a letter informing them of the relationship. Karen at our next session presented a well-written letter which she proposed to send to the parents and it is my understanding that she did so . . . .

. . . In my dealings with Karen Thompson I was impressed with her concern for Sharon's needs and did not see her concern as selfish. I evaluated her motives as very sincere and caring.

. . . I have been informed that based upon Sharon's performance on a subtest of the Stanford-Binet Intelligence Test she has been described as functioning at the level of a six or seven year old. I have never evaluated Sharon, nor have I seen the test data or the report submitted to the court which describes her level of functioning. I can say that it is generally very inappropriate to place an age estimate on someone in Sharon's condition based upon one subtest from one test. Any such test results presume that the subject is capable of responding in a reliable manner. Brain-injured patients typically respond with much variability, and their performance differs greatly depending on the nature of the task being requested. To make any global statement regarding neuropsychological functioning based on one such subtest is usually considered very inappropriate by neuropsychologists in general. Furthermore, to then describe such a patient as functioning at a particular chronological level, with the same emotional needs as a 'normal' person at that age level, would seem especially inappropriate.

When I had gone to see Dr. Chmielewski, I knew I didn't have all the answers and that I needed help with Sharon's parents. It hadn't been easy for me to get help, but I saw it as a really healthy decision.

I was especially disturbed that the arguments about counseling and emotional stress could be used both ways. The Kowalskis' attorneys used my seeking counseling against me, while Della Kowalski's emotional state was used as 'evidence' in support of Kowalski's motion to have Sharon moved closer to their home.

Since Spellacy expressed concern that the nature of our relationship had never been litigated, I convinced Beth Ristvedt that we must have a court record supporting it. At the first two hearings on the guardianship, witnesses were prepared to testify about our relationship; however, when we settled out of court and made Donald Kowalski guardian, their testimony was never entered into the record.

For this most recent hearing we submitted affidavits from four witnesses whom Sharon had told about our relationship in the four years preceding the accident. One friend, who had camped, fished and skied with Sharon and me for years, testified:

❖   . . . that I have been a long-time friend of Sharon Kowalski.

     . . . Sharon Kowalski talked with me approximately five years ago about being gay. She also talked with me [about] being in love with Karen Thompson.

     . . . Sharon Kowalski has talked with me about living with Karen Thompson in a gay relationship and exchanging rings as a symbol of their commitment.

     . . . I visited with Sharon Kowalski on November 11, 1984, at the Park Point Manor in Duluth and saw her respond to the following questions by pointing to the answer on a sheet of paper. After pointing to her answer, she then touched the other answer upon request to demonstrate that she could tell what it was and that she could in fact touch that answer also. In some of the questions the position of the answers (i.e., yes or no) was reversed to insure that Sharon understood what she was communicating. Sharon responded to the following questions:

a. When asked if she would rather be in St. Cloud or Duluth, she touched "St. Cloud."

b. When asked if she wanted to go to court on November 30, and indicate to the court what she wanted, she touched the word "yes."

c. When asked if she wanted to make her own decisions, Sharon touched the word "yes."

d. When Sharon was asked who she wanted to be her guardian she touched Karen's name.

e. When asked if she wanted to be able to go out to her and Karen's house, Sharon touched the word "yes."

f. When Sharon was asked if she and Karen were gay, she touched the word "yes."

g. When Sharon was asked if she and Karen are lovers, Sharon touched the word "yes."

Sharon's roommate from college testified to the same first three points and added, "Sharon Kowalski and Karen Thompson have talked with me about the house they had bought. They considered it their home and were very excited about it."

One of our best friends also testified to knowing about our relationship and our home together, adding, "Approximately one week before the accident Sharon talked with me about accepting a golf coaching position at St. Cloud State University for the coming spring. She was very excited about it. During the course of our conversation, she also told me how much she still loved Karen."

Sharon's work supervisor from Sherburne National Wildlife Refuge gave the following testimony:

❖   . . . I have been a friend of Sharon Kowalski for approximately three years prior to Sharon's accident, and worked with her as her supervisor at the Sherburne National Wildlife Refuge.

. . . Sharon Kowalski talked with me some time ago informing me that she was gay and in love with Karen Thompson. She also discussed with me that she was living with Karen Thompson in a gay relationship.

. . . Sharon wrote me the summer before the accident about the house that she and Karen had together. Sharon was excited and happy about it and considered it their home.

. . . Sharon talked with me about buying the house. Sharon stated that she was happy at the house and enjoyed it.

My attorneys also submitted copies of the life insurance policies we had taken out to cover the price of the house should either of us die. A copy of a United of Omaha life insurance policy for $50,000 named me as Sharon's sole beneficiary.

As further proof of the relationship, I submitted a card and letter Sharon had written to me. The front of the card said "I love you," and had a verse on it. Sharon said, in part:

     Karen:
       You never forgot the 'little' things that say things so much better. Guess I started to take things for granted. I want you to know that even if I don't always say or do things that I still love you just as much. I had forgotten how much fun it is to get your cards and write.
       The book that I got you says things much better than I can—pretend it's me saying it . . . .
Love you,
Sharon

HEARING TO CLARIFY
VISITATION SCHEDULE

After making the decision to go public, I had written a letter to the Minnesota Civil Liberties Union explaining the whole case and asking if they could do anything on Sharon's behalf to protect her rights. They responded quickly and asked me to come to Minneapolis to talk with them and to bring them more information, including the videotape of Sharon and me working together. I met with two staff members for a couple of hours. They seemed appalled at the whole case, but when I left, I had no idea what, if any, action they could or would take.

The day of the hearing arrived. As we were entering the courtroom, a brief of amicus curiae was hand-delivered to the court from the MCLU. It stated:

❖   The November 30, 1984, hearing on the motions brought by Donald Kowalski and Karen Thompson raise fundamental questions concerning nursing home residents' and visitors' rights to free speech and association as guaranteed by the First Amendment to the United States Constitution and Article I, Section 3, of the Minnesota Constitution.

In its brief of amicus curiae, the MCLU wishes to underscore for the court its obligation to give paramount consideration to the interests of the ward in any proceeding involving or affecting guardianship, and to remind the court that the enforcement, by a nursing home or other resident health-care facility, of an order contrary to the wishes of a ward may be the functional equivalent of state action violative of the constitutional rights of such ward.

After stating the issues of the case, the MCLU document went on to say:

❖   To understand how such state action could occur, and could violate Ms. Kowalski's constitutional rights, it is necessary to consider how an order of this court might be enforced. Although an order might not expressly require enforcement by the institution to which Ms. Kowalski is confined, as a practical matter such enforcement is necessary if the order is to have any force and effect. Assuming, *arguendo* and for the purposes of illustration, that the court issues an order limiting the visiting rights of a party, enforcement of that order cannot be left entirely to the other party. That party cannot be expected to stand at the door to Ms. Kowalski's room to prevent visits that would violate the order. Instead, enforcement would perforce fall to the institution entrusted with the ward's day-to-day, and hour-by-hour, care. If it is assumed further that the terms of visitation set out in the order are contrary to Ms. Kowalski's wishes, then the institution would necessarily be placed in a position in which it must deny Ms. Kowalski the right to see visitors of her choice, or to communicate with persons of her choosing.

The appearance of the MCLU brief expedited the hearing tremendously. The whole mood of the courtroom changed. The judge quickly decided to limit the motions heard. The motion to remove my rights to equal access and give Donald Kowalski full power as guardian as well as my opposing motion to remove Donald Kowalski as guardian were both postponed to a hearing later scheduled for May 3, 1985. The petition for a change of venue was denied, and the visitation schedule was revised, assuring that "[a]ny time not hereinafter specifically assigned to either party is open time and either party may visit during such time by scheduling the same 24 hours in advance with Park Point Manor Nursing

Home . . . If either party is out of town, all times are considered open."
Furthermore, the judge ruled that I could hire someone to re-evaluate
Sharon at my own expense.

A few days later, the counsel for both parties and the judge
conferred by telephone. This resulted in an agreement regarding the
postponed motions. ". . . Donald Kowalski hereby withdraws his motion
of October 30 for various amendments to the Court's Order of April 25,
1984, upon the condition that Karen Thompson shall forthwith withdraw
her motion for removal of Donald Kowalski as guardian . . . ." During this
conversation, Della Kowalski's hospitalization for a nervous breakdown
was introduced to the court as part of the rationale for why our motion
should be dropped. Since nothing was in writing about the phone hearing, Ristvedt wrote the following letter clarifying our position:

❖   Dear Judge Johnson:
        I wish to clarify and set forth our position regarding the
matters which were discussed during the telephone conference of
December 4, 1984 regarding the outstanding Motions in this
matter:
        1. While it is lamentable that Mrs. Kowalski is currently
having some psychological problems which have resulted in her
hospitalization, that is not a factor which should determine this
Court's actions. The consideration for decisions in a guardianship
should always be the best interests of the ward, in this case,
Sharon Kowalski, and not that of other persons though they may
be loved ones of the ward.
        2. We are willing and do hereby move to withdraw our
pending Motion for a change of Guardian on the express understanding of all persons concerned that we are in no way indicating
that we will not proceed on the matter, as that is not the case. We
do intend and will present those issues to the Court at a later date
when those issues can be dealt with fully. I certainly do not want
Mrs. Kowalski to be misled that our withdrawal somehow means
that the whole matter will go away. To do so would in my opinion
only make it more difficult for her when the Motion is brought.
Judge Douglas recognized that the parties involved needed professional help back in April when in his Order he recommended
but did not order psychological help. The Kowalskis and their
attorneys attempted to exclude my client on the basis of her
contact with a psychologist in order for her to deal with some of

the issues involved in these proceedings. Now they are seeking action from the Court based upon Mrs. Kowalski's nervous breakdown and her failure to psychologically handle this entire situation. I appreciate that this situation has been difficult for the Kowalskis because they have been unable to handle the entire situation. This situation has, however, been equally difficult for my client in that the parents have sought to exclude her from the person with whom she had made a life-long commitment.

3. It is our feeling, for what it is worth, that the mere withdrawal of our Motion is not going to make Mrs. Kowalski psychologically well. Until the Kowalskis are able to confront reality and accept their daughter as she is and has been, there will continue to be problems. My client is, as she has always been, ready to discuss this matter and try to resolve the differences between the parties. My client is not, and has never sought to exclude the parents.

This is where things stood as I prepared to visit my own parents for Christmas, as yet unaware that the case had preceded me to Ohio.

CHAPTER 8

A Base of Support

I went home for Christmas determined to come out to my parents in person. I was afraid they would read about the case in a newspaper article. I had told them earlier that I was filing for guardianship of Sharon, but I had tried to make it sound like I would do it for any friend and that Sharon really needed my help. My parents had met Sharon several times when she had visited me in Ohio. And they knew that I'd always been the sort of person who would give the shirt off my back to a friend who needed it.

The day after I arrived, I was in the garage helping Dad work on my car when he asked me out of the blue, "How are you doing financially?" This was especially surprising because I rarely had conversations with my dad about personal things.

After a pause of panic, wondering what had precipitated that kind of question, I answered, "Well, Dad, actually I'm in over my head at the moment."

"Can I help out in any way? You know I do have some retirement money . . . ."

"I really appreciate your offer, Dad. It means a lot to me. But you could give me all the money you had and I'm afraid it wouldn't solve the problem of my legal fees. I would like to talk with you about some things but I'm not sure you really want to hear them."

Then Dad shocked me. "I know everything."

I instantly got a knot in the pit of my stomach. I wondered what he meant by 'everything.'

He went on, "I received an anonymous letter from someone in Minnesota who explained their version of the story and viciously attacked you."

He had hidden the letter in the garage so Mom wouldn't see it. He got up and gave it to me to read. It contained a newspaper article with nasty accusations and insinuations written in the margins. Looking at the postmark, I could only think of two people in northern Minnesota who would have any idea I was even from Ohio, let alone my parents' names and address. They were Don and Della Kowalski. I remembered very clearly Della's threat to get even with me and wondered if this was what she meant.

Dad and I talked about the whole situation. I told him how much I loved Sharon and a little about our life together. He was very angry that someone would write such a letter about me and offered to support me in any way he could.

I looked at him and wished that I had a way to reach out to him and tell him how much his love meant, instead of standing there across a car, not touching. I had known that somehow my family would stick by me, but I didn't know what form it would take.

Dad told me that Mom didn't know and he didn't think she should be told. Since my sisters and Dad agreed on this, I decided against telling her.

I was relieved that Dad knew, but was really sorry that he had found out in such a shocking and horrible way. As I drove back to Minnesota, I had a nagging fear that Mom would also find out, especially since there would be more publicity about the case. I was sorry I'd agreed not to tell her. Though I badly wanted her support, I wanted to be there when she heard and to help her deal with it.

❖

In my desperation to get help for Sharon, I had begun to reach out to different people and organizations. Because of my fears about 'coming out' as a lesbian in a public way, I made a special point to get Julie's advice. I had kept in touch with her off and on and I was hoping she would have some ideas about gathering support for the case. Julie started by writing a letter describing the case briefly and asking for any affordable donations. After a few other faculty members signed the letter with her, she sent it to individuals who had donated to support the sex discrimination suit on campus.

That letter became the basis of our initial fund-raising attempts and our beginning efforts to let other groups that might lend us support know about the case. Julie established an account at a local bank for the Karen Thompson Legal Fund. We were rewarded with about $650 from the first letter—only a beginning since the bills were already approaching $15,000. But I hadn't known that anyone would ever donate to support the case. I found myself experiencing both relief and embarrassment that I had to ask for help.

I also found that some of my support was double-edged. Shortly after an article appeared in the *St. Cloud Daily Times,* almost a year after the accident, the associate pastor of the First Presbyterian Church, which I belonged to, asked to see me. He wanted to assure me of his support and asked if there was anything he could do to help. I told him of Sharon's and my struggle about being gay and Christian, and that I had worked with Reverend Peg Chemberlin on sorting it out. He told me that he agreed with Peg's interpretation and mentioned that there was even a support group within the Presbyterian Church. He asked my permission to communicate with the Presbyterians for Lesbian/Gay Concerns (PLGC).

When the associate pastor spoke to me, I felt a sense of belonging again, and I began to think that maybe I could go back to my church. The time I had been away from the church had left an emptiness. The church had been a fellowship and a family for me. I had to believe that there was a bigger plan for us, or I wouldn't have made it through a single day. There was something out there that kept me taking the next step and that never gave me more than I could handle.

Another member of the church came up to me after reading the newspaper article. Early on, this woman had been very supportive of all I was doing for 'my friend.' Now, she couldn't believe I was really gay. "Don't you think you probably have just an agape love for Sharon where you love others in Christ? You must have allowed Satan to twist the love you had for Sharon into something else to try to get you away from Christ."

"Not everybody believes that," I tried to reason with her. "Not everyone interprets the Bible as you're interpreting it. Sharon and I struggled with whether we could be Christian and gay. I searched through the verses in the Bible with a minister at Newman Center and there's nothing in the Bible that condemns a committed, loving relationship with another human being. I found that Christ never once refers to homosexuality, and if it's so high on the 'sin meter,' you'd think Christ would mention it." My excitement was reflected in my voice. "Even our assistant minister believes that Sharon and I were not living in sin."

Evidently she quickly conferred with the minister, because he called to arrange a meeting with me. "Your neighbor came to see me," he admitted. "She thought that there was a good chance you could be swayed away from your lifestyle if you had not received support from me. I hope you understand that while I do believe there is nothing in the Bible that condemns you, I must maintain my ability to minister to all the groups within the church. So while I want to support and help you any way I can, I would appreciate it if you wouldn't use my name to others in the church. There are certain factions within the church that simply wouldn't accept this."

I felt like I had been kicked in the solar plexus. I hadn't shared the information to cause any problems within the church. I hadn't thought that he had spoken to me in confidence. He had initiated the conversation and volunteered his support. I had hoped that he would help others accept me as a member of the 'family of the church.' I felt betrayed once again. Knowing I didn't have the strength to handle another emotional crisis, I felt I had no choice but to leave the church. No one reached out to me.

The minister had followed up on the Presbyterians for Lesbian/Gay Concerns, however. Their newsletter printed the letter Julie had written. Suddenly, little sums of money began to arrive from all over the United States. At a time when everything else seemed so bleak, the letters and checks buoyed my spirits. They came from people who didn't know Sharon and me at all. Some sent a dollar, along with a note of support. The total amount wasn't as significant as the caring that was behind it. But every bit was needed. Within a few months, we had received a total of $1,500 and applied this towards the outstanding bill with Beth and Peter.

In addition to the support for us, some of the letters told of similar personal experiences and struggles to be with loved ones during times of crisis. One gay man wrote me about his partner who was dying of cancer and how they were separated because of their fear of 'coming out' to family and medical professionals. He thanked me for fighting it out in the open and he shared his grief that when his partner needed him the most, he wasn't there. He said that he had lost the home and other personal possessions they owned together. When I read his letter, I sobbed. I was beginning to see that what Sharon and I were experiencing was not just an isolated instance. I wondered how many others were struggling through similar tragedies. I hurt for him and for all the lesbians and gay men who must survive these experiences alone.

Another woman wrote of her partner who was dying of complications from a kidney transplant. Her story was very similar. They were closeted and couldn't let anyone know how much they loved each other at a time when they needed to express that love the most. She, too, appreciated that I was making these issues public. She expressed the hope that if I won, maybe others wouldn't have to experience the same hell we had been through.

I began to wonder: if someone else had fought for their rights, would Sharon and I be suffering now? It seemed as though we were suffering more from society's homophobia and handicapism than from the accident itself.

For the first time, I was understanding that lesbians and gay men do not have equal rights under the law. Our relationships cannot be 'legitimized' by traditional marriage, leaving us vulnerable to the whims of every relative, professional and institution. These letters made it very clear to me—if I didn't fight and win, how many others would have to go through this as well? It had to stop. My resolution strengthened and I determined to do everything necessary to press for change. I began to realize that I would have to reach a number of groups and individuals in order to move in that direction.

Two other people contacted me as a result of reading the article in the Presbyterian newsletter. Char and Gus Sindt wrote that their son, David, was gay. They wanted me to know how much they empathized with me and wondered if it might help if they tried to reach out to Sharon's parents as people who had experienced similar feelings. I explained to them that I had tried to obtain counseling or mediation with her parents to no avail, but I couldn't see how their attempt would hurt.

The Sindts wrote a very sensitive letter to the Kowalskis about how they understood the initial shock and distress at learning their daughter was a lesbian. They explained their journey to understand and love David, their gay son. They expressed their feelings that Sharon, now more than ever before, needed the woman she loved to help with her rehabilitation. They asked if they could possibly meet with Don and Della to talk.

Obviously, the Kowalskis turned the letter over to Jack Fena because the Sindts immediately received a response from him. He questioned where they had gotten the information that Sharon was a lesbian. He asked them to mind their own business and stop harassing his clients. When shown a copy of Fena's response, I was still able to be shocked that this man could be so insensitive to such an honest reaching out, from one set of parents to another. The Sindts were sorry that their letter hadn't been helpful, but wanted me to know that their thoughts and prayers would continue to be with me.

❖

At about this time, I recontacted Kathy Wingen, the Director for the Handicap Services Program of Tri-County Action Programs, Inc. I had previously spoken with her about home living before Sharon was transferred to Country Manor. This time I gave her information on Sharon and asked for help in protecting Sharon's rights. Soon after that, Handicap Services became involved with Sharon. Kathy described their activities in a letter to the court which she submitted at the February 15 hearing:

❖   In deciding whether or not the Handicap Services Program staff could be of further assistance to Sharon in enabling her to become actively involved, as a human being in the community, a visit with Sharon was requested by our staff.

This first visit to Sharon took place on Thursday, November 15, 1984, at 3:30 p.m. Staff was surprised at how well Sharon responded to this visit, since there were earlier indications that she often had a tendency to sleep most of each day. On the day of the staff's visit, she appeared to be very aware and alert, and in our opinion, actively interactive in the entire conversation. Most of the two-hour visit was spent in getting to know Sharon, and at the same time allowing Sharon to familiarize herself with us and our services. Although she had no verbal communications at that time, in the opinion of staff, she was able to communicate effectively and consistently by other means. Those means include use of finger movements on right hand, facial expressions and head movement. Before ending the visit, Sharon did attempt to make verbal sounds. Finding that this individual could communicate, staff asked her a number of questions to which she consistently responded. As an outcome of the first visit, Sharon had two definite requests for Handicap Services staff. These were: 1) She wanted the staff to check into available services which would benefit her; 2) Sharon expressed a strong desire to see and visit with us again soon. Karen Thompson was present during about the last half-hour of our visit, at the request of staff. It appeared that Sharon's general mood brightened upon seeing Karen. This, perhaps, proves that outside stimulation is a very important factor in Sharon's rehabilitation program.

Staff visited Sharon again on Thursday, January 24, 1985. She was sleeping on arrival of staff. When asked by Park Point Manor staff if she wished to see us, her reply was "yes." Through use of her communication systems, Sharon said she was upset with us because we had not been back to see her sooner. However, when asked if she would like us to leave, rather than talk with her, her reply was "no." Sharon then agreed to get out of bed and "talk" with us through use of a typewriter. For this purpose,

Handicap Services staff had written up a set of questions prior to leaving for Duluth. Attached hereto and made a part hereof, is a copy of the questions written by Handicap Services staff, asked by Carla Hansen, answers typed by Sharon Kowalski and notes written by Carla Hansen . . . . The only area of questions which Sharon seemed to be confused about were questions in regard to her actual accident, which we've found, from experience, is quite normal. During the typewritten conversation, Karen Thompson was present, but not within eyesight.

We would like to make it known that the Handicap Services Program and staff have become involved in an attempt to ensure Sharon's civil rights, as well as her well-being, as a handicapped individual citizen. In short, we are only looking out for Sharon and her best interests.

Based on the knowledge we have of existing laws, Handicap Services staff feels that many of Sharon's rights, as a handicapped individual, are being violated.

Handicap Services went on to summarize the federal and state laws which prohibit discrimination on the basis of a handicap. They further described state and federal resources available for Sharon's rehabilitation.

Handicap Services submitted their questions, Sharon's typed responses, and their notes regarding her responses as part of their testimony to the court in February. It was wonderful to have documentation from a non-partisan group that Sharon willingly responded to difficult questions.

Sharon's responses to their questions were revealing:

❖ January 24, 1985
1. "Do you know what city you are in right now? Please type the name if you do."
yes st cloud
"Where is Park Point Manor?"
duluth
2. "Have you been in your wheelchair yet today?"
no
3. "What is your place of residence?"
st cloiud
4. "What type of work did you do before your accident?"
tech
"Did you teach?"

yes
"What did you teach?"
pe health
5. "What is the name of the place you last worked at?"
bug lake
(bug lake—finger pushed u harder than i)
6. "Where were you living at the time of your accident?"
stcloud
7. "Did you have a roommate at the time of your accident? If so, what was the person's name?"
kt
(kt—Karen Thompson)
8. "Who are your parents?"
d d
(d d—Don and Della)
9. "Where do your parents live?"
naswauk
10. "If you have brothers or sisters, what are their names?"
mark debbie
11. "Where do you want to live? Duluth, St. Cloud or Nashwauk?"
s
(s—St. Cloud)
12. "Are you gay?"
yes
13. "Do you have a lover? If yes, what is the person's name?"
karen t
14. "Has Tom Hayes, your attorney, been to see you since you have lived in Duluth?"
no
15. "If Tom has been to see you, when was he last here?"
(not applicable according to 14)
16. "Are you satisfied with the way Tom has been representing you in court?"
no
17. "Would you like to have another attorney represent you?"
yres
(hit r by accident)
18. "What type of accident did you have?"
car
19. "When did the accident happen?"
august

(isn't aware of things that happen about the accident)

20. "Was anyone with you at the time of your accident and whom?"

no

(same comment as 19)

21. "Do you get any therapy, and what kind?"

no

"Don't you like the therapy you're getting?"

n

"Did you like your therapy better somewhere else?"

cm

(Country Manor)

22. "Do you want an electric wheelchair?"

yes

23. "Are you happy at Park Point Manor?"

yes

"Do you want to stay here?"

no

24. "Where did you spend Christmas Day?"

Karen

"Was Karen the person you wanted to spend Christmas with?"

yes

"Where did you spend Christmas Day?"

n

(Nashwauk)

25. "Would you like passes to spend time in the community?"

y

(yes)

"Would you like passes with Karen?"

y

(yes)

"Would you like passes with your parents?"

n

(no)

26. "Would you like to be present and contribute information at future court hearings regarding your guardianship?"

yes

27. "Are you able to ride in a car?"

n

"Do you like riding in the car?"

n

"Did you ride in Karen's station wagon since your accident?"
yes
"How did you go home for Christmas?"
car
28. "Do you feel you can make your own decisions?"
yes
29. "Do you wish your parents and Karen Thompson could get along better?"
y
(yes)
30. "Are you afraid to hurt your parent's feelings?"
yes
31. "Are you afraid to hurt Karen Thompson's feelings?"
yes
32. "Do you realize you may be handicapped for life?"
y
33. "Are you having a hard time accepting your handicap?"
y
34. "If you must have a guardian, who would you like it to be?"
karen
"Would you want Karen to be completely responsible for you?"
y
35. "Is there anything you would like me to check into for you? Such as attendant care, accessible housing, electric wheelchair, recreation, transportation, therapy, etc."
yyyyyyy
36. "Is there anything you want or need? If so, what?"
nothing
37. "What is your full name?"
sharon k kowalfski
38. "Where were you born?"
gr
39. "When was your birthdate and how old are you?"
aug8 56
40. "Do you want me to continue to be a part of your recovery?"
zo
(zo? Not clear)
"Do you want me to continue to check options of living situations, housing, attendant care, guardianship, etc.?"
yes
41. "Do you own any type of vehicle? If so, what?"
var

(var—hit v by accident)
"Do you own any other kind of vehicle?"
mc
(motorcycle?)
42. "Do you want Karen Thompson to continue to visit you?"
yes
43. "If decisions must be made for you, do you want Karen Thompson to be a part of those decisions?"
yes
44. "4+6=" *10*
45. "7-2=" *5*
46. "2×2+3=" *7*
47. "24÷4+1=" *7*
48. "Is there anything else you want to tell me?"
no
49. "Would you like to take part in the 'Ms. Wheelchair Minnesota Pageant,' which will be in St. Cloud, Minnesota on May 3, 4 & 5, 1985?"
yes
"Do you want Karen to continue to try to help you?"
yes
"Would you like to go home to St. Cloud as soon as possible?"
yes

Sharon had lots of problems with short-term memory. She couldn't remember much about the accident and she usually didn't know what day of the week it was. What the Handicap Services interview showed was that Sharon still had very clear wishes about where she would live and with whom. These were the questions that were at the crux of the guardianship case. The Handicap Services interview and report was a great lift to my spirits. So many people had told me over and over that my plans for home care were unrealistic. Even though I knew of people with greater disabilities than Sharon's who lived at home, I felt my faith was often undermined. Because we had a really vital relationship in the present, I believed that Sharon and I could cope with the problems that would come up, or that we would have the resources to get the help we needed. Handicap Services found Sharon's capabilities to be greater than most people had judged. They saw Sharon with the same potential I viewed her as having. Once again, I believed that what I envisioned for Sharon and me was not so far out of reach.

❖

Still looking for a group that would advocate for Sharon, I contacted numerous other disability rights groups. I would meet or talk with them for hours and show them the videotape and other court evidence. On the whole, they appeared to think that Sharon's rights were being grievously violated. Some promised to contact other groups and individuals that they were sure would intervene on Sharon's behalf. Others promised to contact me regarding specifically what they would do. I would be tremendously excited only to have weeks pass with no response. In one instance, I was informed by one disability rights advocacy group that they had enough problems without getting involved in a gay rights case as well. Some individuals from these groups did get involved and have continued to be involved throughout.

Meanwhile, Julie and Peg organized an initial meeting of a group of people in St. Cloud who were willing to help. It was a diverse group of men and women, activists for a wide range of issues. At the first meeting, they decided on the name, Committee for the Right to Recovery and Relationships (RRR). The Committee decided to focus on getting information out about the case to counteract some of the negative and homophobic coverage by the mainstream press. They also decided to ask for monetary support to defray my rapidly increasing legal fees. Peg began to work to find a non-profit group who would take on the case as a sponsored project, making donations tax-deductible.

The Committee for RRR also compiled a list of Lesbian/Gay and Disability Rights publications in the United States. A few feminist and other general alternative publications were added to that first list as well. Julie's early letter was revised and updated and sent off in the mail. Within a few days, reporters from various parts of the country began calling Julie and me.

I had always been a person who hated to talk on the telephone and found meeting new people difficult, so I was terrified to get phone calls from Boston, New York, San Francisco and Chicago. But my desire to help the reporters understand the case overcame my fears; once started, I had plenty to say. A few articles began to appear and I was sent copies. It seemed so strange to read about Sharon and myself in these articles. Who was this person who sounded so strong, assertive and confident? Somehow the public 'me' seemed so vastly removed from the private 'me' who cried myself to sleep every night.

I had always been taught to give, to nurture other people; I had never really learned how to ask or receive help in return. All of a sudden, a number of people were willing to help. In many ways I didn't allow myself to really accept or feel the support that was available. For a long time, I still felt very alone in my struggle.

There were times I felt I couldn't keep doing this day after day. The main thing that kept me going was knowing that Sharon might never get better, might never get free if something happened to me. And finally I was realizing that many people cared what happened to Sharon and me, and were willing to act on those feelings with moral support as well as financial support. It was beginning to sink in that I wasn't alone.

I had such mixed feelings about accepting financial help. I was the type of person who had paid my own way all my life. I had never understood how people could be in debt; I had always saved and paid cash for things. Now my whole financial status was drastically changed. That kept me awake nights too. The reality that I needed others to keep going required a radical adjustment in my thinking. But, thank God, they were there!

CHAPTER 9

Sharon's Depression

Even though I had been making every attempt to see Sharon five days a week, she still wasn't doing well. She slept a lot. She wasn't as alert and it was much more difficult to motivate her. I couldn't seem to get her to laugh or to make jokes. I felt as though my hands were tied, since I couldn't offer her the variety of activities that we had had available in St. Cloud.

By the time I left my classes and spent three hours on the road, it would be evening when I arrived at the nursing home to see her. I couldn't see her throughout the day to catch her most alert times and work with her on her time schedule. Even though some of our best work sessions had previously been in the evening, now it was rare to have sessions I felt good about. I never saw improvement—I was just fighting to help Sharon maintain the skills she had already demonstrated. It was a losing fight.

Sharon kept typing that she wanted to go home to St. Cloud, or she wanted to go out to church or to basketball games. I could only reassure her that I was doing everything possible to take her on outings and eventually bring her back home. I became even more convinced that she was experiencing a depression, but no one else seemed to care.

At the last hearing I had received permission from the court to have Sharon tested for competency. I began to fear that she wouldn't be able to pass a competency test so I wanted to get it done as soon as possible. She was rapidly losing ground, especially with short-term memory. However, the person we had originally asked to do the evaluation was unavailable. Finally, near the end of January, 1985, we located another psychologist, Catherine Anderson, from the Human Development Center in Duluth.

I talked with Sharon about the forthcoming evaluation. I wanted her to be prepared and as relaxed as possible. I hoped she would understand that she could answer the questions openly and didn't have to hide anything, including our relationship. I wanted her to know how important it was that she do the very best that she could.

The judge had indicated that more weight might be given to the evaluation if I weren't present during the testing, but that I could set it up however I wanted. After talking with Beth Ristvedt, I decided not to be present during the testing.

On January 31, Cathy visited with Sharon and me to establish rapport and learn the best ways to communicate with Sharon. The second visit occurred on February 6. Cathy wanted me to stay until Sharon was set up properly in her wheelchair with the typewriter—not an easy task.

However, before we were ready to begin the testing, a nurse rushed into the room insisting that I leave because I was not allowed to be in the room while the testing was occurring. Cathy told her that the testing hadn't begun and that she would ask me to leave when the time was appropriate.

We were still checking to see if Sharon was at a good angle to reach the typewriter and were trying to restore a relaxed atmosphere when a nurse's aide came into the room demanding that I leave and implying that I was deliberately violating orders. Cathy again pointed out that the testing hadn't begun yet and that I would leave as soon as she requested me to.

Once more we tried to reassure Sharon. I left when Cathy asked me to.

While the testing only took 45 minutes, it seemed endless to me. I waited anxiously until Cathy appeared, worrying about how Sharon was doing with the test.

"How did Sharon do?" I asked immediately.

"It is somewhat difficult to reach any conclusions based on Sharon's response today," Cathy answered. "She responded erratically. Sharon even indicated that she lived in Nashwauk before the accident."

I immediately felt defeated. "Oh, no! I know why she says that. Her parents have told her that if she says she lived in Nashwauk they will get more money for her. It's like brainwashing her. She never typed Nashwauk before that came up. And now it makes her look inconsistent and incompetent. It's extremely frustrating!" I was so disappointed with the results and with Sharon's performance that I was close to tears. Too much seemed to hinge on this one visit.

"But she wasn't sure whether she was now in St. Cloud or Duluth either," Cathy went on.

"How could she know?" I blurted out. "She hasn't been able to go out on any passes to see any of the sights in Duluth. Park Point Manor isn't supporting Sharon's right to be out on passes like they would for other patients. We haven't been able to do any of the things that we were able to do in St. Cloud to help with her orientation. She's been like a prisoner here."

"Well, I'll write up my report and send you a copy as soon as possible."

It was amazing how differently this whole discussion between Cathy and me was interpreted by a nurse who was in the room across from the lounge at the time. Unbeknownst to me, she hand-wrote a furious note to the Head Nurse of the rehabilitation unit.

   Ann:

     I had informed the NA's [nurse's aides] that Karen was not to be in room with Sharon's eval. & to please see that she stayed out. While I was at supper Kristi La Dean had to go in & ask Karen to leave the rm—Karen tried to tell Kristi, she was only helping set up, but Kristi said that wasn't true, Karen was helping with the typing.

     Also—when Cathy Anderson came out, & I was in med room, much discussion between her & Karen. I couldn't hear much of what Cathy said, but Karen was agitated, stating, "she's being held prisoner here" & various other things about this NH [nursing home] being wishy, washy & not taking a stand & Sharon is being brainwashed by her parents. Kept stating "Her parents tell her to say she wants to be near Nashwauk because she'll be getting lots of money," etc. I can't remember it all, but I found it extremely disgusting. Sounded like Karen is about to lose her marbles. Also is VERY VICIOUS.

     As for the psychologist she had been told, no one was to be in with her. I'm sure you can tell by the hand writing that I'm angry—
Jane

The letter was given to Jack Fena, who presented it to the court many weeks later as evidence supporting the elimination of my rights to visit and relate to Sharon. As a result of that letter, it became necessary to get Cathy Anderson's view of the incident in an affidavit.

❖ . . . I am a licensed psychologist and performed a psychological assessment of Sharon Kowalski on January 31, 1985 and February 6, 1985.

. . . On February 6, 1985, when I arrived at the Park Point Manor Nursing Home I asked Karen Thompson to come into Sharon's room with me and make sure everything was set up properly for the testing session, including the positioning of the typewriter and Sharon's positioning. I informed her that I would tell her when I would like her to leave.

. . . At my arrival a nurse told me that Karen Thompson was not supposed to be present during the testing and I assured her that she would not be.

. . . While we were still in the process of getting Sharon set up and insuring that Sharon was able to reach the typewriter and respond with it a nurse's aide came into the room and said that Karen Thompson was not supposed to be in the room. At that point we had not yet started testing and I had not yet asked Karen Thompson to leave. We informed the nurse's aide of that fact.

. . . When I was ready to begin the testing I asked Karen to leave the room and she did so immediately.

. . . After leaving Sharon's room and completing the testing, I talked with Karen Thompson regarding the results. It was my opinion that Karen was frustrated and hurt that Sharon had not seemed oriented to her surroundings and was not alert or very responsive. I did not interpret anything which Karen said or the manner in which she said it as being "very vicious" against the nursing home. Karen made a statement that Sharon was in a prison which I interpreted as Karen's frustration at not being able to take Sharon out to interact with her environment, even though Sharon was medically able to go out and needed that stimulation. It was my opinion that Karen was frustrated with the entire situation and her statements were not directed at anyone or anything specifically.

I now wish with all my heart that I had talked to Cathy in a private room or later by phone. I'd never tried to hide any of my concern for Sharon, and it simply never occurred to me that others would think I was trying to influence Cathy. I knew perfectly well that Cathy was going to report exactly what she saw.

I obviously cared deeply about Sharon and was under extreme duress. But unlike the professionals, any time I showed any emotions, I continued to be labeled sick or crazy. Fortunately in this instance, Cathy Anderson's affidavit supported my viewpoint.

A few days after the evaluation I received Cathy Anderson's report, which said:

❖ Mental Status: Sharon was able to type her name and those of her immediate family members. She exhibited some confusion on her current place of residence, on one occasion typing Duluth and on another occasion typing St. Cloud. Her time awareness was the most significantly impaired, with her getting both the dates and the day of the week wrong. Sharon showed evidence of higher cognitive functions. She was able to perform several simple one and two step math problems. Sharon was also able to identify and categorize familiar objects in her environment. Long-term memory was relatively more intact.

On one occasion, Sharon established eye contact but was unwilling to do so subsequently. When asked if she was depressed, she typed "yes" and identified that emotion as "sad." She denied any suicidal ideation when asked. The only spontaneous affect which Sharon displayed during the evaluation was when, after discussing her present living situation, she hung her head and refused to interact any further for approximately three or four minutes.

Observation of the videotape of Sharon from August, 1984, showed evidence of a significant range of interactional capabilities and intellectual processes which were not evident at this time. On that tape, Sharon demonstrated foresight and planning ability, maintained eye contact, and showed purposeful spontaneous activity. The suppressed skill level which she is presently demonstrating must, therefore, be viewed as an inadequate testing of limits when compared with her previous skills and her variable interactive level.

These variable skills, together with Sharon's contention of sadness, appear to indicate that Sharon is currently experiencing a major clinical depression. Therefore, it is recommended that Sharon be evaluated for medication by a psychiatrist who is skilled diagnostically with neurologically-impaired individuals.

Furthermore, it is recommended that she be provided with psychotherapy to help her grieve her numerous losses. Further assessment will be necessary to determine the degree to which her depression is precipitated by her separation from Karen Thompson, although that pattern does appear to be substantiated.

Sharon's depression may be further situationally precipitated by her confinement within a convalescent environment. Therefore, it is recommended that she be allowed out on passes on a much more frequent basis to facilitate her interaction with her environment.

Even though Sharon didn't 'pass' in terms of competency, the report still had many positive aspects. Cathy was the first professional person willing to acknowledge Sharon's regression, as opposed to accepting her condition as static. Unlike the evaluation at Miller-Dwan's Polinsky Institute, she noted the substantial difference in Sharon and began to question why it was occurring. She also recommended grief counseling, which I felt was crucial to Sharon's recovery. But the only response to the reports of her depression was to give Sharon medication.

❖

Meanwhile, I continued to have major concerns about the nursing home. Park Point had a Young Adult Rehabilitation Ward and it is not uncommon for brain-injured patients to be violent or loud. It was not possible for nurses and nurse's aides to watch all the patients all of the time, so ambulatory patients, most of whom were men, would come and go from room to room. Sometimes they would walk right up to Sharon, grab her arm and yell things at her. It would startle and scare Sharon. She couldn't tell them to let go of her or leave her room. On many occasions I saw patients walking out, and I'd go in to find Sharon upset and not know really what had occurred. Other times they would walk in while I was there, and I had to ask them to leave. Sometimes I had to take hold of their arms and walk them out of the room. They even scared me, since they were unpredictable and occasionally violent.

During my visits to the nursing home, I would sometimes see patients tied to a wheelchair and the wheelchair tied to the wall. Later, I discovered that some of those patients were ambulatory. Nurses and nurse's aides told me that it was easier to keep track of them in a chair. They didn't have the staffing to constantly be looking for patients who might wander off the unit. Questions about these practices that might not have occurred to me a few months before kept coming to mind. When people don't walk for long periods of time, wouldn't they lose the ability to walk? Were they making people more dependent than they really needed to be? Why couldn't the nursing home hire more staff?

Thank goodness in the midst of this turmoil a support group had developed in Duluth. A gay bar owner in Superior, Wisconsin, just across the lake from Duluth, made sure I had a place to stay and introduced me to many people in the Duluth area. He volunteered his club for fund-raisers. An auction held there raised over $1000 for the legal fund. Getting an amount like that really was a lift, even though my bill was growing much faster than money could be raised. I didn't know how I would have gotten through the year without the Duluth support group.

I flew home to Ohio for spring break because I increasingly felt the need to talk to my mom. I felt sure it would only be a matter of time before she found out about the case and my relationship with Sharon. I wanted to be sure to tell her in person so I could give her what support I could. We were sitting together on the living room couch when Mom gave me the ideal opportunity to discuss it by saying, "It really upsets me when people keep things from me."

After a short pause, I jumped into the feared topic. "Sometimes people don't tell you something because they don't want to upset you and cause unnecessary pain. There are things I've wanted to talk with you about for a long time, but I was afraid you would be hurt."

Mother immediately blurted out, "You're a lesbian!" I think it was the worst thing she could think of that I wouldn't be able to tell her.

Before I even confirmed it, I said, "Once I do talk with you about this, there's no way to take it back, Mom. Do you really want to know?"

"Yes, you might as well tell me," she responded nervously.

"Yes, I am a lesbian," I said. "And there's no way you should feel badly or responsible because I'm okay. The happiest four years of my life were the years I spent with Sharon. I finally put the missing pieces of my life together. Mom, my choice was to be a workaholic all my life and wonder what was wrong or accept my love for Sharon and start living for the first time." I went on to tell her everything that had happened since the accident.

Although I was sure she would have preferred that I wasn't a lesbian, Mom made it very clear that she loved me and wanted me to be happy. She was worried about how this would affect my job, how public it would become, and if someone would try to hurt me. She was worried about my living so far out of town alone now. Would someone try to harass me or damage my home?

I realized that I never should have tried to 'protect' her from the truth. Mom dealt with the information better than any of us expected. It didn't seem to affect her health negatively either. She took this in stride.

My mom is a very special person who has survived for 30 years with a serious kidney disease. I think of her and her strength as a role model for me. She's taught me persistence and patience and her love has always been very precious to me. It felt so good to be able to be honest with my whole family. I didn't have to pretend or guard what I said. When I felt like I was taking on the weight of the world, it was great to know my family was behind me and would do anything they could for me.

As we talked, I felt the depth of my love for Mom. I finally felt free to tell her how much I loved her. A barrier had been removed which had not only kept me from receiving her love but from expressing my own. I realized that when you can't share the most important things going on in your life, your relationships remain shallow. Because of what had happened to me and Sharon, I was given the opportunity to build a new and deeper relationship with my family. I was eager to tell Sharon about my family's reaction when I got home.

❖

During this same time, not trusting or liking Cathy's evaluation, Fena and the Kowalskis asked that Sharon be evaluated by someone recommended by their doctors. Jerry Henkel-Johnson, a psychologist working with Park Point, evaluated Sharon over a period of time without my knowledge. His assessment, introduced at the next hearing, reinforced the conclusion that Sharon was experiencing a depression:

❖ . . . It is speculated that Sharon is undergoing a depressive reaction. Specific symptoms include allowed response time, social withdrawal and non-responsiveness to people, difficulty in decision-making, insomnia (especially at the 2:00 a.m. bedcheck), and frequent poor eye contact. Also, this is substantiated by a report by Catherine Anderson, M.S., Licensed Psychologist, and Ryan Jagim, Ph.D., Licensed Consulting Psychologist, Human Development Center. This report occurred from testing on 1/31/85 and 2/6/85. The conclusions of that report were that Sharon seemed to be experiencing a major clinical depression. I would agree with these findings, and emphasize the need for psychiatric assessment for medication management.

Both reports substantiated my conclusion that Sharon was indeed experiencing a depression. Neither report suggested anything negative about my interactions or my relationship with Sharon. However, once Fena and the Kowalskis had to accept that I was right about the depression, they set about trying to establish that I was also responsible for it. That was the major thrust of the next hearing.

CHAPTER 10

Testimony

May 3, 1985, was a gloomy day even for spring. I entered the courtroom thirty minutes before the hearing to remove my visitation rights was scheduled to start. By now, I was quite familiar with its features. The judge's bench, on a raised platform, placed him far above the proceedings. A much smaller area was allotted for the lawyers' tables, and a wooden railing separated the rest of us from the action in the court. Linda and Theo sat beside me. We sat on hard benches, provided for the courtroom 'audience,' immediately behind the table where Beth would be sitting. I was sure that our case was so strong and Fena's so weak that we had to come out well, but I was nervous because Beth would be calling on me to testify. As the hearing progressed, Fena's presentation added to my nervousness. My knowledge of Sharon and the surrounding facts was so contrary to how he was presenting things that I kept suppressing the physical urge to jump out of my chair and object to the contradictions he was introducing.

FENA'S CASE FOR THE KOWALSKIS

Fena's case, which tried to establish that I was responsible for Sharon's depression and should be eliminated from her life, relied almost exclusively on 'evidence' he solicited from a Dr. George Cowan. (Later he solicited the opinions of two other doctors, Dr. Julie Moller and Dr. Steven Goff, to shore up his sagging argument. They all rendered opinions about Sharon's contact with me, but not one of them had ever seen us interact. And none had observed Sharon before and after visits with me to determine what effect, if any, those visits had on Sharon.)

Dr. George Cowan was a psychiatrist practicing part time in the Duluth area. He was the only doctor Fena called to testify at the hearing. Dr. Cowan said that he had only seen Sharon two times. He was not one of Sharon's regular physicians and in his own words, "from a psychiatric standpoint, there was no type of therapy I could offer her." He saw her at the request of Mr. Fena. The first time he saw her was on October 4, 1984, when he saw her briefly and she did not respond to him. The second time he saw her was the day before the hearing, May 2. Once again, Sharon did not respond to him. At no time did Dr. Cowan administer a psychological test to her.

Based on these contacts, Dr. Cowan determined that Sharon was suffering from a "reactive depression, largely based upon her reactions to statements that she heard from Karen Thompson." Dr. Cowan testified that he knew for a fact that it would be devastating for Sharon *if* she knew that her parents were told that she was a lesbian, or *if* I had made negative comments to her about her parents. As a result, Sharon might withdraw and be depressed. He said that *if* these things were true, he would write an order "forbidding Karen Thompson from visiting this gal."

But these were only hypothetical 'if's. Fena never even tried to prove that such conversations between Sharon and me had actually occurred or to identify what, if any, information Sharon had requested.

Beth, in her cross-examination, was able to cut through the weaknesses in Fena's case. When she asked Cowan if there weren't many reasons why brain-injured people could be depressed, Dr. Cowan admitted that there could be a variety of reasons for Sharon's withdrawal. He agreed that it was possible that since she had been a very active, athletic young woman prior to the accident, her present physical limitations could logically result in a depression. (Other experts would testify that depression is an almost universal response to the type of injury Sharon suffered.) He also agreed that Sharon could be depressed because a loved one had departed.

Then, when Beth asked Cowan how he could tell, without having done psychological testing, the exact reason for Sharon's depression, he refuted his prior testimony. "Well, in the state that she is in, I think it would be impossible to find out the reason." He further conceded that if I didn't discuss with Sharon the homosexuality issue or the controversy between myself and Sharon's parents, there was no reason I could not visit. "If her visits were on a neutral basis without discussion of a personal nature . . . and if she could guarantee that, sure, let her visit."

Personal nature! Neutral basis! Of course, I talked with Sharon about court proceedings, but only if she wanted to know. After all, it was affecting her life as much as mine. I would ask her, "Do you want to know what's going on in court, Sharon?" She would indicate either "yes" or "no." Usually it was "yes." Then I would say what was going on and ask what she thought or what she needed in the situation. In this case the question would be something like, "They are trying to eliminate my right to see you. Is that what you want?" She always typed or indicated "no" to that question. She also knew from the beginning about the publicity. I asked her if she wanted to know about articles regarding the case, and I even read some of them to her when she asked. Sharon's depression did not start until she was moved to Duluth, many months after I had begun discussing the guardianship case with her. Beth would make this point very clear to the court when she later called me to the witness stand.

However, Cowan's contradiction—that a person who was presumed cognitively 'incapable' of even being in a depression could, at the same time, comprehend the complex conversations that he was now identifying as the basis of the problem—went unchallenged even by Beth.

When Cowan finished his testimony, a very odd thing happened. As he stepped down from the witness stand, the court recorder stood up. At first I thought he was going to ask the doctor for a clarification. Instead he shook Cowan's hand with a nod of the head that indicated he had done a great job. It was obvious to me that the court reporter agreed with the tone of Cowan's testimony. I was shocked. Yet no one else seemed to notice, nor did anyone mention the incident.

At this time Fena entered into the record the testimony of Ann Pelman, the head nurse of the young adult rehabilitation ward at Park Point. Her testimony had been taken by deposition earlier. I had brought my concerns about Sharon's care to Ann many times. We had a system set up by which I addressed those concerns only to her and she would pass them on to the staff. The staff had found my suggestions helpful and made changes in Sharon's care as a result of them. In her deposition, Ann substantiated that Sharon wanted to see me at times when she would refuse to see other friends. In contrast to the doctor's conclusions, Ann refused to say I should be kept away. More than any other professional, she had observed me with Sharon on an ongoing, daily basis. When asked if she had an opinion as to whether I should be kept away, she said it was her professional opinion that any time you are looking at long-term rehabilitation, significant others should be an important part of the patient's care.

Even though her testimony turned out to be supportive, it was very carefully noncommittal. Because she was Fena's witness and we weren't sure where her allegiance was, we decided against depositioning her ourselves.

It later became frustratingly clear that we should have depositioned Ann for more testimony. One day, after a visit with Sharon, I ran into her on my way out of the building and we talked for more than an hour.

"I don't understand your relationship with Sharon," she volunteered, obviously uncomfortable. "But I've never seen the depth of love you show for Sharon. It's difficult even for family members to stay involved with brain-injured patients on any long-term basis. No spouse has ever been more supportive than you've been with Sharon. You work so well with her, and she responds to you."

I had to ask her, "If you think I'm good for Sharon, why didn't you say more in your deposition?"

"I would have if I had been asked the right questions," she defended.

But *why* wouldn't the medical professionals speak out on their own for what was best for their patient? It made the frustration all the worse when they would tell me in private that they were supportive but would not risk supporting me in public or in court.

Because my attorneys didn't object, Fena was allowed to monopolize court time with testimony that was not pertinent to the question of my visitation rights. For instance, Fena had Debbie DiIorio, Sharon's sister, testify about her opinion as to what Sharon's plans were before the accident and how my visitation affected Sharon now. She testified that Sharon was either planning to move back with her parents or move to Colorado because she was unemployed.

Fena used Debbie to try to reinforce his argument that I was the cause of Sharon's depression. The cross-examination by Tom Hayes, Sharon's court-appointed attorney, revealed the lack of substance in her testimony.

Hayes asked, "When you do get responses from her [Sharon], are they, by and large, always appropriate, given the circumstances and the type of question you have asked?"

"No."

"How frequently are they not appropriate?"

"I would say 50-50."

Hayes later picked up this line of questioning again. "Would you estimate that in the past thirty days, the appropriateness of her responses was about 50-50?"

"In the past thirty days, I haven't gotten any responses out of her."

This answer was particularly surprising, since Sharon's responsiveness had been increasing for more than a month. I had noticed it, and the medical staff had noticed it. Sharon was finally pulling out of her depression. It seemed as if either Sharon wasn't responding to her sister and other members of her family while responding more to me and the staff, or Debbie was trying to make it look like Sharon was still in the depression to justify my removal.

Hayes asked Debbie, "In response to a question posed by Mr. Fena, you indicated you believe that Sharon has become depressed?"

"Yes."

"Would you please describe for us your basis for that opinion—what you observed?"

"Well, I have gone there after Karen has been there. I met her coming out of Sharon's room at one time, and whenever I have gone very recently, Karen has been there and she doesn't—she seems almost to hide from—like she will turn away and close her eyes and kind of curl up."

"How many times have you visited with Sharon immediately following a visit by Karen Thompson in the past three months?"

"In the past three months, probably once," Debbie said.

During Debbie's testimony, I alternated between wanting to jump out of my seat to say she was lying and feeling totally crazy, as though everyone else had a different reality from mine. Yet, if Sharon really was close to Debbie, why didn't she tell her that she had accepted a position at St. Cloud State University just a few days before visiting her family? Why didn't she know that we had life insurance policies on each other? If, as Debbie claimed, Sharon didn't want to be around me, why would she have gone to the trouble of driving hours to bring her niece and nephew down to our house? For that matter, why would Debbie allow her children to come if she had heard such terrible things about me?

Fena had planned to call four witnesses—Dr. Cowan, Debbie, and Don and Della Kowalski—"for some hopefully brief testimony." However, the first two witnesses took more than two hours of the three-hour court session. It was Fena's usual practice to monopolize the time with testimony that didn't seem to have substance or relevancy. For instance, he spent quite some time showing Debbie pictures of Sharon in which she appeared very happy. She was with family and family friends during one of the very few outings the Kowalskis took Sharon on. Then Fena tried to draw a relationship between these pictures and the newspaper articles about the case that he alleged were 'damaging' to Sharon's mental health.

Fena was a master at this tactic, clouding the issues and taking up time with a number of irrelevant tangents. I felt that Beth should be objecting and wondered why she wasn't. By allowing Fena to take up most of the scheduled court time, we were forced to submit much of our material by affidavit. And, therefore, I think our case was never fully developed, since much more information can be brought out when questioning a person face to face. In that way we failed to preserve testimony that may have been essential to the case.

Fena concluded his portion of the testimony by saying that since time was running short, he would turn in Don and Della's testimony by affidavit later. (As mentioned earlier, Fena would also turn in letters from Drs. Goff and Moller, although he didn't indicate at the trial that he planned to do so. And the court would allow this very unusual procedure. Fena, who had not worried about time up until then, may have known he needed to go after more evidence. But I could only speculate about his motives.)

RISTVEDT CALLS

KOWALSKI TO THE STAND

Beth was finally allowed to call her first witness, Donald Kowalski. Following up on Debbie's testimony, Don confirmed that they, too, had gotten only inconsistent responses from Sharon. Taking another direction, Beth asked Don, "Do you believe that Karen is a loved one of Sharon?"

"No," he answered

"As a general statement, do you believe that loved ones are important in Sharon's recovery?"

"Yes."

"Under what circumstances would you come to believe that Karen is important to Sharon? Is there anything that could convince you?"

"I haven't seen anything."

Beth questioned Don as to whether he had ever discussed any of the 'concerns' he had with me. He indicated that he had never made any attempt to talk with me or my attorneys nor had he asked the nursing home to talk with me. He believed that the only solution was to bring a motion in court for my removal without ever trying to work through any of the 'problems.'

Beth asked, "Since last fall, you brought three motions to remove contact between Karen and Sharon, is that correct?"

"That is correct."

"If you are not successful today, will you continue to work toward that goal?"

"I will."

By his testimony, it was clear that under no circumstances would he ever consider me important to Sharon and that he would do everything possible to eliminate me from her life.

Tom Hayes asked Don, "Do you feel that at this point in time, the level of care of Sharon is wanting in any way?"

"No, I think she is getting excellent care there."

"If you continue on as guardian of Sharon, would it be your intent, at least for the foreseeable future, to have her remain at Park Point Manor?"

"Yes."

I was astonished that he could really believe Sharon was getting excellent care there, when from the first day there had been problems that I had to bring to their attention. Didn't her parents notice the lack of baths? The tube problems? The wheelchair problem? Sharon's regression to being tube fed only? Her loss of flexibility? They were so committed to establishing that this was the best place for Sharon that they had even refused to acknowledge their own daughter's depression until I had struggled to have her tested.

When Fena got up to cross-examine Don Kowalski, he pursued a line of questioning that I felt once again clouded the issues. He asked Don things like, "Were you ever able to visit your daughter alone in that [St. Cloud] hospital?"

"No . . . never. She [Karen] wouldn't leave for five minutes to let us have time alone," Don answered.

I didn't understand what this had to do with the motion at all. This line of questioning had been covered in every hearing we had had. They were trying to establish that I was this pushy, controlling person. Even if it were relevant, it wasn't true that they never had time alone with Sharon. I was teaching and coaching full time that year. While I spent a lot of my time with Sharon, I deliberately used the time when her family or friends were there to catch up on my work, since I knew that someone would be with her. Besides, I was still trying to cover up our relationship at that point, so I didn't want them to know how much time I actually spent with Sharon.

Don testified that Dr. Moller had told him Sharon didn't really "realize what gay is. To her, it is just a gay time . . . ." Later, he testified that he believed that Sharon was embarrassed by comments I made about being gay. How could Sharon be embarrassed by discussions of being gay if she didn't understand what it meant or thought it meant to have a gay time? These types of contradictions permeated the testimony.

At one point in the testimony Don's (as well as Fena's) views of disabled people became very clear. Fena asked why he wanted to remove me from Sharon's life. "Are you doing it just because she [Karen] said she is gay? Do you really care?"

Don answered, "I don't care. It really doesn't mean much to Sharon now what she was."

"Is she in diapers?"

"She is in diapers."

"She has to be turned every two hours?"

"Every two hours."

"She can only have limited movement of her right hand?"

"Her right hand, and she moves her right leg but not under any control."

"She is a totally helpless person?"

"Totally helpless," Don answered.

Both Donald Kowalski and Jack Fena seemed to believe that disabled people no longer have any identity, let alone sexuality. I found it appalling that anyone could describe Sharon as being 'totally helpless.' There was so much evidence about what she *could* do. I had learned that being in diapers and having to be turned every two hours does not make a person less human, less able to feel, to care, to love, to think, to dream of a future.

DR. GAIL GREGOR CALLED TO THE STAND

Beth called Dr. Gail Gregor as a witness. Dr. Gregor is a physiatrist—a rehabilitation physician—at Sister Kenny Institute. Her testimony reinforced the importance of all loved ones being involved in the rehabilitation process, and reiterated that there are always unique, special relationships that are very important.

When Beth asked whether depression is common in brain-injured patients, Dr. Gregor responded, "It is very common and also universal . . . ."

"Can the treatment of a brain-injured patient with depression be [affected] by the absence or departure of a loved one?"

"Very definitely . . . ."

"Do you find that outings or passes out of the nursing home are beneficial for a patient?"

"Very. They are usually the highlight of a person's existence."

I was so upset—to hear a professional stressing the importance of outings. I had fought so hard for the right to take Sharon out from the very beginning and now, because her outings with me were canceled, Sharon seldom got out. No wonder Sharon was in a depression!

Tom Hayes questioned Dr. Gregor as to whether there might be an occasion to limit or cut off visitation by an associate or friend.

Dr. Gregor responded, "I can't imagine any circumstances why anyone would want to exclude any person wanting to continue to be involved with a brain-injured person."

When asked about the best way to deal with cases of conflict between loved ones, she responded, "The medical model for that is to attempt conferencing and counseling for the family members."

During cross examination, Fena raised once again his hypothetical, unproven premise that it was negative to give Sharon information about the dispute, court proceedings, etc. Dr. Gregor stated, "You can't eliminate conflict and information if it is important in the relationship [and] the interactions."

Fena then tried to discredit Gregor's statements by asking what medical records she had read. This was especially interesting since she could specifically identify which medical records she had read, while his physicians could never remember.

Fena then asked her if she would be concerned about the handwritten letter from the nurse, Jane Russell, to the Head Nurse regarding the incident surrounding the psychological testing by Cathy Anderson. Dr. Gregor said, "It would give me two concerns. One is about the professionalism of the nurse communicating that information in that way . . . and how that was dealt with in the nursing home structure . . . . That is not a typical way for a nursing staff to communicate concerns about patients . . . . My understanding of that note was that it was not part of the official nursing record . . . . The second concern would be that the loved one was having some difficulty with the adjustment and needed help."

Fena baited her with Cowan's assessment that "it would be devastating for Sharon to hear her parents condemned by Karen Thompson. Do I take it you don't agree with that?"

"I think I would disagree with the previous medical expert [Cowan] on the cognitive abilities of Sharon, and the cognitive abilities of Sharon are the necessary medical information to determine a devastating reaction, or any reaction to sensory input, social or informational."

Fena tried to have this statement stricken from the record and was denied. He tried to turn it around, asking if it would then be helpful for Sharon to hear negative things about her parents from me. By continually repeating the phrase that I said negative things to Sharon about her parents, it began to take on the *appearance* of fact, even though there was no evidence to support his contention. Again, my own lawyer made no objections to this line of questioning.

Dr. Gregor answered, "I think a brain-injured person would be sheltered into an unrealistic environment, so if Sharon is beginning to comprehend and understand what is going on around her, I think it is beneficial to be actively involved and informed, positive and negative."

After Fena's questioning, Beth questioned Dr. Gregor. She asked, even if Fena's statements about the impact of my discussions with Sharon were true, would she completely eliminate the contact of that loved one?

"No, I don't think that is medically indicated in Sharon's case."

"What would seem to be the next step?"

"To work at all possible medical and legal and interpersonal social measures to reconcile differences between concerned loved members or loved ones who are significant people in Sharon's life so she can benefit from maximum stimulation and opportunity from all spheres of her life."

I tried to separate myself from my 'side' and look at it from a neutral perspective. Whose opinions were more reliable and valid? Whose competence was more evident? Who would the court believe? Sitting in the courtroom listening to Dr. Gregor, I was certain that the court would be persuaded to deny the motion to exclude me. Maybe now the court would order some counseling to occur between the Kowalskis and myself to examine the real issues. Dr. Cowan's unsubstantiated 'medical evidence' paled in comparison to the highly professional basis for Dr. Gregor's conclusions.

KAREN THOMPSON CALLED TO THE STAND

Beth called me to testify next. I was nervous but felt confident I could explain the fundamental issues I had identified as important for Sharon's recovery, how Donald Kowalski had broken the trust invested in a guardian because of his prejudices, and how my actions were founded on my love for Sharon and what she wanted.

In order to prove Fena's accusations were wrong, Beth asked me if I had any idea why anyone might think my discussions with Sharon were negative or caused her depression. I answered, "I don't believe any of the things I tell Sharon are negative. I believe it is all a matter of interpretation. I do try to explain the facts to Sharon, especially when she is asking me why something is happening."

"What type of things have you talked to Sharon about?"

"Okay," I began, "I am going over an orientation with Sharon: 'Sharon, do you know where you are? . . . ' She will sometimes say, 'Why am I here?' Then I will tell Sharon that she is here because the court order places her in Duluth and that that came about as a result of where her parents wanted her to be. I will follow that up with, 'Where do you want to be, Sharon?'

"These are examples of questions I would ask Sharon so they consider that as being negative towards the parents.

"Sometimes she tells me to 'take me out,' you know, 'Please get me out of here.' Then I say, 'Where would you like to go, Sharon?' Sometimes the response is 'anywhere.' Sometimes it is 'take me home.' So I would say, 'Would you like to go out on a pass?' Sharon might say, 'Yes.' And I would say, 'Do you understand, Sharon, I am not allowed to take you out on a pass?' Then she would say, 'No.' Then I would say, 'There is a court order preventing me from being able to do that, Sharon. Do you know that there is a court order on that?' The answer is 'no.'

"So I have explained to Sharon that that is what her parents want and 'is that what you want? Do you want me not to be able to take you out?' Sharon's response always is [that] she wants me to take her out and she gets very upset with me if I don't take her out."

Beth asked, "Has Sharon ever indicated to you that she was upset with you?"

"Yes, she has."

"And have you ever asked her or discovered why she was upset with you?"

"I discovered numerous causes."

"And what did she respond to you?" Beth urged me to go further.

"All right, Sharon is upset with me because I won't take her out. That is one of the most frequent ones. When she types 'take me home,' and I try to explain to her that I am doing everything possible to take her home, and I even ask her, 'Where is home, Sharon?' She tells me, 'St. Cloud.'

"Then I try to explain to her what is going on and sometimes Sharon seems to understand and believes I am trying to take her home. Other times Sharon totally turns me off and she doesn't want to hear that I am trying and that she is still [in the nursing home] and she just gets frustrated with it."

I paused to take a breath, "If I talk about taking her out on passes, she has been frustrated with me and has turned away from me when I have said, 'I can't take you out, Sharon.' Sharon has been frustrated with me when there have been other people in the room and she has typed or hand-written, 'Karen, make love to me,' and then if, in fact, I have to reject Sharon, yes, she turns away from me and is very upset with me."

As I was testifying, my thoughts went even further but I didn't dare express them. How awful not to be able to reassure the person I love most that I still love her, even more now since I didn't take things for granted. She wanted reassurance that I still found her attractive and wanted her in every way, but I was not allowed to show her that for fear of someone falsely accusing me of sexual abuse.

I continued, "Yes, our relationship has become very strained at times because Sharon doesn't understand why I used to do things with her and now I no longer do them with her."

"When did you notice Sharon starting to withdraw?" Beth asked.

"I noticed she withdrew completely when she was moved to Miller-Dwan Hospital for the period of time during that testing. She responded very little. Then when she was moved to Park Point Manor, I talked with her again and I don't consider anything that I said was negative input.

"I said, 'Sharon, you have to try. You have to make every attempt no matter whether you want to be here or not. You have to make every attempt to do everything you can for yourself. I am doing everything I can to help you and I need your help.'

"That was the kind of approach I had with Sharon and Sharon did start to come back. She did start to try to do things. I think up until Christmas time, I noticed a fairly steady progression where she was alert and I felt I got valid, accurate responses from her. Also, she was starting to be willing to do more things with me again."

Beth let me go on. "A few days before Christmas, Sharon said, 'Take me home again.' I said, 'Sharon, I can't take you home.' Through questions and answers, I found out that somehow in Sharon's mind, she had established she would be home by Christmas and I think Sharon's real regression, even though it didn't show up, it was a very slow start and started at Christmas time. When it became really noticeable was the second or third week in January that I think she became totally just helpless and hopeless and she almost had given up that she was ever going to get out of there."

Beth asked, "When you noticed this, then in mid January, what did you do about it?"

"I talked with Ann Pelman whom I had been instructed to address my comments to, and when she was there in person, she asked me to talk with her, and if she was not there, I would leave written notes for her that I had requested that Sharon be allowed to have some counseling.

"Sharon had told me she wanted to work through some problems. One issue that was bothering her was being handicapped. She constantly typed, 'handicapped.' I said, 'Sharon, are you upset about being handicapped?' She will reply, 'Yes.' She has responded this to other people too. So I know that this is an issue that she needs work with. Yes, Sharon needs work with the whole issue of the relationships of all people who are important to her.

"I have constantly told Sharon she needs the love and support of her parents and of her family. I have constantly, you know, stated that to her, but Sharon is concerned about choosing between people. Sharon is concerned that every time I leave, she thinks I'm leaving for good, that I won't come back."

Beth asked, "What is Sharon's [reaction] when you tell her it is time for you to leave?"

"Generally speaking, she grabs hold of my hand so tight that I literally have to pull my hand out of hers, then she will turn her head away and she then won't respond to anything else I am saying."

"Can you see her withdraw or appear to withdraw?" Beth followed up.

"Yes, she is very upset."

Beth changed to another issue. "Has anyone, Ann Pelman, or anyone else ever talked to you or approached you with any complaint about your behavior or anything you said to Sharon?"

"No, they have not."

She pursued the issue. "Prior to the time of the deposition last Wednesday, had you heard anything from either the nurse's aides or the nursing home administration, or the guardian, or anyone else involved in this matter regarding any complaints?"

"No."

Beth asked me what kinds of things I had brought to Ann Pelman's attention. I talked about Sharon having no wheelchair and, therefore, not being out of bed for two weeks. I explained that they hadn't been bathing Sharon because they had no handicapped bathtub and thought that Sharon couldn't take a shower. And I brought up my concern about weight-bearing transfers so Sharon would have the exercise and stimulation of bearing her own weight.

I went on, "I've asked about the passive stretch program and has Sharon ever been stretched besides what myself or other friends or family give her. She has not. She gets half as much physical therapy as she received at Country Manor where she would get 30-40 minutes there at a period of time. I have gone through their therapy sessions and they may spend the whole time working just on her trunk, or just on her head, or just on specific parts of the body and that means she might go days without some parts of her body ever being stretched."

At this point, my testimony was interrupted by Fena's concern about being "pressed for time." The hearing was continued on May 9.

CONTINUATION OF

MAY 3 HEARING ON MAY 9

The courtroom had the same cool, impersonal atmosphere as six days before with one exception: two women in wheelchairs, representing the St. Cloud Handicap Services, were stationed in the aisle. I welcomed their visible support, especially because I was still very nervous about my testimony. I felt like so much of Sharon's future was at stake, and I wanted to do well.

When Beth called me back to the witness stand, I began by explaining my concerns about other patients wandering into Sharon's room and scaring her. I spoke of my concern for her safety since there had been violent episodes in the nursing home and Sharon had no call button that was located where she could reach it. And we discussed Sharon's methods of communicating.

Finally, Beth asked me about being gay. "Have you and Sharon ever discussed the issue of being gay?"

"Yes, we have."

"Were you present in the courtroom last Friday when Sharon's father indicated that, based on information that he had from doctors and his personal information, he did not feel that Sharon was capable of knowing what that meant?"

"Yes."

"Have you and Sharon ever discussed the meaning, and do you feel she knows what she is talking about when she refers to the word 'gay'?"

"Yes, I do believe she knows what it means when we use the word 'gay.' I think it has been very important for me to establish whether or not Sharon understands that, and exactly where Sharon and I are. I will ask Sharon what our relationship is and she will either type 'gay' or 'lovers.' On occasions, if she types 'lovers,' I will ask her, 'Are we gay?' Then she will type 'yes.' Then I [will] say, 'What does it mean to be gay?' Then normally her response is 'us.' Then I will say, 'Okay, we are gay, what does it actually mean?' On two or three different occasions, Sharon typed the word 'queer.' Then I said, 'Do you really believe we are queer, Sharon?' She typed 'no.' Then I said, 'So can you actually define it for me, Sharon? Tell me what it means to you.' What she has consistently responded has been 'lovers, same sex.'"

Beth pursued it. "Is this something that is fairly recent that you have discussed with Sharon?"

"I discussed it again last night."

"Do you recall when approximately it would have been the first time that you and Sharon discussed your relationship after the accident?"

"Last summer."

"When did you first discuss the situation regarding the press with Sharon?"

"I first discussed going to the press with her, should I or should I not, what were her feelings on that. I went over the pros and cons with Sharon and asked if she felt, if this was necessary, did I have her permission to do that and she said, 'Yes.' So I have talked from the very beginning before I went to the press at the end of September or beginning of October and I discussed every article with her from then on. I had taken them in to her when the articles came out in October—I took them in and read them to Sharon.

"I asked her, 'Do you want to see the article? Do you want me to read it to you?' If she responded 'yes' then I would do it and we have been over it. I asked her if she understood and if she wished me to continue with this and her response has always been 'yes,' she wants me to do whatever is necessary to get her back to St. Cloud."

Beth asked, "When did you begin discussing the court proceedings with Sharon?"

"I would say, the first one we had in September. I would explain them to her in detail and describe what was going to be going on at that hearing."

"Did Sharon express interest in knowing what was going on?" Beth continued.

"Yes. I never pursue any conversation with Sharon until she answers 'yes,' she wants to hear this information or 'no,' she does not. If she doesn't, we drop it and if she says she wants to hear it, then we go into the entire situation."

"I believe you testified earlier in your deposition that you saw Sharon's depression becoming evident in mid to late January, is that correct?"

"I would say it is definitely mid January. It started occurring before the end of January, yes."

"Okay, do you also recall that the nurses that testified indicated that they, too, saw Sharon's depression beginning in mid to later January, I believe?"

"Yes."

"Is there anything that you have done differently with Sharon since mid January to the present?"

"No, because I started the reading of the articles to her, talking with her about the court hearings way back before that and she continued making progress at that time," I explained.

Beth asked me to describe a conversation that nurse Mary Kay Hewitt had overheard and labelled 'courting.'

". . . [W]hen people walk into the room, I will say, 'Sharon, do you want me to drop whatever conversation we are on and wait until they leave?' That frustrates Sharon with her short-term memory problem. Lots of times she forgets and Sharon has indicated over and over again that regardless of who comes and goes, she wants us to complete whatever conversation we are having. Mary Kay came into a conversation on dating, a conversation we have frequently, that Sharon wanted to go out on a date. We talked about 'where would you like to go on that date?'

"She would like to go for a drink, and you know, we had established she would like a frozen strawberry daiquiri like they have at the Ground Round. Okay, we would go out on a date. So what would you do on a second date and Sharon's response to that normally is 'make love.' I would ask her, 'Do you do that with everybody on a second date?' She would say 'no' and she would just point to me."

Beth asked me to tell the events that led to my writing the letter to Sharon's parents telling them of our relationship and finally asked, "Have you heard the allegations that you have made statements condemning Sharon's parents?"

"Yes."

"Is that statement true?"

"No, it is not."

"What have you said to Sharon, if anything, regarding her parents?" Beth pursued.

"When in the course of the discussions something comes up that involves her parents or what her parents' actions are, I have always prefaced anything I say to Sharon [with] 'You know I want you to love your parents.' She responds, 'Yes, I know that.' I say, 'I know you need their love and support.' She responds, 'Yes.' 'Do you realize, Sharon, you can separate people's actions and you can either like or dislike their actions without disliking the person?' I have been very clear and very consistent throughout this whole time making sure that Sharon understands that I may disagree with what is being done, but that does not mean that I, in any way, am trying to put down or trying to hurt her parents."

The last topic Beth wanted to get into the record was the information about Sharon's job. "To your knowledge, was Sharon planning to leave the Sherburne County area at the time of the accident?"

"No."

"Did she have any prospective employment in the area?"

"Yes, she did."

"Can you describe what that was?"

"Yes, Sharon had decided she would take some part-time jobs until she could get a full-time job, and one of the positions that had been offered to her was a golf coaching position at St. Cloud State University. She . . . had a meeting with Gladys Ziemer, the Women's Athletic Director, just a little over a week prior to her accident. Sharon stopped at my office to say how excited she was about taking the job and she was also planning to look into some instruction time at the driving school. The coaching position was for the spring of 1984."

At this time Beth submitted an affidavit from the Women's Athletic Director documenting that she had offered Sharon the position and Sharon had accepted. I felt sure this fact would lay to rest the suggestions of Fena's witnesses that Sharon wanted to leave the St. Cloud area.

Stepping down from the witness stand, I felt good about how the testimony had gone. I hoped that the court would see the special way I interacted with Sharon. I hoped that they would see that I always treated Sharon with respect, as an adult with feelings, capabilities and something to offer. And that would then make them see how important it was for me to continue to see Sharon.

CHAPTER 11

Fena's Ploys

Fena had perhaps recognized that Cowan's testimony was weak and hadn't reached the desired conclusion—that I should not be allowed to see Sharon anymore. Therefore, between hearings he had solicited 'evidence' from Dr. Moller, dated May 7, and Dr. Goff, dated May 8, in letter form, not under oath and after his part of the case had been closed on May 3. He submitted these letters, that he just happened to receive in less than a week, before my testimony on May 9.

Beth objected to the letters on the basis of timeliness and underhanded maneuvering. "Both of these were prepared in anticipation of this hearing. I think if this had been done and presented several weeks ago to us, we could have [had] an opportunity to depose these doctors if we felt it necessary to do so. Last Friday we had a doctor here [Dr. Gregor] [who] could have perhaps commented on the opinions and the results of these physicians' opinions."

Beth was outraged. "I think that this is clearly something that has been staged to be presented at the last minute. I didn't receive it until we sat down today at the counsel table, until we were ready to begin. I think clearly this is a grandstand approach to get the doctors who are obviously under Mr. Fena and the family's control to come up with an opinion that supports their opinion."

Tom Hayes did not object, but he did point out, ". . . number one, it was filed on a late basis. Number two, it is not filed under any oath. Number three, it is filed in such a manner that it would not permit cross-examination."

Nevertheless, the court accepted the letters into the file, granting Beth permission to investigate the contents by deposition (that is, she had the right to examine the witness in person, over the phone or in writing and the witness had to comply with her request for testimony).

Fena then gave his closing statement. Tom Hayes followed by summarizing his position. He asked the court to permit continued visitation by me, and that all visitation be continued according to the court-imposed scheduling; to limit discussion by both parties concerning the guardianship or the other party; and to retain Donald Kowalski as guardian.

Beth, for her part, asked to submit a trial brief. She had decided on this course because it would give her an opportunity to make a statement after she had taken the depositions from Fena's late arrivals. At this point, then, other than the material from Beth, the record was closed and all testimony and exhibits were *supposed* to be complete. Beth immediately made plans to take depositions from the doctors who wrote the letters.

❖

In the meantime, the Gay/Lesbian Support Group at St. Cloud State University was planning a dance fund raiser for the case. It forced me to strip away another layer of my own homophobia. Not only did it still astound me to see same-sex couples dancing together, but they were dancing in the same room with mixed couples! The great part was that it was a consciousness raiser for more than just me. The group was so proud that they had raised $600 in such a supportive atmosphere.

Financial help on the legal expenses wasn't the only gift I received at this time. I was absolutely broke with no possibility of money coming in for the summer. I had no idea what I was going to live on without going further in debt, which only added to my anxiety. To my surprise, I miraculously received a check for back pay as a result of the sex discrimination suit against St. Cloud State. I was tremendously relieved. I would have the money to pay my next month's mortgage and gas bill.

At the same time, I felt ashamed about receiving the back pay at all. I had done nothing to support the case since I simply didn't understand how I had been discriminated against as a woman. I really had believed that the system did its best for me, as an individual, regardless of my gender. Yet here I was benefiting from the years of hard work by the feminists on campus. At the time I could only believe that the money was a sign from God that I was being looked after and that I was meant to go on with the fight. (Later, I joked with Julie about how offended she must have been that I gave God credit for her hard work.)

It took almost a month to make the arrangements for the depositions. The first deposition was of Dr. Julie Moller, a general practitioner, who never met me nor observed me working with Sharon. She did not testify at any of the hearings in the case, but did have her deposition taken on June 3, 1985, in response to her May 7 letter submitted by Fena to the court.

Dr. Moller first saw Sharon in 1984. At this time Moller wrote a letter to Jack Fena stating that "[i]t appears that she likes her mother, her father and Karen Thompson and enjoys their company. She thinks of Karen Thompson as a good friend."

Yet in the letter that Fena had introduced at the hearing, Dr. Moller wrote that she had conferred with nurses at Park Point who said to her that they "consider Miss Thompson's visits as abusive to a vulnerable adult." When pressed in the deposition taken by Ristvedt, Dr. Moller could not remember the names of any of the nurses who told her this. A detailed review of all the nursing notes undertaken in connection with various appeals shows that *nowhere* in the Park Point nursing notes is there any statement that my visits were detrimental to Sharon.

Dr. Moller herself could not state from her own observations that any visits between Sharon and me were harmful. Her testimony was simply hearsay. Nonetheless, Dr. Moller's letters have been cited time and time again by Donald Kowalski in defense of his restriction of contact between Sharon and me.

Moller's ignorance of Sharon's capabilities and mental state became clear when her letter was compared to her deposition. In her May letter she states, "In our local newspaper I have read that Miss Kowalski types sentence-long messages to Miss Thompson on her small communicating machine; I seriously question her ability to do so spontaneously. I saw Miss Kowalski use this tool in December, 1984, and it was cumbersome for her to type out short single words; at that time she was unable to type out her own name."

Less than a month later, in her June 3 deposition, she contradicted herself by saying, "It's my impression that she uses the typewriter fairly well." When asked about the contradiction, she said, "Well, you know, I think at that point I wasn't aware of the typewriter . . . . I am aware that she is able to write short sentences."

Dr. Stephen Goff, a specialist in rehabilitation who evaluated Sharon at Miller-Dwan's Polinsky Institute, wrote the other letter submitted by Fena, dated May 8, 1985. Though he had not testified in court, Goff's letter was cited throughout the subsequent litigation. The letter almost exclusively relied on statements allegedly made to him by Dr. Cowan and Dr. Moller. By definition, this letter was also full of hearsay. In the deposition that Beth took, his testimony called into question many of the opinions stated in that letter.

For instance, in the letter, Goff gave his opinion, based on what Drs. Cowan and Moller had told him, that my visits were harmful to Sharon and a cause for her depression. By the May hearing, it was generally agreed that Sharon was out of the depression. Occupational therapists' and physical therapists' notes clearly indicated that Sharon was more alert and responsive. Yet I was spending the same amount of time with Sharon doing the same things with her that I always had. In his deposition, Goff concurred that she had regressed since January but that she was recently picking up again.

Goff also admitted that even the testing physician, Jerry Henkel-Johnson, had not identified the cause of Sharon's depression. Goff actually stated he knew that as a result of my time with Sharon "there was some very good interaction, that there was some stimulation, that there was caring and good nursing care, and that there was an active participation, a desire to include . . . outside activities and so on." He admitted that Dr. Cowan did not give him any evidence or support for the opinion that I should be kept away from Sharon. I had even tried to call Dr. Goff on several occasions, as I was legally entitled to equal medical information, and he testified that he deliberately ignored my calls.

Beth questioned Goff about his normal approach to family visitation:

"In your practice, would you normally recommend that a husband or wife be excluded from visiting without first having—if there was a problem, first having given them the opportunity to—to discuss the problem with yourself?"

"No. I would normally try to discuss the problem and . . . find out what were the contributing causes. I am—I believe in this case that I had a significant amount of secondhand information that—that I didn't need to do. However, I would have been glad to do it upon request."

"Did you ever indicate to Karen Thompson that you wanted to discuss anything with her—"

"No."

"—regarding the situation?"

"I did not."

He concluded, "I think that this whole proceeding is very detrimental to this lady, this girl . . . . My recommendations are not directed against the personality, they are simply directed to try to end this conflict, which I feel is very detrimental."

Dr. Goff continued to maintain that the only way to end the conflict was by cutting out one of the parties, which he admitted he normally wouldn't have done (agreeing with Dr. Gregor's testimony). He based his recommendation to remove me on Dr. Cowan's statements to him, even though those statements had been contradicted by Cowan's own testimony at the hearing.

ANOTHER FENA TACTIC

As part of his determination to imply that I somehow abused Sharon and his strategy of mounting a personal attack on my character, Fena submitted an affidavit dated May 27 (long after the records were 'closed') to the judge from a patient at Park Point Manor who claimed that I had bathed Sharon behind closed doors. How interesting that the patient just happened to observe this (through closed doors?) on May 12 and then felt such a sense of moral obligation that he sought out the guardian, Donald Kowalski, to make this urgent report. Fena addressed this matter in a letter to Mr. James Ingison, attorney for Park Point Manor, dated May 16·

❖   . . . Donald Kowalski was informed by one of Sharon's fellow patients at Park Point Manor that Thompson was in the bathroom behind a closed door for half an hour, apparently bathing Sharon, with no one else in attendance. Donald Kowalski came to me with this information and a copy of the regulation [following] . . . . Resident care is done by facility personnel. State regulations prohibit family members from providing resident care while the resident is receiving skilled care . . . .

He [Donald Kowalski] was concerned, in view of not only his own feelings, but based on the medical opinions of the three doctors regarding Thompson's contact with Sharon Kowalski, especially the one referring to Sharon as a vulnerable adult.

Part of Fena's strategy seemed to be to send the judge copies of his correspondence which might reinforce any point he wanted to make in court. These letters then became part of the file even though they were never properly submitted as evidence. Fena's letter to Ingison was sent to the judge along with the patient's affidavit. While nothing was ever brought up in court about it, Fena used the letter in several situations to his advantage *even after* he received the following answer from Park Point Manor's attorney:

❖ . . . [O]ur client's investigation of this matter revealed that there was proper monitoring by a staff member during the bath in question and that the door to the bathing room was not shut. Further, there was no evidence of abuse of Ms. Kowalski during the time in question.

Since that time, I have confirmed that there is no regulatory prohibition against family members or friends providing resident care. Unfortunately, this statement is included in an outdated pamphlet prepared several years ago . . . . To date, with regard to Ms. Kowalski, Park Point has no evidence that there has been any abuse and neglect of Ms. Kowalski by any person.

MINNESOTA CIVIL LIBERTIES UNION

At the same time that 'evidence' was mysteriously piling up on Fena's desk, the Minnesota Civil Liberties Union began to take a more active role on Sharon's behalf. When Sharon had signed a statement back in November asking the MCLU to represent her, they had filed an amicus brief on her behalf. On May 30, Janlori Goldman, Assistant Director of the MCLU, visited Sharon to personally reconfirm her desire for representation. During that visit she asked Sharon questions to which Sharon responded by typing answers.

Among other questions, Jan asked Sharon, "Do you want me, as a representative of the MCLU, to visit you?"

Sharon typed, "Yes."

"Do you understand that if the MCLU represents you, we can only represent you on the constitutional issues involved in your case such as your right to counsel and your right to receive visitors of your choice?"

"Yes."

"Do you feel that your wishes are being made known to the court?"

"No."

"Do you want your wishes to be made known to the court?"

"Yes."

"Will you tell me what your wishes are?"

Sharon typed, "Yes."

During that visit, other subjects were also discussed. In response to the question, "What are you and Karen?" Sharon typed, "Gay." When asked what 'gay' meant, Sharon once again demonstrated her ability to understand by typing, "Love same sex."

On June 12, Janlori returned to see Sharon, along with Amy Bromberg, a volunteer attorney for the MCLU. Sharon was asked many of the same questions and answered them consistently, the same as the previous visit.

"Do you understand that there is a court proceeding going on where decisions are being made about who you get to see and where you live?"

"Yes."

"Do you feel that your wishes are being made known to the court?"

"No."

"Do you want me to help to let the court know what you want?"

"Yes."

"Did you exchange rings with Karen Thompson?"

"Yes."

"Why?"

Sharon clearly typed out, "Because we love each other."

Based on these communications, Amy Bromberg and Brian O'Neill, volunteer attorneys for the MCLU, requested the right to represent Sharon Kowalski as counsel on June 20. Ironically, Jack Fena responded June 25, in another irregular correspondence with the judge. ". . . I welcomed her [Bromberg's] entry into this case, even though all of the evidence has been submitted and final arguments made to the court."

The MCLU then asked the court to have Sharon tested before reaching a conclusion on the May hearings. Depending upon the results of the testing, they argued, it might be advisable to obtain Sharon's own testimony before making a ruling that might drastically affect her life. In this instance, the court denied this request because the record was closed and it was untimely. Fena's timeliness, however, never seemed to be in question.

Beth had already responded to some of Fena's correspondence sent to the judges. She wrote a letter to Judge Douglas:

❖   Since our last hearing in this matter I have received copies of at least six letters from Mr. Fena which he has directed to various parties and attorneys involved in this matter. In these letters Mr. Fena has attempted to present further testimony based on his own opinion, based on the opinions of his clients, and that of other persons. In any event these two- to three-page letters have been replete with nothing but additional argument he has submitted in his letters. *To then receive a letter and affidavit of Mr. Fena requesting that his own correspondence be treated as evidence and be considered as such by the Court in making its decision is not only contrary to any rules of evidence which I have had experience with, but is precisely the situation which I was referring to at our last hearing in which I stated that this matter could go on ad infinitum. Mr. Fena has raised several new issues and allegations against my client which must apparently be dealt with and resolved now that he has presented them to you.* [Author's emphasis]

In Fena's numerous letters he has raised issues and allegations against my client which are wholly improper to be raised before the court in the manner in which he has done. Mr. Fena has repeatedly made allegations that a rally which was to be held in Duluth regarding Park Point Manor was my client's rally. He has repeated this on more than one occasion based only on hearsay information. Mr. Fena did not take the time to contact me to learn any truth regarding this rally until the date of the depositions on June 3 which was subsequent to the time he raised the rally in letters to both yourself and Tom Hayes. As I have now informed Mr. Hayes, Mr. Ingison and Mr. Fena, it is true that my client knew of this pending rally and had been contacted by persons in connection with it. This rally was not Karen's rally, or held at her instigation. In fact, she was asked by some of the organizers to refrain from participating in that the organizers did not wish the issue, which was proper patient care, to be overshadowed by a possibility that news media would turn it into a gay event. My client at their request did not participate.

There are other persons and organizations who have concerns regarding the care of patients at Park Point Manor and those persons organized and held this rally. As a result of Mr. Fena's allegations and insinuations, I am enclosing copies we have obtained from the office of Health Facility Complaints for the past year. It is clear that there have been other persons who have made complaints against Park Point Manor and this has been true prior to the time that it was even contemplated that Sharon should be at the facility.

During this entire time, I continued visiting Sharon almost daily in spite of school, court hearings and constant fear about the upcoming decision. When school was out, I stayed in Duluth for days at a time, living out of my car, moving constantly so I wouldn't be a burden to the strangers who had offered support. I was displaced, at loose ends. At home I had no time, and when I had time, I wasn't at home. Since Sharon had come out of her depression, she was beginning to make progress again, but it was slow and she had a long way to go to catch up with her previous accomplishments in St. Cloud.

The weather was beautiful, but I couldn't take Sharon any of the places she wanted to go. I would wheel her out into the courtyard, but that soon got old. I was totally frustrated by not being allowed to take Sharon on an outing. The stagnation was wearing on us. I kept thinking that the accident had happened to the wrong person. Sharon was always so much more creative than me, so fun-loving—she should have been directing our activities. Still, in spite of all the barriers, we continued to share our love and grow together. I became more and more sure that we could work through the problems caused by the accident if we would just be given the chance. I believed even more strongly that Sharon could come home and we could make a new life together.

COURT RULING ON
KOWALSKI GUARDIANSHIP

On July 23, 1985, the court order was filed and my worst nightmare became reality. Donald Kowalski was given full guardianship with unlimited powers. I had lived in fear that I would be denied visitation with Sharon since that terrible evening in January of 1984 when Don told me friends shouldn't visit so often. I had listened in court to Donald Kowalski stating that nothing could convince him I was a loved one of Sharon's and that he would do everything possible to separate Sharon and me. I knew what he would do.

Some of the court's key findings were:

❖ 1. The ward was unable to attend the hearing by reason of medical condition as evidenced by written statements from licensed physicians.

2. The ward lacks sufficient understanding or capacity to make or communicate responsible decisions concerning her person . . . .

11. Donald Kowalski is the most suitable and best qualified among those available and willing to discharge the trust.

12. The ward's ability to respond or communicate had been inconsistent and, at times, unreliable, which situation may or may not improve.

17. The ongoing conflict between Don and Della Kowalski and Karen Thompson adversely affects the welfare of Sharon Kowalski at the present time; and elimination of that conflict and its adverse affect on the ward is in the best interest of the ward at the present time.

Therefore, it was ordered:

❖   . . . [t]hat the appointment of Donald Kowalski as guardian of the person and estate of Sharon Kowalski be and hereby is confirmed and continued in all respects with all the powers . . . without limitation and condition.

. . . [T]he guardian . . . shall have the power to determine who may visit Sharon Kowalski, and the times and duration of such visitation. The guardian shall consider, regarding all visitation decisions, that the primary consideration is the best interest of the ward and any reliably expressed wishes of the ward, both of which may change from time to time. The guardian shall also consider regarding visitation, the recommendations of medical and health care personnel and the needs and desires of the institution wherein the ward resides.

Within 24 hours of receiving the court order, Park Point notified my attorneys that Donald Kowalski had denied visitation to anyone not on his list. It was made clear that the nursing home would not allow me to see Sharon. Later I found out that Donald Kowalski also prohibited visitation by Tom Hayes, the MCLU, disability rights groups and many of Sharon's friends. They were not on his approved list and he would never add them.

Even though it was clear we could appeal the decision, I was devastated. How could this be happening? Crying couldn't express the depth of my anguish. Nothing brought relief. My mind was in a constant whirl. I couldn't think straight. I hadn't even had a chance to explain to Sharon why I wouldn't be there. It would be like I had just dropped out of her life. She would think I had left her. I kept saying over and over to myself, "What can I do?" Yet even in my most panic-stricken moments, I believed my attorneys would eventually be able to get me back in to see her.

There was no justice or logic to the decision, starting with Sharon being declared medically incapable of being in the courtroom when we had presented so much evidence to the contrary. And how, in God's name, could they find Donald Kowalski the most qualified person to be Sharon's guardian when he didn't know the first thing about Sharon's care or how to look out for her daily needs? Was it because the court thought that, as a man, he could handle the financial end better? And that paying for Sharon's care was more important than the quality of her care?

Beth's final argument at the hearing had said it all:

❖ The guardian, aside from his request for an exorbitant amount of compensation for himself, appears to have handled the guardianship of the estate adequately, but he has totally failed as the guardian of the person because he will not accept his daughter as the person she is and was. It is no surprise that he does not discuss with her what he seeks to do on her behalf. He argues on the one hand she wouldn't understand it, but on the other hand that she is devastated by the publicity. If she understands one, she understands the other.

But we will never know why Don Kowalski was granted full guardianship because the court gave no reasons, and it didn't have to.

MEDIA COVERAGE OF THE HEARINGS

When reporting the guardianship decision, the *St. Cloud Daily Times* headlines read, "Lesbian Bitter Over Decision." The article, reducing the case to a level so simplistic that the real issues were totally distorted, reported as a fact, "Psychologists say she [Sharon] has the mental capacity of a six-year-old." However, they did include a few things I had told them, for instance, "If Sharon and I were a man and a woman, we'd be married and this couldn't happen to us, and therefore we're not protected equally by the law."

But these few points were overshadowed by the headline and Fena's allegation, "Thompson may be seeking guardianship for financial reasons. Settlement is pending on a multimillion dollar lawsuit . . . ." They quoted Fena further, "They're [the Kowalskis] very pleased that they have their daughter back and they'll get back to a normal life . . . . [T]hey're grateful that the facts were found to be as they believed from the very beginning—that their daughter, who is helpless physically as well as mentally, belongs under their care, custody and control."

Fortunately, Julie immediately wrote a letter to the editor challenging the misinformation in the article and the homophobia of the press. She responded point by point:

❖   First, Karen Thompson cannot possibly benefit financially from any settlement in regard to Sharon Kowalski. She has filed for guardianship of the person, not guardianship of the estate . . . . On the contrary, Karen is in debt more than $25,000 in legal costs . . . .
     Secondly, Karen never even would have filed for guardianship if the Kowalskis [had] communicated and worked with her. Karen, personally and through her attorneys, has continually asked Sharon's parents to discuss the situation and work together for Sharon's benefit . . . .
     Homophobia (the fear and hatred of lesbians and gay men) runs deep in our society. Sharon's parents continue to deny, against all evidence, that Sharon and Karen loved each other. While they have refused to cooperate with Karen, Karen has worked thousands of hours to help Sharon recover muscle coordination, speech skills, etc. . . . Because of homophobia, Sharon's parents, now backed up by the court, are blocking the person most likely to help Sharon's chances of recovery . . . .
     Finally, the media are not immune to homophobia and certainly have a great influence on public opinion. In this instance, I challenge the use of the term 'bitter' in Wednesday's headline. Bitter implies that someone is twisted, acrimonious or reacting more strongly than he or she has a right to. Society is not sympathetic to bitter people. Bitter is not an objective term, it is a judgment.

For the most part, the mainstream press coverage continued to portray Sharon as a totally helpless person, to question my motives for wanting guardianship, and to play into stereotypes about lesbians. Article after article described me as the 'alleged' lover, or 'the woman who claims to be her lover.'

A poll taken by the *St. Cloud Daily Times* was an excellent case in point. The question asked of the 209 adults polled was: "Some time ago, a St. Cloud woman was disabled in a car accident. She now requires permanent care by a guardian. The court appointed the woman's father as guardian rather than a female homosexual friend who claims she had maintained a marital-type relationship with the disabled woman. In cases like this, do you think the guardianship should be awarded to the parent or the relationship partner?"

It was very unclear to me why the paper had chosen to poll readers. That they set up the responses by the question was predictable. Who, given the general social prejudices, would vote for a "female homosexual friend who *claims* . . . a marital-type relationship"? I was surprised that only 48.8 percent voted for the parents while 25.8 percent voted for the "homosexual friend" and the other 25.4 percent were undecided. It seemed an outright victory given the biased presentation.

At this point I was still shocked that no media had been willing to do a real investigative report on a case so significant to everyone's rights. I thought if I could just get all the well-documented facts to the reporters, they certainly would present them to the public. I couldn't believe they never checked on the veracity of Fena's accusations. If this case was indicative of a pattern of reporting, what kind of information was the public receiving on other important issues? Many of the beliefs I had functioned under for so many years of my life were falling by the wayside. My belief in the 'objectivity' of the press was now just one more.

❖

Within 48 hours of receiving the order, Donald Kowalski had Sharon moved from Park Point Manor Nursing Home in Duluth to Leisure Hills Health Care Center in Hibbing. He had testified under oath that he had no plans to move Sharon and that they were very satisfied with the quality of her care at Park Point Manor. The court had earlier ruled that Sharon must be in a nursing home with a young adult rehabilitation ward. Leisure Hills did not have such a ward. This was the nursing home that the court had passed over the year before in favor of Country Manor in St. Cloud.

I was in anguish at not being able to see Sharon. I knew that she would be suffering from the move; each of the moves had been harder and harder on her. My not knowing the staff, not being able to even visualize the room she was in, not being there to help her get oriented all made me feel more helpless than I'd ever imagined I could feel.

On August 5, the volunteer attorneys for the MCLU tried to get a temporary restraining order, which would have restored my visitation rights. It was postponed. On August 7, they filed an appeal of the July order to the Court of Appeals of the State of Minnesota. By Minnesota statute, when an order is under appeal, it is suspended until the appeal has been decided. Therefore, I expected to be able to continue visiting Sharon.

With a copy of the appeal and the Minnesota statute in hand, I anxiously drove to Leisure Hills to see Sharon on August 8. Since I was teaching summer school, I got there in the evening. The only thing the staff would tell me was that Sharon wasn't there. They told me to come back the next day to speak to the administrator. I tried to leave the papers with them so everything could be cleared by the time I returned, but no one would take them.

When I returned the next morning, I was told the administrator was out of town and wouldn't be back for a week or so. I asked, "Who can I talk with, then? Who is in charge?" I finally talked to the assistant administrator who would not make any decision without speaking to the administrator. I had a legal right to be with Sharon, and they were breaking the law by refusing me visitation. After talking to several different people, I was told that I would have to leave the premises or they would call the police.

Frustrated to the core, I left and called Beth Ristvedt. One more time, Beth was unwilling to bring the force of law behind my rights by pursuing other ways of getting me in. She recommended that I drive back to St. Cloud until we got things cleared up. I drove back, crying all the way. During the time the nursing home was blocking my legal right to visit, Fena was trying to obtain a special order from the appeals court to remove the statute so I would be prevented from seeing Sharon ever again. His first attempt failed, and finally on August 13, the nursing home could no longer delay my visitation rights. By the time I'd heard from my attorneys, it was too late to drive to Hibbing on the 13th, so I had to wait until after classes on the 14th. I drove up with a friend, Paul Reichert, so that if there were any further problems, I would have a witness.

I was so excited to see Sharon and yet anxious because I wondered what her reaction would be. Would she be mad at me because I hadn't been there for three weeks? Or would she be glad to see me? We arrived in the evening. Another man and woman were visiting Sharon, who was sitting with her head slumped to the side, showing no sign of interaction. When I walked into her room and said, "Hi, Sharon," she lifted her head and her whole face lit up. With her reaction, a weight lifted off of my shoulders, and I'm sure my face lit up, too.

Paul and I acknowledged the others in the room but they did not speak to us. So I sat down beside Sharon and began talking to her. The tension mounted as I tried to carry on a normal conversation with her while they made asides to each other in low voices. I asked the man and woman if Sharon had a typewriter. At first they sat and glared at us, then responded nastily in a way that gave us no information. Paul went to the car and brought in a typewriter we had brought. (I later discovered that the Kowalskis had left my electric typewriter at Park Point and had provided her with no other means of communication.)

When 'open' time came, other friends of the family came into the room immediately. I could see this was planned and that nothing constructive for Sharon would be accomplished by my trying to stay longer. I told her goodbye and that I would see her the next day.

When I drove up after classes the next day, Thursday, I planned to stay through the weekend. Fortunately, no one was there during my visitation periods for the next four days. I spent every minute with Sharon during those days. I asked the Director of Nursing if she would observe Sharon and me during one of our work sessions. The director agreed to sit in with us, and Sharon expressed her willingness to work in front of her. We went through different stretching exercises and typed conversations. The Director of Nursing appeared shocked and volunteered to me, just out of Sharon's hearing, that she had seen Sharon do nothing since she had been moved there. What's more, she never expected Sharon to be able to do the kinds of things she demonstrated.

I asked permission to attend occupational therapy with Sharon and I discovered the same thing. Sharon had responded very little since being moved there. I asked the therapist if we could show her the types of things Sharon was used to working on. She was very receptive to learning as much about Sharon as she could. We had a fun session in which Sharon typed all kinds of responses including compound math problems. The therapist seemed very impressed, thanked me for coming to the session and made me feel welcome to return.

I also checked on Sharon's physical therapy schedule and learned that in the three weeks she had been there, she had never been out of her room for physical therapy, but they "were planning to start it next week." I was disappointed that it was taking so long to get the sessions started.

Even though Sharon still responded to some questions and exercises—which totally surprised the staff—her condition was noticeably worse to me. Her reaction time was much slower and she labored over skills she had performed routinely before.

She was seriously disoriented in many areas. Her short-term memory was the worst I had ever seen it. I would leave the room to get a drink of water and she wouldn't remember I had been there. She had so many questions. She didn't know what had happened, where she was or why she was there. She was eager to know and grateful to have someone explain it. Obviously, she had not been getting the constant, repetitive attention that was necessary to maintain, let alone improve, her memory.

It was heart-wrenching to see her struggle to understand and remember simple things.

I prepared to leave on Monday night to drive back to St. Cloud, since I had no visitation on Tuesday. It was hard enough for me to get ready to leave, but Sharon seemed panicked at the thought.

She pleaded with her eyes and typed, "Help me. Get me out of here."

Once again I tried to explain why I couldn't take her out but assured her that I would be back on Wednesday. Fighting tears, I told her my visitation time was up and I had to leave.

She typed, "Please take me home with you."

Looking at the love and trust in Sharon's eyes, I could hardly bear to leave her. It made me feel like a traitor, like I was betraying her by leaving. This was the most difficult parting we had ever experienced, even though at the time I had no idea it would be the last time I would see her. I had no idea how long that look in Sharon's eyes would haunt me.

On August 20, my attorney was notified that, based on a doctor's order, my visitation would no longer be allowed. Even though the statute gave a legal right to visit, the nursing home was required to follow doctor's orders. Once again Fena's orchestration became apparent. The letter from this Dr. Wilson was addressed to him and began, "As per your request." Normally such correspondence would be directed to the nursing home or placed in Sharon's medical file. The letter read as follows:

❖   Dear Mr. Fena:

As per your request for a medical report on Sharon Kowalski concerning her current medical and psychological condition and her ability to deal with visitation from Karen Thompson, this report is based on an extensive review of her medical and psychological evaluations since her accident on November 13, 1983. This would include reports from Dr. Goff at Polinsky Institute in Duluth and her attending physician Dr. Moller, from the Duluth Clinic and psychiatric reports form Dr. Cowan in Duluth. It is also based on previous court testimony and depositions from various parties involved in this case. It is also based on my direct observation of personnel at Leisure Hill Nursing Home.

. . . Ms. Thompson has apparently been visiting Sharon on a regular basis for approximately the past week at the Leisure Hills Nursing Home. According to affidavits and statements from individuals who have observed this interaction at Park Point

Manor, it has come to my attention that Karen Thompson has been involved in bathing Sharon Kowalski behind a closed door for a prolonged period of time. It has also come to my attention that Ms. Thompson has alleged a sexual relationship with Sharon Kowalski that existed prior to the accident.

Based on this knowledge and my best medical judgment concerning Sharon and her welfare, I feel that visits by Karen Thompson at this time would expose Sharon Kowalski to a high risk of sexual abuse and I also believe that such visits would again expose Sharon to recurrent bouts of reactive depression that have greatly impeded her recovery in the past. I also have been made aware that Karen Thompson has, at times in the past, been involved in directly administering physical therapy to Sharon Kowalski. Because of Sharon's physical problems, I feel that such therapy administered by a non-professional could be extremely dangerous to her health and long-term recovery. Thus as Sharon's physician, I have directed the Leisure Hills Nursing Home staff to not allow Karen Thompson to visit Sharon Kowalski under any circumstances and that Sharon is to receive physical therapy only from a qualified therapist. These orders are based on what I feel is in Sharon's best interests from a medical and psychological standpoint.
William L. Wilson, M.D.

I couldn't believe that a doctor would write such a homophobic and ridiculous letter. It was very apparent to me that he had written this letter based on select materials. Even more obvious, he had not read the medical notes nor talked with the Director of Nursing from Leisure Hills about my visits.

In the medical notes subpoenaed to prepare our new motions, Ms. Stone, the occupational therapist, had written,

❖❖   Patient seen five times this week in O.T. Her attention to task and level of cooperation varied greatly. Monday Sharon was seen with former roommate present. She appeared highly motivated and typed responses to questions, did head and RUE movements on request. She correctly answered compound math problems, typing the answers (example: 64÷8+3.) She utilized hand signals appropriately for yes/no. When asked, she stated she was not aware of place or time, and R.O. was given. The rest of the week Sharon was seen with only therapist present. [Monday was the last day I was allowed to visit with Sharon.] She did minimal typing on Tuesday, and responded with hand signals to four or five questions. The rest of the week Sharon did not respond with head shake or hand signals to approximately 90 percent of requests. She put chin to chest and right hand to face when not responding.

This constant documentation which should have supported our being together had been twisted around to serve as a rationale for why we should be kept apart. I thought for sure the upcoming appeal would overturn that decision since there were so many clearly documented facts which supported our position.

CHAPTER 12

The Appeals

My attorneys decided to write a letter to Doctor Wilson, raising the contradictions in testimony and citing other medical information "to try to change his mind." I was totally exasperated with this 'reasonable' approach which meant that my rights continued to be violated while precious time for Sharon's rehabilitation was passing. Why couldn't we take some bolder, more immediate action? Fena always did. Because my attorneys recommended a conservative strategy, we were constantly fighting a defensive battle and continuing to lose ground.

I tried to express my frustration to Beth Ristvedt and Peter Donohue. They simply repeated the rules by which everything must be done. I was always made to feel that they knew what was best and that I should just follow their advice. But at this point I had lost confidence in them and wondered if I should seek other counsel.

Peter's letter wasn't sent for nine days. I was in agony the entire time. Now that summer school was over and I had several weeks to spend with Sharon, we were kept apart from each other. Half of the anguish I felt resulted from the knowledge that this entire situation was so unnecessary, such a waste of everyone's time and energy. Sharon's suffering was compounded by the interference of self-serving institutions and individuals.

Peter's five-page, well-reasoned letter laid out all of the information that Wilson had neglected to consider. He included the opinions of Sharon's neurologist in St. Cloud, Dr. Larson, who said I had a special relationship with Sharon and nothing should be done to separate us. He included the names of all the therapists and nurses from all the places

Sharon had resided testifying about the positive impact I had on Sharon. He wrote of the documentation of Sharon's communication skills and asked if Wilson had tried to ascertain what Sharon's wishes were. He asked if Wilson had seen the response of the nursing home about the 'bathing incident.' And he asked Wilson to examine the lack of medical evidence tying the depression to my visits. Wilson never bothered to respond. So much for reason.

While Peter was writing his letter, I tried direct action through another channel. I contacted the Minnesota Office of Health Facility Complaints and asked them to investigate Sharon's rights to visitors of choice under the Minnesota Patient Bill of Rights. This bill guarantees patients certain rights—among other things, the right to choose one's visitors.

After reviewing the formal complaint, a special investigator for the Office of Health Facility Complaints made "an unannounced visit" to Leisure Hills Nursing Home on September 11, 1985. He reviewed Sharon's medical record and interviewed staff. Then he

❖   . . . visited the patient, accompanied by the Director of Nurses, and with the permission of the patient, interviewed her regarding her desire to have the identified individual visit. Because of the patient's diagnosis and handicap, the interview was conducted using two systems, the first in which the patient indicated yes or no by raising her right thumb and the second system whereby the patient typed out her answers on a portable electric typewriter.

Using the first system the patient raised her thumb to indicate that she would permit the investigator to visit and ask questions and also raised her thumb to indicate that "yes" she would like the identified friend to visit. During this time the patient was able to lift her head and did maintain eye contact with the investigator. With the second system the patient was asked her age and she responded by tapping out the numbers two and four (the patient is actually 28 years old). The patient was again asked if she would like the identified friend to visit with her and she responded by typing out "yes." The investigator visited for a few minutes more and then left . . . .

It should also be noted that the patient has demonstrably been able to communicate using both of the identified systems (raising her thumb and the typewriter) for some time now. Both administrative staff and supervisory nursing staff could give no reason why these visits have been terminated and saw no detriment to the patient if they were to continue.

The attending physician was also interviewed and stated that he wrote the order to protect the patient from possible abuse, but that if the facility could provide evidence to him that the patient could be sufficiently protected he would not object to the patient having visitors of her choice.

Conclusion: Substantiated—In violation.

A Suggested Method of Correction: If such an order is necessary for any patient, adequate documentation could be entered into the medical record to support the order. If no such documentation is available, such order could be refused or rescinded. Policies addressing this matter could be developed.

Time Period for Correction: Five days

Sharon had communicated with them! What a relief to know Sharon was still fighting from her side. And the Office of Health Facility Complaints had taken a very strong stance on Sharon's behalf. In the meantime, I had decided I had to change attorneys, as difficult as that process seemed. I had been inquiring about what attorneys in Minneapolis/St. Paul might be qualified in human rights law—especially disability rights or lesbian/gay rights. It was also important that they know I had no money and be willing to do some, if not a lot of, pro bono work. Julie and I drove to the Twin Cities to interview various attorneys. On the drive home we discussed the advantages and disadvantages of each. We reasoned that maybe we should hire a nice white male who would be more acceptable to the system we were dealing with. But that reasoning went against everything I believed in and my beliefs were about all I had left. There were times when I wondered if I should have left some scruples behind if doing so would free Sharon sooner or improve her chances for a fuller recovery. For instance, I had refused to base our case on anything that would have publicly attacked the Kowalskis' lack of qualifications to make decisions about Sharon's care. I didn't think that was what Sharon would have wanted and I've never believed that the ends justify the means.

After we had discussed attorneys, Julie launched into an enthusiastic explanation of the settlement of the sex discrimination suit against St. Cloud State University. One of the provisions was to require each full-time faculty member to attend eleven hours of an Affirmative Action Education Program. She was ecstatic. "Can you imagine? We'll actually have eleven hours with the entire faculty to address affirmative action issues!"

"I have too much to do already," I grumbled. "I hardly have time to get my work done as it is."

"Oh Karen," she began patiently, looking at me as much as her driving allowed, "don't you see that these issues are related to the very foundation of what your case is all about? Sexism, sexual harassment, racism, ageism, handicapism, all the issues are related." Her hand made a circle in the air. "Certain groups benefit when they might not even intend to. It's important to study all types of oppression so we can see how they relate. I'm sorry for the lecture but try to keep an open mind, okay?"

"All right, I promise you I'll go to the affirmative action workshops and not complain. I don't really understand what it has to do with my case, but I'll do it for you." At this time, I really didn't see the connections. I would get glimpses of the injustice, and I could clearly see it in my own situation. But only later did I realize how deeply these issues had affected my case from the very beginning and how similar it was to other types of oppression.

A few days later, I decided to retain Sue Wilson and Toni Pomerene as my new attorneys. They had worked on a number of custody cases for lesbians. Peter and Beth were exhausted and very willing to turn over the case to a fresh team. By the middle of September Sue Wilson filed as my attorney.

APPEALS TO REVERSE THE JULY 23 ORDER

By this time the MCLU, Tom Hayes and my attorneys had all filed separate appeals of the July 23 order that had given full guardianship to Donald Kowalski. The first appeal to be filed and heard was the one filed by the MCLU in August.

Don Kowalski countered with two motions. The first addressed the Minnesota statute that prohibited a court order from going into effect while under appeal and would have restored my visitation rights. Although Dr. Wilson's letter, as enforced by the nursing home, continued to keep me from seeing Sharon, Fena, on behalf of the guardian, was still trying to remove the statute in case we successfully challenged the letter. The guardian's next move was to ask the court to dismiss the MCLU appeal as having been brought by counsel "without standing" to represent Sharon. (That is, the MCLU had never been recognized by the court as having a legal right to represent Sharon.)

On September 13, the court of appeals ruled on the guardian's motions, granting both. One of the three judges, Judge Doris Huspeni, gave a dissenting opinion, stating emphatically that the Minnesota statute *should* apply. "The statute clearly suspends operation of the order 'until the appeal is determined or [this court] orders otherwise.' Minn. Stat. #525.714. This trial court did not find the ward was endangered by liberal visitation and I discern nothing in the record before us to support a finding that operation of the statute will endanger her. I would apply the statute and suspend operation of the July 23 order until resolution of this appeal." This was the only time that Judge Huspeni sat for this case, though the other two judges were present for all three appeals hearings.

SECOND ROUND OF APPEALS

The MCLU responded by filing Writs of Prohibition and Mandamus to the Minnesota Supreme Court asking for further review of the Court of Appeals' decisions. The Writs, which are documents asking for extraordinary and immediate relief, argued that Sharon had the right to be represented by the attorney of her choice. They were summarily denied on November 4. The MCLU filed a motion asking for reconsideration, which was also denied. Undaunted, the MCLU took their appeal on the right to represent Sharon to the United States Supreme Court. In their petition, they stated:

❖   The Court has held that even those accused of a crime have a right to be represented by their counsel of choice . . . . The handicapped have a need for protection greater than those accused of crimes. Subjected to legal proceedings not dissimilar from criminal proceedings, they are often voiceless. In addition, the impaired are disenfranchised through no fault of their own. The impaired ought to have rights greater than those accused of crimes.

The United States Supreme Court, however, refused to hear this petition, "without prejudice." (Meaning that though the court was refusing to hear the case at that time, it did *not* mean that the case lacked merit to be heard.)

When the MCLU was denied the right to represent Sharon by the Minnesota Court of Appeals, Tom Hayes asked permission to associate the MCLU with him in representing Sharon. The law clearly states that attorneys may associate with other attorneys to guarantee clients the best possible representation. However, the Court of Appeals denied *this* association, stating that it was too late to associate while the case was under appeal. This was another extraordinary and arbitrary ruling, especially since later the court would allow Jack Fena to associate with Harry Seiben on both the personal injury and guardianship cases.

Nevertheless, the MCLU was allowed to submit an amicus brief for Tom Hayes' appeal, in support of Sharon's civil rights. Their brief dramatically summarized their position on Sharon's behalf:

❖   The Minnesota Civil Liberties Union submits this brief as amicus curiae in accordance with this Court's order filed September 17, 1985. We still believe that we represent Sharon Kowalski.

In her brief, Ms. [Thompson] notes that the probate court found that Karen Thompson and Sharon Kowalski have a "significant relationship." We note that the evidence below established that Ms. Kowalski and Ms. Thompson were involved in a lesbian relationship and had made significant personal and financial commitments to each other over an extended period of time. The dispute in this Court is a result of that commitment: Ms. Thompson will not abandon her loved one and Donald Kowalski will not accept Ms. Thompson as a loved one of his daughter.

The decision below resulted in a unique kind of deprivation—the termination of a relationship between two individuals, against their wishes, without a finding that such deprivation was necessary, medically or otherwise. The decision below is patently unconstitutional.

This case presents issues of fundamental importance . . . rights that are intrinsic to our concepts of human fulfillment and dignity, rights that deserve zealous protection by the courts. . . . Sharon Kowalski is a case in point. The convicted criminal loses only his or her liberty; Sharon Kowalski has lost the right to choose who she may see, who she may like, and who she may love.

Once declared incapacitated, the ward or conservatee is often subject to gross condescension. He or she frequently is treated without dignity as though of a lesser status than the competent. Sharon Kowalski is again a case in point. Her guardian and the court below presume that she is unable to decide whether or not she wants to see her friend, and have given no weight to either the decisions she made while fully competent or the wishes she has expressed since the accident.

In addition, the incapacitated often are subject to the whims of their guardian, including the guardian's prejudices and private biases. Again, Sharon Kowalski is a case in point. The reason for her guardian's zealousness in terminating her relationship with Ms. Thompson is obvious—he harbors deep-seated prejudices against homosexuals and cannot accept the choice his adult daughter made. While we cannot control such prejudices, neither can we tolerate them.

The rights to choose who you talk to, who you visit, who you befriend, and who you love are the most basic of constitutional and human rights. They are fundamental to our concept of what it is to be a human being . . . .

The order of the court below violated Sharon Kowalski's constitutional rights. The court terminated one of her most basic personal rights, her right to choose her friends. And it gave that power to Mr. Kowalski who had stated under oath that he was determined to cut Ms. Thompson out of Ms. Kowalski's life. The court below took these drastic actions and stripped away Ms. Kowalski's dignity without making the constitutionally and statutorily required findings.

First, the court below made no finding that it was medically necessary to terminate Ms. Kowalski's relationship with her friend although that was the obvious result of the order . . . .

Second, assuming that such a finding had been made, the court should have explored the alternatives available to address the medical need, and determined which alternative was least restrictive of Ms. Kowalski's civil rights and liberties. The court did not do so.

Third, even if the court below was predisposed to abridge Ms. Kowalski's rights after steps one and two, the court should then have ascertained what Ms. Kowalski would have done. That would not have been difficult in this case. The court had before it evidence of Ms. Kowalski's decision to live with Ms. Thompson for the four years immediately preceding the accident, the exchange of rings, and Ms. Kowalski's life insurance policy which named Ms. Thompson as beneficiary. In addition, the court had before it evidence of Ms. Kowalski's wishes expressed *after* the accident. Mr. Kowalski cannot point to a single instance in which Ms. Kowalski indicated that she did not want to continue seeing Ms. Thompson. The evidence is overwhelming that Ms. Kowalski wants to see Ms. Thompson.

Fourth, the court should have issued specific findings of fact detailing the clear and convincing proof of medical need, the exploration of alternatives, the reasons for rejecting various alternatives, identification of the least restrictive alternative, Ms. Kowalski's preference, and the reasons for rejecting her preference.

No such findings were made. The findings made were summary, conclusory, boilerplate findings. The probate court's findings of fact were inadequate to justify the deprivation of constitutional rights which resulted.

Today, the rights to privacy and personhood ensure that incapacitated people may die with dignity. Surely these rights also ensure that incapacitated people may live with dignity and continue to choose their friends. We respectfully submit that they must.

It was wonderful for me to read the MCLU brief. Not only could they see the same issues I saw, but they were able to cut through all the court language and put into writing what was humane and important. While the court was ruling against us time after time, seemingly against irrefutable fact, it was nice to know there were some sane institutions still in existence.

❖

With each day I was unable to see Sharon, I tried every means I could to bring the case to other people's attention. I clung to the hope that some group would be able to open the door to Sharon's and my freedom. Hating to talk on the phone, I literally made hundreds of phone calls. For every call I crossed off my list, ten more were added. I never caught up. I called disability action groups, lesbian and gay organizations, feminist activists and returned phone calls from alternative press reporters. Everyone had ideas which required more time on my part and, in some cases, expertise in areas that I hadn't developed.

The most successful calls were to alternative press publications. For instance, the MCLU's *Civil Liberties News* published Amy Bromberg's article on the case. It was entirely different from mainstream newspaper articles:

❖ Although she [Sharon] has been declared "incompetent" by a Minnesota District Court judge, it is clear to some observers that Kowalski is able to make her wishes known by typing, writing, pointing to words others have written and using hand signals. Kowalski's situation is complicated by the fact that she only communicates freely in the presence of her lover, Karen Thompson.

... [When visited by representatives from MCLU] Kowalski was able to respond to questions of both an objective and subjective nature. For instance, she told Goldman that her favorite bird is an eagle, that she lived in St. Cloud prior to her car accident, that she is physically handicapped and may be for life, that she is gay and has had a gay relationship with Karen Thompson and that she wants the MCLU to represent her to ensure that her wishes are made known to the court.

Even *Ms.* magazine printed a short article in the September, 1985 issue describing the case and its relevance for gay and lesbian couples. But by far the most impressive and detailed coverage occurred in the lesbian and gay press. They covered the case from the east to the west coasts when no one else would. And they followed up with me, calling back month after month to find out about any new developments. With each new article, I received letters of support and donations. Most of the donations were small, around five to twenty dollars. Some people even sent one dollar. It meant so much that people stretched their budgets to include Sharon and me.

❖

In addition to the phone calls, I wanted to get out in person and speak to any group that would have me. I had started by speaking to Human Relations classes in Julie's program at St. Cloud State. Each occasion was a nerve-wracking experience, since I had never thought of myself as a strong public speaker. But I began to realize that the case was having far greater impact on people when they heard about it from me, in person.

Sometimes I was asked to speak when I least expected it. For instance, at the Take Back the Night march in Minneapolis, Emma Hixson, the Executive Director of the Minneapolis Human Rights Commission, had arranged to have a table to distribute flyers about the case. While I was sitting with her, Karen Clark, an openly lesbian Minnesota state representative, stopped to talk to us.

After some discussion about how the case was progressing, Karen said, "You know, you really should be a speaker here today. In fact, I'll go see if it can be arranged." I was paralyzed with nervousness and torn between being glad about the possible opportunity to put the story out to thousands of people and wishing someone else could do the actual speaking. What would I say? Could I get *anything* out? Karen came back to say it was all arranged. I would have two minutes to speak. Oh great, I thought, now I'm really in trouble. What could I possibly say in two minutes to help people understand our case?

When the time came, it was even worse than I imagined. I could hardly walk across the stage. I didn't think I could get to the microphone without tripping and falling over one of the electrical cords. I fervently prayed I could get through these two minutes without making a fool of myself. I couldn't breathe. Finally, I managed to spill out a few sentences and then rush off the stage. I hadn't even used the two minutes! At least, I figured, I'd never face that large a crowd again! But that evening was my first lesson that no matter how inadequate I was as a speaker, the case spoke for itself. The crowd responded enthusiastically, and many people came up to me afterwards for more information and to offer support.

From this experience I began to realize the importance of channeling my pain and anger into action. But many times it didn't work. I continued having difficulty sleeping, and severe headaches plagued me almost daily. I lived on aspirin and tried to suppress my feelings so I could survive each day. I would see Sharon's eyes pleading with me that last time I saw her. I couldn't shake the feeling that I had failed her. Sometimes, talking with friends, I could no longer hold back my frustration and grief, and would break down in sobs. My despair was so deep that I couldn't be consoled. I simply had to go through it until I was too exhausted to cry any longer.

The next day I would get in gear again to try another approach, call another person. Would it ever end? Would I ever have a normal life again? The only place I could escape from my pain was in the classroom. I slipped into my teacher role and few would guess I had other concerns in my life. Teaching was my salvation. There, I felt I was accomplishing something. For a little while things could be under control while the rest of my life was so completely out of control.

I went to see Peg Chemberlin again to see if she had any suggestions. I'd already tried many different approaches to seek a solution outside of the courts. The first letter I had written to Sharon's parents had asked if we could sit down together and talk about what was best for Sharon. Then I had asked the court to require counseling, again to no avail. The Sindts had written to ask if they could talk to the Kowalskis. Peg suggested trying to reach them through the church. She was willing to write a letter to their priest in Nashwauk to see if mediation could be arranged. The priest responded that while he didn't know them very well, he would check on it. We never heard from him again. Another dead end.

Then a woman I had met at the Take Back the Night march called me. "I'll be visiting Hibbing. Would you like me to try to get in to see Sharon?"

Excited at the prospect of getting some information on Sharon's condition, I responded, "That would be great! Be careful, if you get caught in her room, you might be asked to leave."

I anxiously waited to hear from her. Finally, she called to say, "I was able to find Sharon. I asked her if she knew why you weren't there and she indicated 'no.' So I tried to explain to her that you weren't allowed to see her. Sharon cried and responded, 'I thought she left me.'"

I was shattered. Sharon thought I had left her when I was doing everything possible to see her. Because of Sharon's short-term memory problem, unless she was told over and over every day, she wouldn't remember why I wasn't there. She would still wonder if I didn't love her anymore. I was totally helpless to reassure her and I was sure that the Kowalskis would do nothing to reassure her for me.

My pain was so intense I felt physically ill. When I stopped in the middle of some daily routine, I would actually feel waves of nausea sweep over me. How did Sharon get through every day? How was she coping with our separation? Would it be better for her to be reminded occasionally that I still loved her and was trying desperately to see her or would it just upset her unnecessarily? In the end, I had to believe Sharon would welcome any expression of my love, no matter how much pain it caused her.

❖❖

While the appeals were going through channels, Sue Wilson was preparing another motion for district court. She wanted to take the deposition of Donald Kowalski, Dr. William Wilson and others. She was planning to bring a contempt motion against the guardian for denying all contact between Sharon and me and needed more concrete information. The attorneys flew to Duluth in October to take the depositions. They had asked me to be there since they were new to the case and I had knowledge that might be helpful, so I drove up from St. Cloud to meet them. Fena, in several behind-the-scenes maneuvers, tried to prevent the depositions before they started. He requested phone conferences with the judge and all the various attorneys involved. Meanwhile, Dr. Wilson, informed that he didn't need to honor the subpeona for the deposition, didn't show up in Duluth. After more calls to the judge, everyone drove to Hibbing to finally depose the elusive doctor.

When Sharon had been moved to Leisure Hills, Dr. William Wilson, the family practitioner who had earlier been treating Sharon Kowalski's mother for depression, became her 'treating physician.' Dr. Wilson had no credentials in rehabilitation medicine. He had seen Sharon on two brief occasions between July 23 and August 20. Neither time did she respond to him. He never attempted to discover who she wanted to visit her because he didn't think she could have any meaningful input. He never saw me at all. At the guardian's request, he viewed selected court and medical documents presented to him by Jack Fena. On the basis of two visits and these selected documents—which he could not remember—Dr. Wilson wrote his letter denying my visits.

In the deposition Sue took from him, Dr. Wilson admitted he had had no communication with anyone other than Fena and Donald Kowalski prior to writing the letter. He saw nothing in the nursing notes or occupational therapy notes that indicated I should not visit Sharon. Dr. Wilson stated he had never seen Sharon depressed and had done no testing of her. While Dr. Wilson thought it was important that he include newspaper articles as part of his medical evaluation, he hadn't bothered to talk with Sharon's attorney before writing the letter.

Dr. Wilson's perceptions of Sharon seemed to be predetermined. He felt that Sharon's chances of improvement were small and accepted as proven that Sharon was cognitively functioning at a six- or seven-year-old level. When questioned about the value of occupational therapy as part of Sharon's maximum recovery, Dr. Wilson stated, "Well, I don't think occupational therapy is at this point critical to her recovery . . . . I guess when you say occupational therapy, well, that would be in a sense an absurdity. She is not qualified to perform any occupation. So the idea of having someone like that have occupational therapy by strict definition would be absurd." Sadly enough, Dr Wilson didn't even seem to know that occupational therapy includes the teaching of daily living skills like brushing teeth, dressing oneself, and the identification of money.

Dr. Wilson's letter, the basis on which my visiting rights were denied, had concluded that any visits with me would place Sharon at a high risk of sexual abuse since we might have had a prior sexual relationship. When pressed during the deposition, he admitted that the only reason he thought there was a high risk of sexual abuse was because of a prior involvement. Sue pursued this with Dr. Wilson. "[A]re you saying that every single person who's been in a sexual relationship and is then injured is at risk of being sexually abused by the person they were involved with?"

"I think that potential definitely exists," he responded.

"For example, if your wife, God forbid, were injured in an accident and was disabled, she would be at high risk to be abused by you sexually?" Sue continued.

"I think the potential is there, yes."

"So you would be concerned that you might abuse her?"

"No, I didn't say that. I can speak for myself, as far as what my actions would be. I can't speak for—the potential in the situation exists."

". . . You're saying that the potential exists for you to sexually abuse her. Then would you say that she should have restricted rights to see you, let's say, only with the door open, with someone else there?"

"Possibly."

"So you would agree with that?"

"Possibly. I can't speak on a hypothetical situation like that . . . ."

Yet Dr. Wilson *had* based his letter on a "hypothetical situation like that" and it stood as a permanent block to my visits with Sharon. As the Office of Health Facility Complaints had pointed out, Wilson's letter was based on no documentable medical evidence.

In the middle of Wilson's deposition, Jack Fena was somehow able to persuade Chief Justice Popovich, of the appellate court, to intervene *by telephone,* calling off the rest of this deposition and all remaining depositions. For the appellate court to cancel depositions ordered by the district court is unheard of. My attorneys were astonished. In this manner we were effectively denied the right to discovery. This prevented us from gaining essential information to challenge the actions of the guardian.

❖❖

CONTEMPT MOTION AGAINST
THE GUARDIAN, DON KOWALSKI

Despite the roadblocks, we filed a motion in district court on December 13, 1985, to hold the guardian in contempt for failing to take into consideration the best interests and reliably expressed wishes of Sharon Kowalski regarding visitation. Furthermore, the motion asked for the guardian to be held in contempt for failure to have Sharon evaluated in terms of medical care as required by the guardianship statute. The motion specifically asked for the right to further discovery (that is, to continue to gather information through depositions).

Finally, the motion asked for the removal of Jack Fena for conflict of interests since he was representing the guardian *against* Sharon in the guardianship dispute, while representing *for* Sharon in the personal injury suit. The law clearly states that attorneys cannot represent two conflicting parties. As representative for the guardian, Sharon's father, Jack Fena argued in court that Sharon, his client for the personal injury suit, ought not to have the right to counsel of choice, nor freedom of association, nor the right to be tested for competency, nor the right to be present in the courtroom. It seemed obvious that Jack Fena was in a classic position of conflict of interests.

Besides filing the motion with the district court, Sue Wilson and I had filed a complaint with the Lawyers Professional Responsibility Board regarding Fena's conflict of interests. The Board asked Gary Bloomquist, the Chair of the Twentieth District Ethics Committee, to investigate. He wrote a response that was so unprofessional itself, it defied the imagination. I thought it highlighted the incredible homophobia which permeated the entire case. In part it said:

❖   In fact, I am getting so tired of people like the Karen Thompson involved in this matter that I herewith submit my resignation from the Twentieth District Ethics Committee and its Chair.

In reviewing the materials you sent me, I see that perhaps another allegation of unethical conduct has been leveled against Mr. Fena which was not addressed in the original matter. I don't care a hoot about this. Perhaps there is some unprofessionalism and perhaps there isn't. I do know, however, that Karen Thompson and her wacko relationship with the poor girl who is the subject of all of this has filled my stomach to the brim and I cannot digest anymore. The other attorney members of the Range Ethics Committee are as follows . . . . If any of these individuals have masochistic tendencies, perhaps you should inquire of them as to whether they want this job.

As a result of Bloomquist's refusal to even investigate the complaint, the Board informed Sue Wilson that since the issue of Fena's conflict of interests was before the court and that the court had much more information, it deferred to the findings of the court. (In subsequent events, the district court merely denied the motion to remove Fena as Sharon's attorney and the appellate court indicated that since the Lawyers Professional Responsibility Board found no conflict, they would concur with that conclusion.) In passing the buck, the real issue about conflict of interests was never assessed by either the court or the ethics board.

The district court hearing occurred in January by telephone conference. Shortly thereafter, the court issued what Sue Wilson called the "shortest court order in history." It made no findings of fact to support any of its decisions. The right to discovery was ignored altogether. Basically, the order reaffirmed Donald Kowalski as guardian and merely reiterated the necessity for the guardian to arrange for periodic evaluations of Sharon "on at least an annual basis." It stated that "[s]uch evaluations should specifically address the ability of Sharon Kowalski to reliably express her wishes as to visitation."

The court denied the removal of Jack Fena as attorney, stating there was no evidence to justify his removal. However, the judge ignored and made no reference at all to the many citations of case law and statutes presented in our motion.

In disbelief and outrage, Sue Wilson appealed this order immediately. Now we had two district court decisions under appeal: the original order naming Donald Kowalski as guardian, and this recent one in which the court threw out our motions that the guardian be held in contempt and Jack Fena be removed. Once again we began the long period of waiting before the appeal was heard and decided. For everyone else the court proceedings were just a process. People kept telling me, "It just takes time." I could understand that, but in the meantime I was being kept away from the person I loved. Each month that I waited for a hearing date, or ninety days for a finding, was excruciating. I experienced the whole gamut of emotions. I was worried about Sharon's actual physical well-being. Was she getting proper care and stimulation? What was she thinking? Did she think I had finally left her? Did she think I didn't love her anymore?

At the same time, I needed Sharon and missed her with all my soul. I felt so alone in the world without her. I felt incomplete. We had shared so much, both before and after the accident. Even during the time she was in the coma, I had felt a connection to Sharon, that there was a special communication occurring.

But now I had some health problems of my own. Since October I had known that a hysterectomy might become a necessity. By December, it was clear that I would have to make arrangements soon, so I scheduled surgery for the middle of January, 1986. I longed to be comforted by Sharon but couldn't talk to her, couldn't reach out to her.

In fact, I kept putting off the surgery because of the possibility that I might be able to see Sharon after one or the other hearing or decision.

Each time, my hopes would be destroyed. I couldn't see Sharon and I still hadn't had the surgery.

But of course, just before my surgery in late January, I found out the oral argument for the appeal of the July 23 order would take place the following week. There was nothing I could do but have the hysterectomy and hope that I would be well enough to travel by then. The operation went as well as could be expected and after a few days in the hospital, I went home to recover. It was hard to be at home. I had never had to stay alone out at the house for any extended period of time, and now I was there all day, every day, with no break. I couldn't exercise; I couldn't seem to read; watching television was a bore. There I was with all this time on my hands, yet I couldn't be with Sharon, couldn't even communicate with her. It was a time of survival. That's all. Survive and get well enough to travel to the appeal. Only six days after the operation, I was lying in the back seat of Julie's car on my way to the hearing in Anoka.

THE MAIN HEARING TO APPEAL
THE JULY 23 GUARDIANSHIP ORDER

Representing Sharon, Gary Pringle (Tom Hayes' associate) argued that the guardianship order be overturned because Sharon's constitutional right of association and the Minnesota Patient Bill of Rights were being violated. He said, "Kowalski is not totally incapacitated, as the Kowalskis' attorney, Jack Fena, says," and argued that Sharon should be allowed to decide for herself who may visit.

Sue Wilson reinforced Pringle's case and pointed out that the judge did not make, "as he is required to do by state statute, a finding that the visits were harmful" on which to base his guardianship order. Sue emphasized, "[w]hat we're saying is whether you're injured or not, whether you're a lesbian or not, you have a constitutional right to associate with whomever you want to. That right can't be taken away from you unless a court, after hearing all the evidence, finds that it is absolutely medically necessary. The court didn't find that. They just gave the father the right to decide. The father had said all along he'd never let his daughter see Karen."

In my opinion, Fena appeared even more ineffective at this hearing than in the past. He primarily reiterated that Sharon had a six-year-old mentality, and that she wanted to get away from me and was leaving the area. In one outrageous statement, he argued that I had cost Sharon thousands of dollars in the personal injury suit settlement by claiming that Sharon was a lesbian. Now he wouldn't be able to argue to the jury that the accident had cost Sharon the capability to have a husband and children.

The panel of three judges had ninety days to make their decision. Once again the precious days passed, days which might have improved Sharon's recovery, days of loneliness for me. It was a busy time for Julie. She wrote regular press releases which were sent out by the Committee on the Right to Recovery and Relationships. She also confronted the misinformation generated by Fena and the mainstream press by writing guest editorials and letters to editors of various newspapers.

It was good that I had a few speaking engagements in Mankato and Willmar, Minnesota to occupy some of the time while I was still recovering and waiting for the appeal decision. At least I could feel like I was accomplishing something.

I finally got my doctor's permission to return to normal activities. As I was preparing my classes for spring quarter in early March, the Minnesota Court of Appeals announced its decision to confirm Donald Kowalski as guardian.

Once again our case was handled in an extraordinary and highly irregular manner. The appellate court is not allowed to make findings of fact. That is, no new findings are to be introduced into the appellate court's opinion; its task is simply to review the merit of the district court's decision based on the facts presented in *that* court.

Regardless, Chief Judge Peter Popovich wrote in his opinion, "[t]he relationship between Sharon Kowalski and Karen Thompson is uncertain." He noted that "while the women had exchanged rings and named each other as beneficiaries of life insurance policies, Sharon Kowalski had closed their joint bank account before the accident and had told her sister she was considering moving because Thompson was becoming very possessive."

He was further quoted by the *Minneapolis Star and Tribune* as stating: "Regardless of the relationship . . . Thompson's contact with Kowalski upsets her and results in her depression."

In fact, Sharon and I had decided a month before the accident to close our joint account. At that time Sharon was making no money to contribute to the house expenses (and the purpose of the joint account was to pay mutual expenses), so it seemed silly to pay bank charges for an account we weren't using. Based on that mutual decision, *I* closed the joint account. Sharon, of course, kept her own checking account, and so did I. But we weren't able to present these points to the appellate court.

The district court didn't find that our relationship was uncertain nor that Sharon was leaving. It didn't find that I upset Sharon or caused the depression. I thought Popovich would certainly be found in violation of the law for going beyond the scope of his charge. I thought the law was the law, the rules were rules, and that someone would hold someone accountable. I was wrong.

What is most appalling in this final decision is that when all the facts were in and everything was said and done, there had been absolutely no attempt to consider Sharon's real interests.

CHAPTER 13

From Disillusionment to Change

Despite everything that had already happened, I was still completely shocked when Jack Fena began contacting college papers. I couldn't understand why an attorney would take the time to personally attack his client's opponent, especially when his client was winning. It seemed to me that Jack Fena had such a stake in this case that he was willing to put lies in writing. He contacted the *Mankato State Reporter* (I had spoken at the university recently) and the *St. Cloud State University Chronicle*.

The *Chronicle* article at my own university hurt the most. The reporter there wrote:

❖ Bringing in the lesbian issue is a red herring, Fena said. "She's been given more rights than a man would have gotten. Was it Thompson's right to come out and talk about the nature of the relationship? . . . What's more private than a person's sexual preference? I think Thompson has inflicted grievous harm."

Fena related a testimony from a psychiatrist who has treated homosexual people. "The psychiatrist said that the worst thing for gays 'in the closet' is to have their parents find out. What a friend," Fena said about Thompson . . . .

Fena said that Thompson demanded rent payments from the Kowalskis while Sharon lay in a coma. Donald Kowalski paid Sharon's bills. When he stopped paying these bills, then Thompson began suing, Fena said. "She had all these rights; she lost them because nursing home personnel said Thompson was preventing recovery and well-being."

"These aren't doctors I hired," he pointed out . . . . Fena also said it was not Donald Kowalski who kicked Thompson out of Sharon's room. It was the doctor on duty who refused to let her in.

Fena has said Thompson's motivations are monetary. She uses the gay rights discussions to get money from gay rights support groups. "I think the gay community has been brainwashed in this case by Ms. Thompson and I believe if they were to view the medical records thoroughly, they wouldn't give Ms. Thompson five cents to continue these attacks on Sharon Kowalski and her family."

Once again, Julie responded, answering in a guest editorial the myths that Fena stated as fact. How could Fena possibly say that the doctor refused to let me see Sharon? The nursing home notes, subpoenaed by Beth in preparation for hearings, clearly state that Jack Fena called and said that I should not be allowed in under any circumstances. Dr. Wilson's letter was not dated until three weeks later.

Fena's articles and letters were more than just demoralizing. Since the general public did not have access to the day-to-day struggles in this case, we were forced to keep challenging Fena's accusations over and over again. The mainstream press was willing to print Fena's side of the story without any effort at investigative reporting. Even some lesbians in Minnesota became convinced by the articles that there was no evidence that Sharon and I had indeed had a relationship.

Every time things seemed bleak, something would happen to pick me up and keep me going. Soon after these articles appeared, I met Richard Schmeichen and his partner, David Hoagland. (Richard was the co-producer of *The Life And Times of Harvey Milk,* which had just won the 1986 Academy Award for best documentary film.) They were appalled by what was happening to Sharon. They were interested in discussing the possibility of a docudrama for television. While I couldn't imagine our personal lives being portrayed on national television, I was desperate to get the story out to the public. To make such a decision was particularly scary because I knew I really couldn't control whether the story would be sensationalized. I decided to wait until the appellate court decision before answering.

With the movie in the back of my mind, I wondered if a book wouldn't be the most effective manner of explaining such a complex case and its ramifications for everyone's rights. Julie and I discussed the possibility, although we thought it was pretty far-fetched. It just didn't seem to be an immediate way to help Sharon.

Then Julie received an unexpected phone call from a feminist singer/song writer from the San Francisco Bay Area she had met earlier. Judy Fjell called to say she would be touring the midwest and would like to do a benefit concert for me. It was short notice, but we were able to arrange a concert to follow a monthly lesbian potluck in St. Cloud. Judy was an inspiration. She wrote a song about AIDS called "Love Is A Dangerous Promise," which asks the question, "Will you be there for me?" Those words haunted me because I was trying so hard to be there for Sharon, yet she had no way of knowing that. That phrase later became a part of my speeches.

After the concert, Judy and several friends stayed at my place, talking late into the night. She asked if I would be interested in coming to California where she could organize a benefit. I had conflicting feelings. One part of me knew I would have to start doing more to get the story out, another part of me was scared to death of traveling to other cities and speaking to strangers. I said yes anyway. At least I would be doing *something* instead of just waiting for the court decisions. Now that I was unable to see Sharon, it seemed the only thing I could do for her.

Six weeks later, I found myself on a plane to Oakland. I was really nervous about the trip and glad that a friend was going with me for support. I'm not sure I could have stepped on the plane without someone with me. This way, I had to pretend that everything was under control. Once I got there, Judy and her lover made me feel welcome. They kept me busy with speaking and media events all around the Bay Area. Besides women's organizations, I spoke at a bookstore, a women's cafe and a college of law. Judy and several other Bay Area performers put on an exciting benefit concert for the case.

I had to ride the BART subway into San Francisco for a speaking engagement. Some people would think this was a great adventure, but I was traumatized. I worried about getting my ticket, getting off at the right stop, finding the person I was supposed to meet. Would I get lost in the city, never to be heard from again? Would I ever get used to new experiences and just enjoy them or would I always be afraid of something different? Somehow, I managed to get to the right place, even though I developed a pounding headache doing it.

Walking in the city, I was shocked to see how many people were homeless. I had never seen a person pushing a shopping cart with all of her belongings in it. Some of them even had pets. I wondered how they could provide for a pet when they couldn't even seem to take care of themselves. Part of me wondered why they were so dirty, why they couldn't keep themselves clean. How had they gotten themselves into such a state? The beliefs I had always accepted sprung easily to mind. They must be alcoholics, lazy, uneducated. I felt sorry for them and thought someone should do something to help them. But certainly not me. I felt that I couldn't worry about anyone else, that I had to stay focused on Sharon; I wouldn't allow myself to see any connection between homeless people and Sharon.

I couldn't process all the new experiences. Despite all the support, I was a nervous wreck inside. The attention felt overwhelming. I was terrified that my naivete about human rights issues or my inexperience as a speaker would be obvious and would detract from the case itself. I was starting to realize that many of the people who were listening were more sophisticated about discrimination issues than I was. When I heard the phrase 'politically correct' for the first time, I wondered if I might have said something to offend some group or another. I was thrust into a new environment of activists, feminists, vegetarians, futons, clothing styles and a freedom to express feelings that was alien to me. I enjoyed the people but not the tofu and avocados!

I came to realize that I could only be myself, so I didn't pretend to be sophisticated, cosmopolitan, brave, relaxed, politically correct or anything else. I just talked to people about who I was and why this case was important. And I prayed—prayed before every event, prayed for the perseverance to be able to get the message to people. I prayed that people would be able to understand how Sharon's rights were being violated despite how I presented it. These prayers sustained me.

Every place I spoke, people responded to Sharon's situation with shock and anger. They asked me what they could do. Caught off guard, I didn't know what to tell them. I asked *them* for ideas. I didn't know the first thing about political organizing. Fortunately, they did, because the nucleus of the first national Free Sharon Kowalski group formed before I left the Bay Area.

Because the response had been so positive, that first trip made me confident that Sharon's and my experience could be told in a way to reach different types of groups, and that I could be effective in telling it. In addition, I brought home several hundred dollars for the legal fund.

Less than three weeks later, I was headed to Boston feeling just as nervous as before. In this case, the lesbian and gay community had organized with disabled activists to bring me there. Once again, people took me into their community and welcomed me into their homes. I was amazed to find that many of the women had almost no possessions. They spent all their extra time and money organizing for causes. They had a real sense of community and purpose. Though I didn't necessarily want to live like them, I began to think that I was missing something valuable, that my life was too shallow.

I realized that I had never spent this much time with women. One afternoon the Boston organizers 'kidnapped' me to drive me to a lesbian clambake. The old me would have felt extremely uncomfortable being with a group of women I didn't know, especially if they were lesbians. But it shocked me to realize that I felt at home. For the first time I understood Sharon's feelings of being with 'family' at the Meg and Chris concert. I was surrounded by women, many of whom were my own age, and I realized how little contact I had with women older than my students.

I had never really thought about women as women. At that clambake, I came to the profound conclusion that women are different. I had always thought that people (not males or females) had different characteristics. But now I felt a special connection with women. I gradually became aware of their tremendous power and resourcefulness. Instead of being totally drained after a presentation, I was learning to become revitalized from being with women.

Shortly after I returned home, the Free Sharon Kowalski group that had formed in Boston called to say they had arranged for me to do a workshop at the Michigan Women's Music Festival, an annual event that attracts thousands of women from all over the country. Although I was grateful for the opportunity, I was not especially eager to go. I had heard that some of the women would be in various stages of undress and I was sure this would make me very uncomfortable. Any nudity, my own included, was embarrassing to me. In fact, Sharon's favorite story about me was that I was the only person she knew who would go into the bathroom fully clothed to take a shower, shower and then come back out fully dressed, even when I was in the house by myself.

A friend and I drove to Michigan together. When I got to the festival, I quickly discovered how unprepared I was to deal with another new experience. As if the huge crowd wasn't enough to discourage me, I could not fathom how anyone could be comfortable sitting on the ground nude or walking around without a stitch of clothing except a back pack. I never got used to staring straight at naked breasts in the food line and being expected to calmly say whether or not I wanted salad. The worst situation was when I gave a workshop to topless, bottomless or nude women. I looked everywhere but at my audience. Then I accidentally ran into one of my attorneys who was also topless. She said, "The problem is, you're just overdressed for the occasion, Karen."

Even with all of my discomfort, the warmth and support was apparent. Many women promised to spread the word back home.

❖

I returned home that August (1986) to news of the court's decision on the contempt appeal. It was the worst decision of the entire case. The appellate court not only upheld all the decisions of the district court, but once again it based the decision on findings of fact that the trial court had not made. Instead, as support for their current decision, they quoted themselves in their previous appellate court findings on this same case which were also irregular.

In addition, the appellate court ruled on the Patient Bill of Rights and the discovery issues which the trial court had ignored. The appellate court even upheld the trial court decision that there was no conflict of interests in Jack Fena's representing both the parents and Sharon. Their decision upheld the trial court's refusal to find the guardian in contempt of court or to remove him for terminating my visitation. This decision was based on its own finding during the appeal of the July 23 order that the record indicated my visitation was detrimental to Sharon. The trial court had made *no finding of fact that my visitation was detrimental*.

Once again, I was shocked by this ruling and the court's willingness to simply disregard the required legal procedures. It hit me that I was expected to conform to the rules and the laws, when our own judicial system was not.

Although the trial court had never ruled at all on discovery, the appeals court ruled that the "[a]ppellant is not entitled to conduct further discovery in this matter." This meant that we could not take any more depositions. They actually stated, ". . . there is no finding by the court that the perpetuation of testimony is necessary to avoid a failure or delay of justice." I sat there wondering how Sharon would feel about that. This finding prevented us from gathering information to support our motions, and made it impossible to advocate strongly for Sharon's rights.

The most serious aspect of this decision was that "a guardian cannot be found in violation of the Minnesota Patient Bill of Rights . . . which imposes duties upon health care facilities and not upon guardians." By this action, the court essentially cut the heart out of the Patient Bill of Rights. Many patients in nursing homes have guardians, and the institutions where they reside are required to follow the orders of those guardians. Because of this ruling, the guardians, through whatever whim, bias or prejudice, can now remove all rights of patients they have authority over.

This ruling set a crucial and dangerous precedent that threatened *everyone's* rights, since anyone could become disabled at any time through accident or illness. I was convinced that disability groups and civil rights groups would flock to challenge this ruling because of the terrible potential for guardian abuse.

❖

I only knew how much hope I had placed in this last appellate court decision when the despair hit me. My usual tendency was to hole up and suffer alone. But when friends called me, sometimes I would just break down and sob. At these times, all of my feelings for Sharon would burst through. Life was empty without Sharon. It had been a whole year since I had seen her. I felt I couldn't stand it one more day. We were being torn apart against our will for no reason whatsoever. The injustice we had endured was far greater than the accident itself. Even with all of my efforts and my speaking, nothing was really helping Sharon. At these times, I wondered if I could go on living.

From the very beginning, Julie had kept asking me how I was taking care of myself. I had been in to talk to Peg Chemberlin and Father Bill Dorn, a gay priest at Newman Center, off and on for two years. Their support kept me going in the worst of times. I knew I should be seeing a counselor on an ongoing basis for my emotional well-being. Still, it was difficult to find the time, the energy, or the right person. I knew I wanted to work with a woman. Eventually, I located Dr. Elizabeth Baraga.

It was hard for me to go to her office because I knew I would have to face, rather than hide, the pain. I thought the tears would never stop, but each time I saw her I felt more and more comfortable. Extremely supportive of my relationship with Sharon and my right to be with her, Elizabeth was a very settling influence. She validated that my feelings and reactions throughout the case were normal. She helped me to accept the extreme changes I had experienced in my personal and professional life. With her help, I found new ways to cope with the stress and emotional turmoil that were constantly there.

Elizabeth also helped me with the grieving process, as far as I could go. I grieved the loss of my sense of the world as I knew it. I grieved the accident that changed Sharon and the activities that we would never again share, and I grieved the temporary loss of our relationship. But I would not grieve that our relationship was over. I remembered all those months at the hospital and the nursing home in St. Cloud, how we had fallen in love with each other all over again. Yes, Sharon was different but I loved this different Sharon. I would not give her up as long as she wanted me. Even though a year had passed without being able to see her, I loved her as strongly as I ever had, and still had faith that she loved me.

I grieved the destruction of my faith in the judicial system. I had held onto the hope that the appellate court would surely see the facts, would see that Sharon's rights had been stripped away. But I saw that people like Sharon, powerless people, are not really the people that the courts protect. After this decision, it was obvious to me that the courts could do anything they wanted regardless of the law. It didn't matter what the facts were. Although I had been forced into this realization, I didn't understand why and I knew I had to find out.

I asked Julie if I could take a class of hers in September. Maybe studying Human Relations would give me some personal answers. Besides, I knew I had to become more informed on the connections between my case and issues faced by other minorities. Julie was excited by my interest.

By this time, I had a tremendous amount of respect for Julie. She was an activist, a feminist and a lesbian, and seemed to have such a good handle on all three. But while I trusted her and knew that I needed a person like her working on the case, I still wasn't comfortable with her ideology. In the past, all of the people I wanted to be connected with had been Christians. Not only was Julie not a Christian, she was an atheist and the language she used sometimes was extremely graphic. While one part of me thought she was dangerous to my peace of mind, another part of me knew she had information that could help me understand how the system worked. I no longer believed that it was just a personal problem that Sharon and I were experiencing. But words like 'multinationals' seemed to have little to do with what was happening in Sherburne County.

Another barrier between Julie and me was my guilt at not being involved in the anti-discrimination suit at the university. Even though Julie didn't seem to hold it against me, I felt like I had unintentionally betrayed the women faculty.

In addition to my guilt, Julie shocked me in many ways, though I tried not to show how much. One day, she began ripping apart television preachers. I didn't know if I should admit that I watched some of them.

"They are just after people's money. And they are selling more than God, that's for sure. Right-wingers. You know, some of them read a letter from Reagan during special rallies. Fascists, that's what they are. Haven't you heard what they say about HOMO—SEXUALS?" she imitated. "They use the fear of gay and lesbian people and the fear of communists as ways to control people. Whipping up emotions to get people to donate big bucks."

"Well," I sheepishly admitted, "since I haven't been comfortable going to church, I've been watching some of those programs while stretching out and riding my exercise bike in the mornings." I had to find some justification. "I think they say some good things. You can pick and choose."

"Karen," she was sympathetic, "listen carefully to their political agenda. You'll start to see that they are selling a whole package that has a lot more to do with money and politics than religion."

We discussed topics like this, sometimes for hours. And we talked about writing a book. Should we spend our time taking on such a big project? What would be our primary purpose in writing it? Would a book really help Sharon? We decided to just try working together to see if it would work, keeping it open for negotiation. We had several weeks in August to begin. We sat at the computer, discussing where to start, or what should come next, while Julie typed. Neither of us knew how to write this kind of a book. We were both good academic writers, which would probably only ensure that the book would be boring. Julie kept asking me, "What were you feeling? We should show the reader the emotional consequences of all you've been made to go through." We debated about the focus of the book. I wanted to get Sharon's story out. She also wanted to make it the story of my changes. We compromised. Facts *and* feelings went into the book. Surprisingly, we worked well together and even had some fun in the process. We became friends as well as political allies.

Julie and her partner of seven years, Mary Anne, became a second family for me. I would stay at their house when I was too tired or couldn't face going home. They encouraged me to take time out to relax, eventually getting me out on the golf course for the first time in years. Mary Anne supported our writing by listening to us, reading drafts, making suggestions, urging us to eat occasionally and calling a halt when we became too tired. She provided needed interruptions to tell us stories and make us laugh.

When I remembered the first day I had sat in Julie's office wanting to dash back out the door, I had to smile at how far I'd come. I never expected that writing this book would give me back a sense of home.

CHAPTER 14

Speaking Out

In September, 1986, I gave a speech in Washington, D.C. Not quite so intimidated, I approached the trip with a plan to include the information and ideas about human rights issues I was learning. I had gained confidence in meeting new people as well. I could feel the energy from this community immediately and I let it soak in. I was grateful but not really surprised when they offered to form a support group, too. With new groups starting, this seemed to be the beginning of a movement, but I was still too insecure to speculate much about where it was all heading.

Just as classes began in the fall, I got a call from two disability activists who were going to Hibbing on business. "We want to try to see Sharon if we can find her," Paul Reichert said. He was already familiar with the nursing home from an earlier visit with me, and probably had the best chance of finding her.

I immediately wondered what was best for Sharon. It had been a year since someone I knew had been able to get in to visit Sharon, and fifteen months since I had last seen Sharon. I knew from the Office of Health Facility Complaints report that Sharon had still responded that she wanted to see me in September of 1985. Now, a year later, did she still feel that way? I didn't know what her family had been telling her or what conclusions Sharon might have come to. If she were to respond that she didn't want to see me anymore, I didn't know if I could bear to know it. Yet, I really wanted to know how she was.

Paul called when he returned. "We were able to find her. She was in bed so she couldn't do any typing, but I told her you still loved her. She just brought her hand up to her head and looked like she was going to cry.

An aide came into the room and volunteered that Sharon was getting therapy and making some progress." Paul seemed somewhat encouraged to find Sharon holding her own.

But I was more skeptical. When I asked what they had actually observed Sharon doing, they could report little. To me, the perceptions of the nurse's aide without any tangible proof didn't mean much. Progress compared to what? What kind of therapy? How often? From all I had been learning about services and techniques, I felt no nursing home could give her the kind of rehabilitation that she needed, no matter how good they were. I knew I wouldn't really know about Sharon's condition until I could spend some time with her. And I still couldn't answer the question whether or not it was good for Sharon to receive information concerning me. Even if I could somehow slip in and see her, what would it actually accomplish? I wanted to spend a lot of time with Sharon; I wanted to work with her on a daily basis to help her explore her full potential. Knowing only a little about Sharon's condition was almost as agonizing as not knowing anything.

Fortunately, I was able to throw myself into school, both teaching and taking classes. The Human Relations classes were a real challenge. I may have looked calm on the outside, but my insides were being scrambled. My whole sense of reality was shaken as I studied about global oppression, militarism, neocolonialism, ageism and more. I had felt I understood what racism and sexism were, but now a much broader picture was opening up for me.

Films on Martin Luther King, the internment of Japanese-Americans, the struggle of Native Americans for control over their land finished stripping away my naive perceptions of the United States. The realization that my tax money was being spent on the military instead of homes for the homeless, food for the hungry and medical care for the ill left me furious and frustrated.

But as my insights grew, I began to see the connections between all these issues. For example, I learned how American interests in Central America reinforce racism and classism in the United States. For the first time, I could see the system from the outside. It became clear to me how many ways I had been oppressed and how I had participated in the oppression of others. I could now apply this analysis to what had happened to Sharon and me. Although the knowledge didn't diminish the pain, it did help me to survive. It gave me a new purpose. Even though my primary motivation was still to fight for Sharon, I could see a bigger cause.

In November, when the Minnesota Supreme Court once again refused to hear the case, I was disappointed but not shocked. What legal avenues were left to us now? We immediately began to investigate the possibilities. I wouldn't give up; I was determined to somehow make the system deal with this case so Sharon would get help, and the horrible precedents these decisions had set would not be applied to others.

I had three speaking trips to make in November, to Iowa, New York and California. Instead of just telling about the case itself, I was able to speak more clearly about the sexism, handicapism and homophobia of our legal system, medical institutions and mainstream media.

I began to stress how others could protect themselves from the same nightmare Sharon and I were experiencing. Any adult, whether lesbian, gay or non-gay, married or unmarried, should consider who they want making decisions for them should they become incapacitated. How would they prefer to live? I talked about the importance of 'coming out' to friends and loved ones if you are gay or lesbian as a first line of protection, pointing out how much Sharon and I had suffered from not being out. Legal protection was the next step. Everyone should have a durable power of attorney, living will, guardianship papers and/or a will, depending upon the requirements of each state.

I told them that Sharon and I were physical educators, athletes who never dreamed anything could ever happen to us. We thought about life insurance, but we never thought that the results of an accident or illness might leave one of us disabled. If it could happen to us, it could happen to anyone.

The two women who organized my trip to Iowa had been together for over twenty years. I was glad to see that kind of commitment and love. They didn't ask me, as so many others did, "Why do you still want Sharon back? Shouldn't you get on with your own life?" Meeting this couple came at a time when I was beginning to wonder if any other couple, lesbian, gay or non-gay, really understood the meaning of love or commitment. How many spouses walked away from their disabled partners? How many parents walked away from their disabled children? It shocked me to discover that many did. I never debated whether I would or wouldn't. It just never occurred to me to leave Sharon. I wanted Sharon home—not out of a sense of duty, but because I loved her and felt we could work out a good life together.

The women in Iowa also decided to form a support group. I couldn't believe how giving and caring people could become about our situation in such a short time. They so readily volunteered to help with whatever needed to be done. The enthusiasm of this group made it easier to anticipate my next trip, which was to combine New York and a return trip to California.

I was in New York for a whole week. I caught my first taxi and rode the New York subway for the first time. It was still frightening enough for me to meet new people and speak in front of groups, without the anxiety of how I was getting there. I felt like I had been cast in the wrong role. I was always reminded that Sharon would have found all this so much easier than I had. With each new experience my hair got a little grayer.

The New York groups responded strongly to my presentations. Another Free Sharon Kowalski group was founded and they immediately shared ideas with me about making this a truly national effort.

While I was in New York, I had an appointment to speak with one of the producers of *60 Minutes*. Terrified at how they might portray the case, yet thrilled at the possibility of finally exposing the blatant violation of Sharon's rights to the general public, I collected myself for the interview. Fortunately, my desire to get the story out was much greater than my fears. At this stage, I still felt any publicity would be better than none.

The interview went extremely well. The producers had looked over parts of the court files, medical records, press clippings and at the videotape I had of Sharon, and expressed their concern about the whole situation. They let me know that they would get back to me in early January of 1987. I felt exhilarated, thinking that through national television Sharon's story would finally be told.

The evening at Albany Law School was one I'll always remember. It was one of those moments when the words flowed easily. There was electricity in the air. I realized on a deeper level how much sharing our story could educate people and change attitudes. At the end of my talk they gave me a standing ovation. Although I didn't have the slightest idea how to respond, I felt we had all shared a special moment. "You made the legal system come alive for the students," a law professor told me afterwards. An experience like that left me aware of how much I missed Sharon and wanted her to be there, sharing the excitement of the evening.

When I returned home from one of my trips, I received a call from *60 Minutes* saying they were going to do the story and would come to Minnesota in February to do the filming. I was ecstatic. Finally we'd have a chance to reach a wider audience and bring public opinion to bear on the case. But after weeks passed and the film crew didn't show up, I realized I had put too much hope on this one event.

After not hearing from *60 Minutes* by the end of February, I called to find out what was happening. They told me they were behind schedule, overbooked and didn't know when or if they would get to this story. Later, I found out that they had contacted the Kowalskis, who had refused to cooperate.

This turned out to be the beginning of a series of major media programs that became fascinated with the story and began the process of investigation, only to back out completely when they were unable to obtain the cooperation of Fena and the Kowalskis.

In March, I was contacted by *West 57th Street* and *The Phil Donahue Show. West 57th Street* said that, although it was unusual, they had received information from a producer at *60 Minutes* who was not going to be able to do the report but thought it needed to be done. Once again, after reviewing the information, *West 57th Street* indicated a strong interest in investigating and presenting the case.

Typically, the producer would ask, "What is this case all about?" As briefly as I could, I would try to explain the major issues of the case. I would tell them of the well-documented facts which were constantly distorted or misrepresented, the violation of Sharon's rights, the legal irregularities and how homophobia, sexism and handicapism were keeping Sharon imprisoned. With each question they asked me, I could feel their interest and excitement increase. They usually told me they could talk only a few minutes and yet they found themselves unable to hang up without hearing the whole story.

"You do understand that I will have to have a representative from the other side in order to receive permission to do the report," they would say.

"Yes, that's all right. I have nothing to hide. I think the facts will speak for themselves," I would respond.

In the beginning, I thought if the Kowalskis or Fena refused to cooperate, the producers would go ahead and investigate the story, saying that the opposition had refused to comment. I had certainly seen other investigative shows where one side or another would not be taped. I actually hoped the Kowalskis *would* be involved, since I would finally have the opportunity to answer some of their unfounded accusations.

When I would finally call, the producers would say, "We don't know if we'll be able to do the story without the Kowalskis. We're trying to find another format."

"You're telling me that if you can't get the other side to participate, then you won't be able to do the report. Why would the other side want to participate? They have nothing to win and everything to lose. They have been winning because the facts have been obscured and unavailable to the public. So even if you think that someone's rights are being flagrantly violated, you won't get involved if the other side won't cooperate?"

Their response was, "We have a commitment to tell both sides of the story."

"What about Sharon's side of the story? Doesn't anybody have a commitment to get Sharon's story out? Did you contact Sharon's attorney or the MCLU? Have you contacted the disability rights group who testified on Sharon's behalf?"

To my knowledge, none of the programs ever contacted anyone who had acted on Sharon's behalf. So after they had pursued me, called me, asked me for further information, and said they wanted to film some things immediately, they disappeared one by one.

I heard from one of the producers at *West 57th Street* that Fena had come to New York and had dinner and drinks with him. The producer repeated Fena's standard accusations, but eventually acknowledged that the evidence *did* seem to support my contentions. Because Fena and the Kowalskis refused to be involved, *West 57th Street* had to find some other way to do the report. Then they dropped out of sight. It took them another year to get back to me.

The Phil Donahue Show, on the other hand, almost materialized. I was shocked when they told me that Sharon's parents had consented to appear. A date was set; then the Kowalskis contacted the program to say that they had decided not to be on the show after all. I was told by the *Donahue* producers that the Kowalskis didn't want to set eyes on me or be in the same room with me. The producer suggested splitting the show— with me on one half and them on the other—in order to meet their wishes, but the Kowalskis still refused and the show was canceled.

When it appeared that none of the programs would materialize, I received a call from *The Sally Jesse Raphael Show* in St. Louis. They offered me a definite time and date and were prepared to send me the tickets. The program was only a half hour and I would be sharing it with a transsexual who had been separated from her son. And although I knew that the transsexual might be even more controversial than me and that my issues might be lost, I decided to appear on the chance that something of Sharon's and my story would get out.

I practiced trying to state my major points in five minutes flat. I thought if I was given five minutes to introduce the case, I could help people to understand its importance. Just as I got started, Sally interrupted me with questions that took the discussion off in all directions. Each time she or a member of the audience asked a question, I tried to get back to the main points. I couldn't compete with Sally, the transsexual and the audience all at once. By the end, I wished the floor could have opened up and swallowed me. I'm just not the sort of person who can outshout others to get attention.

Profoundly depressed about national television, I flew back to Minnesota. I decided that the best way to get the story out was through the book and my speaking. At least then I knew for sure what would actually occur and that I had some control over the format, setting, length of time and how questions were handled. All the investment of emotion, time and energy in the major media, only to spend months waiting and having nothing materialize, had left me drained. Each show of interest seemed so promising that I set my heart on it. Then, when I realized it was another dead end, it would take me days to recover the spirit to go on.

Fortunately, I was getting more and more invitations to speak. I always made arrangements to go, no matter how inconvenient it was or how tired I was. I pushed myself to the limit, afraid to miss any opportunity. Each one just might be the time or the connection that could lead to a breakthrough for Sharon, who was lying there day after day in the nursing home.

Now it was essential for me to take the next step in my political analysis. More and more organizers were asking me to address specific human rights issues and speak about constructive social change. They wanted to know what role they could play to prevent similar violations from occurring to other people. I continued to take Human Relations classes and team-taught a class in order to strengthen my understanding. It was my salvation. Literally, I learned something one day and used it on the road the next.

The National Gay and Lesbian Health Care Providers conference in Los Angeles challenged me to use everything I had learned so far. As the closing speaker, I was to use our case to demonstrate how health care providers could meet the needs of the entire human community, address racism, sexism, ageism, classism, handicapism and homophobia, and prevent burnout in the process. I had 30 minutes to accomplish this. What an assignment!

Whether they learned as much from my involvement in the conference as I did from attending their workshops is debatable. For the first time, I met people with AIDS face to face, adding more depth to my understanding. I felt and shared the commonality of our struggles.

More and more I was seeing that even if I wasn't successful yet for Sharon, I could make an impact for others. At one university conference, a woman came up to me and said, "I couldn't imagine why they let you talk here and I only came because there was nothing else scheduled. But now I'm so moved by all this, I just have to stay for your whole workshop." Though I remember her clearly, she also represents to me hundreds of people who have been touched by this case enough to begin making changes themselves.

Coming back from Los Angeles, I felt that I had survived the most difficult assignment. However, a letter awaited me that reminded me once again not to assume that I had faced my biggest challenge. I was invited to be one of the Grand Marshals of the New York City Gay Pride Parade. I had such mixed feelings. I was honored to be invited but I couldn't imagine why they would have asked me. I had never even participated in a gay pride celebration. The Take Back the Night march had been my only experience of a demonstration of any kind. I was so new to dealing with my own sexuality and all the related political issues that it would have been a thrill just to *attend* such an event. But instead I was asked to be a leader. With both anticipation and fear, I accepted.

❖

By the spring of 1987, my life had taken on a split personality. At St. Cloud State, I was just another faculty member, not that well known outside my own department and the Human Relations program. Then, on Thursdays, I would fly off to one coast or the other to speak. Sometimes on Monday mornings I would wonder if I really had just been in Boston or Oakland.

I was willing to work new issues into my talks at the request of organizers, as long as I could maintain my integrity to Sharon and our relationship. While I wanted to do my very best and meet everyone's expectations, I was afraid that I would be made into someone I was not. I just wanted to be an ordinary person like everyone else. There were many things I wish I had done differently in my life, both before and after the accident. I certainly had made my share of mistakes. I didn't want anyone to think I was suddenly perfect, a hero or a celebrity. I knew I couldn't live up to those kinds of expectations.

I prayed before every presentation no matter how big or small, even though I was no longer sure of who or what 'God' was. Ever since Peg had called God "She," I had been bombarded with a variety of forms of spirituality and religion. I had to put my spiritual struggle on hold because I just couldn't try to sort out one more personal area. My whole perception of the world had been radically changed, and I wasn't prepared to delve into the spiritual realm as well. Yet, though I had no clear name for it, a spiritual presence had remained with me throughout this separation from Sharon.

I was no longer sure who 'I' was, I had changed so fast. I needed time to digest the changes and really integrate them into my life. I still joked about "Who, me? The activist and feminist?" People were calling me that and I felt like a fraud. These people had been activists and feminists for longer than I had even understood the meaning of the words. Yet they wanted me to say something inspirational and make connections for them!

It didn't help my inner struggle when I received a phone call from the Minnesota National Organization for Women asking if I could come to their annual state convention to accept an award. I was to receive the Charlotte Streibel Long Distance Runner Award, for perseverance in pursuing a feminist issue. When they called, I was embarrassed that I didn't even know some of the people who had been long-time leaders in the movement. For instance, at the ceremony, a woman recognized me and came up to talk with me about the case. I felt that she was someone special but I had no idea who, and I didn't want to show my ignorance by asking. Only later did I find out that Ellie Smeal was the national president of NOW.

I was so grateful to Minnesota NOW for their public recognition and support. Their newsletter, along with a report in the *National NOW Times,* carried the story to a new group of activists. I was very honored to receive the award. I soaked up knowledge from individuals and workshops and I left their convention with a stronger understanding of feminism.

Up until then, I had been able to make a progression with every new talk. It never occurred to me that I might be asked to leave out part of the analysis I was developing. The North Como Presbyterian Church Disability Concerns group asked me to speak as an advocate of disability rights on Sharon's behalf. When the minister called, she warned me, "Please stay strictly with disability issues. We have talked about homophobia in another session and don't want you to talk about homophobia during this class."

"They are all intertwined throughout the case," I protested. "It would be very difficult to explain the case without touching on all of them. I do strongly make the point that it's a disability rights case."

"But for this session, we want to keep the issues separate because I think the class will be able to deal with it better," she stressed again.

Since I had agreed to try, I started off as requested and immediately felt strange. I told of the accident, and of the hours and days I spent willing Sharon to live and working with her. But how could they understand if I couldn't tell them I loved Sharon? How could I explain the parents' actions? None of this made any sense even to me.

The speech was flat. Inside I was censoring every word, every expression. I felt like I was in the closet again, pretending, playing a game.

I couldn't believe it. Several times I almost stopped, wanting to fill in the missing pieces and begin making the real connections so they could understand why this was happening. But the other side of me said I had promised to keep to disability issues. And I did, to the bitter end, knowing it wasn't right. I decided never to agree to that again. Either they would take my whole case or nothing.

This resolution had even more meaning for me when I went to Washington, D.C. to speak at the Gay Pride Rally. Despite the fear of speaking to several thousand people, it was good to be myself—to stand there, a whole person. I had been asked to stress the necessity of being public about our relationships and our rights. I tried to explain how important it was for everyone there that day to return for the major national lesbian and gay demonstration of the decade, the October 11 March on Washington. I don't know whether I convinced others of the necessity of being visible in large numbers to advocate for our rights, but I certainly convinced myself.

CHAPTER 15

"The Silent Ordeal"

I returned from Washington to discover that an article I had been dreading had been printed in the *St. Paul Pioneer Press,* one of the two Twin Cities papers. This article covered two whole pages in the Sunday edition of the paper, complete with color photos of the Kowalski family, who for the first time had made themselves and Sharon accessible to the media.

An earlier, and much shorter, article in the religious section of the same paper had covered a disability rights speech I had given to the Episcopalian Urban Caucus. This brief article was the first mainstream press coverage anywhere which portrayed Sharon as a vitally alive human being with many capabilities.

Now Jack Fena had convinced the *Pioneer Press* to present *their* side of the story in full color on Sunday morning. I was not surprised that the article was titled "A Silent Ordeal" because I thought it was going to be Sharon's story. Instead the lead paragraph stated:

"Karen Thompson has made her custody battle for accident victim Sharon Kowalski a nationwide gay rights issue. Now, consider the other side of the story, the anguish of parents Don and Della Kowalski, who have won in court, but lost their peace of mind . . . ."

It continued, "Don and Della Kowalski also have borne the emotional burden of their daughter's paralysis. Their savings, their peace of mind and their plans for a leisurely retirement all have been lost.

"Week in and week out, they have known despair as they dutifully travel the ten miles back and forth to the Hibbing nursing home, where their eerily silent daughter lies trapped in her twisted body . . . ."

After extensively portraying Sharon as a helpless victim, and me as an incomprehensible person preying on her helplessness, the article ended with a brief description of the reporter's visit with Sharon:

"But for the first fifteen questions I ask, Sharon slowly types out one-word responses. She especially startles me when, because I was told she loved flowers, I ask what her favorite flower is, and she laboriously types out 'columbine' . . . .

"The family says hope is thin that Sharon will ever progress much beyond what she can do now. As Della says, 'Sharon is never going to be Sharon.'"

The article sent me into a tailspin. How could I counteract the impression that hundreds of thousands of people would get from it? I was sickened by the way I was portrayed with the same old tired arguments about my character, my desire for money and my being the cause of Sharon's depression.

I was even more devastated by how Sharon was described. I feared people would believe that Sharon really was "trapped in her twisted body," and think that the nursing home was the best place for her, that I was being unreasonable to want Sharon living at home. But the article had the opposite impact on some. I received calls from disability activists who were infuriated. They promised to write letters to the editor.

Julie immediately wrote a response trying to counter the impressions and misinformation contained in the article. But it was never printed. I felt deeply discouraged that there seemed to be no way to get a fair hearing in the media.

It's impossible to assess all the effects of such widespread negative mainstream press coverage. Early in the case, Sharon and I seemed to have less support in Minnesota than in any other state, and I couldn't help feeling this was caused by the barrage of distorted information in the Minnesota press. Unless someone heard me speak in person, there was no way for them to have any idea of who Sharon really was or what had happened to her.

After discussing the article with my attorney, I decided to write a public letter asking the Kowalskis to agree to a third party for mediation, in hopes that maybe they were ready to deal with the issue outside of the courts. I sent my letter to the newspaper. I wanted people to know that I disagreed with the article but was mainly trying to appeal to the Kowalskis. I wrote:

     I am writing in response to the lengthy article [of] June 14 concerning my attempt to have continuing contact with Sharon

Kowalski, who had been my lover and housemate for four years prior to her accident in 1983. *I was led to believe that this was going to be an investigative report yet several key people with information vital to the case were not even contacted. While I do not agree with much of the information contained in the article, it is not my intent to address those issues at this time . . . .* (Author's emphasis)

These sentences were deleted from my letter when it was printed. Since they were the only two that questioned the integrity of the article, their deletion left the impression that I had nothing to contest. My letter continued:

❖   The litigation between Sharon's parents and me has been costly to all sides, both financially and emotionally. I propose that, instead of continuing to battle in the courts, we hire a professional mediator to help us resolve our conflicts and to focus on what is best for Sharon.

I love Sharon very much, and I have no intention of abandoning her. I will continue to pursue our right to see each other as a matter of love and conscience.

I see what has occurred here as a genuine human tragedy, starting with Sharon's sudden and debilitating accident, and through all the court battles and the bitterness they have caused. I believe Sharon's parents love her. I believe they have a great deal to offer her, as do I. I think Sharon should have the benefit of everyone's love.

I do not see the point of continuing the battle in court, but I have no other alternative if the Kowalskis persist in their position that Sharon and I can never see each other again. *Everyone has lost enough, and Sharon has lost more than anyone.* [This sentence was also deleted.] I urge Donald and Della Kowalski to contact me, so that we can mediate our differences.

Two weeks after the original article, the edited version of my letter was printed. Though many letters supporting me had been sent to the paper, they printed only my letter and another short letter of support. The same day they printed a long and vicious letter from Jack Fena. Fena's letter said:

❖   As attorney for the Donald Kowalski family of Nashwauk, Minn., I
want to set the record straight.

Karen Thompson, as Sharon Kowalski's instructor at St.
Cloud State University, used her position of power and authority
to take Sharon over and influence her and dominate her. It is
common knowledge that teachers have power over their students.
For some reason, this never appears in the press. If this were
Johnny Thompson instead of Karen Thompson and Johnny had
entered into a sexual relationship publicly with a student, what
would the effect be then?

Since day one Karen Thompson has had a field day with
the press. Totally lacking in all of the stories, including your
stories, are the following facts, all set out in the court records and
findings after a long, detailed trial:

1. The relationship of Sharon Kowalski and Karen
Thompson has never been totally clear. Sharon cannot talk nor
reason. The uncontroverted evidence indicates that Sharon
Kowalski was leaving the St. Cloud area; she had closed her bank
account, made plans to move to Denver, and one of the reasons
was that Karen Thompson was trying to totally dominate her life
and possess her.

2. Four medical doctors gave their opinions that Karen
Thompson's association and actions in regards to Sharon
Kowalski were damaging Sharon, preventing her from recovering,
and actually putting her into a deep depression.

3. All four of these doctors, none of whom had known any
of the parties prior to this accident, indicated their opinions to the
court that Thompson's association with Sharon Kowalski should
be terminated.

4. The court, after hearing all of the evidence, did in fact
terminate any association by Thompson with Sharon Kowalski.

5. After Karen Thompson's removal from any contact with
Sharon Kowalski, Sharon quickly recovered from her depression
and today is as happy as she could be under the circumstances of
her physical and brain injuries.

In short, Thompson's claims have been found by all of the
courts to be false and her claims remain false.

Exactly what I had feared occurred. My letter didn't challenge any
of the misinformation of the article and it was pitted against Jack Fena's
letter containing even more inaccurate accusations. Once again, I won-

dered what Jack Fena's personal stake was in all this, and why he was never held responsible for these kinds of statements.

After much discussion with the editors of the *Pioneer Press,* Sue Wilson was finally allowed to submit an abridged letter that argued with Fena's assertions point by point. Sue's letter appeared Saturday, August 8, almost two months after the original article. It said:

 Dear Editor:

As Karen Thompson's attorney, I want the opportunity to correct the gross misrepresentations of fact in Jack Fena's letter June 28. The following are facts either misrepresented or omitted by Mr. Fena (attorney for the Donald Kowalski family):

1. Karen Thompson and Sharon Kowalski made a commitment to each other while Karen was a full-time student at Ohio State, two years after Sharon had taken a course from her. Sharon was 23 years old and initiated the relationship; her personality hardly lent itself to being 'dominated and possessed.'

2. One week before the accident, Sharon had accepted a position with St. Cloud State University. She had no intention of leaving the area.

3. Sharon's relationship with Karen has been documented by affidavits from Sharon's friends and employer. Sharon has typed out for the MCLU that she was gay, that gay meant loving someone of the same sex, that Karen was her lover, and that she and Karen had exchanged rings because they loved each other. Sharon named Karen as beneficiary on their life insurance policy.

4. Karen was the first person to point out that Sharon was in a post-accident depression and to seek help for her. No longer being able to deny their daughter's depression, the Kowalskis have tried to blame it on Karen. However, by the time visitation was stopped by Mr. Kowalski, Sharon had been out of her depression for months.

5. The doctors recommending termination of Karen's visitation were hired by the Kowalskis, and never saw Sharon and Karen together. One doctor visited Sharon twice briefly, and Sharon was unresponsive. From those visits, he concluded that Sharon was suffering from a depression based upon her reaction to Karen Thompson. On cross-examination, this doctor completely backed off this position. Testimony from two other doctors was totally based on statements from this first doctor. The [fourth] doctor had no communication with anyone except Mr.

Fena and Mr. Kowalski prior to writing a letter recommending denial of Karen's visitation.

6. The court did not find that Karen's visits were detrimental to Sharon, and did not terminate visitation. The court merely gave Donald Kowalski full guardianship powers. Within 24 hours, he alone ordered no visitation.

7. Medical notes from every institution Sharon has been in document that Karen's interaction is positive and elicits a higher level of response from Sharon than from any other person. The Minnesota Office of Health Facility Complaints documented that Sharon has consistently indicated her desire to see Karen. Because this desire has not been honored, the nursing home was cited with a violation of the Patient Bill of Rights.

The real issue in this case is whether or not a young lesbian woman, who had never told her parents about her sexual orientation, should be denied the right to continue to see a person significant to her recovery and to continue the relationship she has chosen, simply because she was disabled by a tragic accident.

The precedents set in this case have sent a shock wave through the gay, lesbian and handicapped communities. Concerned people report to me their horror that the First Amendment right of free association seems to have been so flagrantly violated in this case. It appears to me that they are right.

CHAPTER 16

Becoming an Activist

Whenever I traveled to other states, I was asked what Minnesota was doing to help the case. While numerous individuals in Minnesota had been active from the very beginning, the original Committee for the Right to Recovery and Relationships in St. Cloud had become inactive. In June, 1987, a few core supporters decided to organize a coalition group to work on the case, including activists from disability, feminist, lesbian/gay and civil rights organizations.

Called 'Bring Sharon Home,' the group brainstormed a wide variety of actions that might bring some results. Besides sharing the functions of the other state groups, the Minnesota group had an additional challenge. As a local group, they had the greatest potential to take direct action for Sharon's benefit. Meetings with state officials, petitions, demonstrations, media coverage of the case were all brought up as possibilities; the new group immediately dug into the work.

That summer was busy. I taught summer school, spoke in various classes at SCSU and traveled to give presentations on weekends. Every spare minute was spent writing the book with Julie. The book had to be mostly finished by the end of August because there would be no time to write it in the fall with my schedule of teaching and speaking engagements.

In the middle of July, I flew to the National NOW Convention in Philadelphia. I had never before spent time with such a large group of politically active women. For the first time, I understood Ellie Smeal's (whom I could now recognize) concept of the feminization of power.

Peri Jude, who had written the first NOW article covering the case, ushered me around during the convention. She took me to the issue hearings to explain my case so a resolution could be considered for adoption. NOW unanimously approved a resolution to support the case.

It felt like a big breakthrough to me to have one of the most visible national feminist organizations support the case. By this time, however, I had learned not to try to predict what results this action might bring; sometimes my hopes had been raised only to be dashed when nothing came of it. But almost immediately after returning home, I received a call from Dade County NOW in Florida asking me to come to speak.

I wondered whether I should go to Florida, since we were pushing so hard to get the book done. Julie was especially worried when she found out I would be missing three writing days.

The trip turned out to be one of the best I'd made. The Dade County NOW group was an inspiration. In the same month they had organized events for me, Pat Schroeder and a protest of the Pope's visit.

No trip I made was without its special insight, something new that I learned. In Miami, all the recent changes in my life seemed to come together. Listening to these feminist activists, I no longer felt like a fraud. I recognized, understood and was wholly in support of the issues they discussed.

I had never been one to join groups, but I realized that I wanted to be an official part of the feminist community. When the Miami group found out that I had been to the state and national conventions without yet being a member of NOW, they decided to make me a member of Dade County NOW. I discovered the excitement of uniting with other women in organizing for change. I was proud to be a member.

This visit also helped me completely accept myself as a lesbian. For some time now, I had acknowledged being a lesbian. My only choices seemed to be to accept that or be very unhappy and incomplete. My struggle with being a lesbian and a Christian was resolved. Yet I had still thought if I had been given a choice, I would have chosen to be heterosexual. I would not have chosen this fight. Now, in the warm, accepting community of the Dade County women, I knew I was glad to be a lesbian, and given a choice, would choose to be one.

I had finally caught up with myself. Having to come out to the nation before I was ready to come out to myself, I had to go through a lot of stages before I became as comfortable with my identity as I appeared. Because I was so visible, many people assumed that I had been to a gay bar or a lesbian bookstore, that I knew the culture and the language. They assumed that feminism was old hat to me—that I knew the history, the issues and their connections. I'd had some wonderful tutors, but some of the connections which had become clear to me intellectually, and were easy to make in my speeches, had not really become an integral part of me until that trip. For the first time, I labeled myself as a lesbian feminist activist, even though I knew I still had much to learn.

Yet a war was raging within me. Here I was, an open lesbian. I could have walked holding hands with Sharon and challenged others to deal with their homophobia. I could have put my arm around her in public. I could have gone to my church with my partner—openly as a couple. And now it was impossible.

I regretted the years I had wasted time struggling over whether it was a sin to love Sharon, fearing that I would have to give her up in order to be a Christian or that someone would find out about our relationship. But even during those years, Sharon had taught me to live fully and to feel emotions I had never known before. We became so deeply connected that now, two years after I had last seen her, I could still physically feel Sharon's presence.

I loved Sharon to the core of my being, and yet sometimes I hated her for the vulnerability this love created. I had never felt this depth of pain before. I knew that physical pain, like the torn ligaments I had gotten playing sports, would eventually lessen. This emotional pain seemed unending. I feel it as sharply today as I did the day I was first separated from her.

Often Julie would ask me what I felt, and, in order to hold myself together, I would answer in a detached manner, as though it wasn't really me feeling it. "It felt horrible," I would say numbly. But some days, the pain would come bursting out. I couldn't stop it. It was a crushing assault that I experienced emotionally and physically. I couldn't stop shaking. I would sink to the floor. I had no idea how to stop it or pull it back inside.

Julie and Mary Anne would sit helplessly by, willing to do anything they could. Once, when Julie pushed me hard to express my feelings, I couldn't keep myself from crying out, "I can't let myself tell you about the feelings because I'm afraid I won't be able to pull myself together again. I exist, I live, I wish away days and weeks until Sharon can come home. Four years of wishing my life away!"

All my carefully hidden feelings were exposed, and I lashed out at these two good friends. "You want me to talk, to say what I'm feeling. What do you want, Julie, to see the me that doesn't want to live from one day to the next?" Each sentence was punctuated with sobs. "Everything is in extremes. One side needs to see relationships like yours and Mary Anne's . . . to know that happiness is really possible. And the other side hates to see it . . . I think of what Sharon and I could have had . . . . One part of me is grateful to Sharon for teaching me how to feel and the other part hates her for making me dependent. I never would have felt this pain if she hadn't taught me!

"And now I've changed so much, I don't even know if Sharon and I would have gotten together anymore. If we were to meet today for the first time, I don't know if we would get together. I haven't seen her for two years! I want to have a normal life again. I want to stay home and worry about things I used to think were problems." My emotions were swinging wildly. "The Kowalskis still have each other. They still have their home. I go home and nothing is normal. I eat by myself, sit by myself, sleep by myself, do everything by myself that I used to do with Sharon!

"It doesn't do any good to let anyone know." I finally became exhausted. "Sometimes I cry hoping for relief but the crying doesn't help. It just ends and the pain's still there, just back inside and nothing has changed. All I can do is get up and answer another phone call, prepare another speech, teach my classes and hope that one day something will change. I just pray that I can get the story out to enough people that someone who has some power will be moved enough to support Sharon, regardless of the political pressure. I just pray that some judge will be fair enough, brave enough or honest enough to apply the law for Sharon's rights. I hope some governmental office will take the risk to at least investigate, that someone will insist that Sharon be tested by impartial doctors. I just have to live my life like that, trying to do whatever I can each day. It's the only way I can keep going. It's the only way I can fight the image of her eyes pleading with me not to leave."

As I slowly regained my composure in the shelter of these friends' love, my resolve returned. Sharon was not free. Still separated against both of our wishes, the fight was not over.

❖

With renewed courage, I actually looked forward to speaking at the Take Back the Night march in Minneapolis. I was a totally different person from the one who had spoken two years before. I had a broader personal and political perspective as I planned my talk. I had only six minutes and maybe no one else would notice the change in me but I was very much aware of it. For the first time, I *was* an activist. I began my speech in a totally new way:

"Why is there an increase in violence against Native Americans, Blacks, other people of color, women, lesbians and gay men? Why would the U.S. rather spend money building bombs than providing for our safety, food, clothing, housing and health care? Why haven't I been allowed to see Sharon Kowalski for two years? Why can't Sharon come home?" I questioned from the platform of the Take Back the Night rally.

"Before Sharon's accident, I didn't understand any of these issues. More importantly, I didn't understand how they are all interconnected. I didn't understand that if I didn't come forth today and fight for anyone's human rights that are being violated, then tomorrow Sharon's and mine might be stripped away.

"I've had a crash course in understanding our rich white hetero-sexual able-bodied Christian male system that oppresses *anyone* who is *different!* This system oppresses Sharon and me because we're women, we're lesbians and Sharon is disabled.

"This system oppresses Sharon and me because we're women and sexism is still deeply embedded in our society today. Our system simply won't give a woman guardianship if there is a man available, no matter how much better qualified that woman is. If Sharon were a man, it would have been much more difficult to strip away her rights. But women's rights have been stripped away for centuries.

"This system oppresses Sharon because she is disabled and han-dicapism permeates all of our institutions today. In one split second you can become disabled, and you become like a child needing the 'uncondi-tional love of your parents' no matter what your age. Like a child, everything a disabled person says is discounted. The court ruled that Sharon cannot be in the courtroom when her own future is being deter-mined, because of her 'medical condition,' even though she can be anywhere you can push a wheelchair. Who are we trying to protect? Sharon? Or ourselves from having to deal with someone who is different?

"The court has ruled that Sharon cannot communicate her wishes in any way, yet she can type words, phrases and sentences. Donald Kowalski said on the stand, 'To take my daughter out on a pass is putting her on display and would be an embarrassment.' To whom? Sharon? Or us? Let's keep the disabled out of sight. The *St. Paul Pioneer Press Dispatch* describing Sharon as the Kowalskis' 'eerily silent daughter lying trapped in her twisted body' is a flagrant example of the handicapism of the press.

"The system oppresses Sharon and me because we are lesbians and homophobia is running rampant. Examples of homophobia run from one end of the continuum to the other. On one end there are the medical professionals who don't want to get involved, or they don't want to take sides. In the middle we have a doctor who had to pray and struggle before giving testimony that I functioned as an effective therapist with Sharon, that Sharon does things for me that she will do for no one else and that he as a doctor would do nothing to separate us.

"At the other end of the continuum we have a doctor who says he understands there might have been a prior relationship between Sharon and me and, therefore, he fears sexual abuse. Based on that, he ordered I should never be allowed to see Sharon again. An especially blatant example of homophobia occurred when a member of the Minnesota Lawyers' Ethics Board wrote, 'I'm sick and tired of these wacko relationships between people like Karen Thompson and this poor disabled girl.'

"So, one by one, Sharon's rights have been stripped away and they continue to be flagrantly violated today. She has been denied:

1. the right to be tested for competency.
2. the right to recovery.
3. the right to the highest quality of life. (What's higher quality of life, a 31-year-old woman living the rest of her life in a nursing home or living in her own home?)
4. the right to counsel of choice.
5. the right to freedom of association.
6. the Patient Bill of Rights.
7. the right to due process and equal protection under the law.

And I could go on and on naming other laws that have been broken or changed for this case.

"But this case is not over. We must win it for Sharon and for everyone. It is extremely important that people understand this case. Anyone, in one split second, could become a Sharon Kowalski through accident or illness. The precedents being set in this case are establishing very bad case law that could impact anyone who becomes disabled.

"I tell you what has happened to Sharon and me not to depress you but to empower you. I have learned that as long as I am invisible, I am vulnerable. I have also learned that one person can make a difference. I can let my pain eat me up and become helpless and hopeless or I can channel that pain and anger into a constructive outlet and become an agent for change. I spoke out and I've been told that thousands of people have taken out durable powers of attorney, living wills and wills to protect their relationships, their loved ones, because of hearing about our situation. I speak out in classes across the nation and receive feedback from students who tell me they can now see the way our system oppresses and that they have changed their attitudes on lesbians and gay men.

"We must fight for everyone's basic human rights. We must make ourselves known. Our voices must be heard in large enough numbers that what we have to say cannot be discounted, cannot be ignored. Nightmares like Sharon's and mine must end and never be allowed to recur. If we don't answer the question 'Why can't Sharon come home,' if we don't win this case, the question tomorrow might be, *why can't you come home?"*

CHAPTER 17

Thoughts of Sharon

Back home from Minneapolis, with a few days to think, I let myself consider what had become more and more apparent—that I had to sell the house Sharon and I had bought together. Between teaching and speaking all over the country, I was rarely able to spend any time there except to sleep, and then only a few nights out of the week. In spite of the fact that I loved shoveling snow, mowing grass and raking leaves, these jobs had become an added burden to my already stressful life.

Slowly, the realization that I needed to live in town became clear. But I was fearful about losing this last link with Sharon. I reluctantly put the house on the market, knowing that if things changed before it sold, I was not yet committed to a final decision. As though my indecision was transparent, I received no offers for almost a year. Yet my loneliness there became more intolerable and my frustration over the house's burden grew. I would arrive home from the airport in the middle of the night to discover my driveway had been drifted in with snow. Other days I might be delayed at school for so long that there seemed little point in driving all the way home just to return early the next morning.

Finally, after lowering the price, I received an acceptable offer and the decision was made for me. It couldn't have been at a worse time. With my speaking schedule, I had only one week to locate another place to live. I was overbooked for the next two months, speaking literally from east coast to west coast. And on top of everything else, *West 57th Street,* who finally had decided to do a 30-minute piece on the case, called to say they needed to film scenes at the house while it still looked the way it had when Sharon and I lived in it. So I rushed home from one trip to have CBS underfoot filming while I was packing. Everything had to be ready since friends would do the actual move while I was away on my next speaking trip.

I returned from a trip that took me from Nashville to Washington, D.C. in one weekend to find our house empty. As emotional as the packing and preparations for moving had been, I wasn't prepared for the onslaught of complicated feelings I experienced as I walked in through the door for the last time. This house had represented to Sharon and me the commitment we had made to our future together. All the images of the joy, laughter and excitement of our first months there crowded into my mind as I wandered through the empty rooms.

Oh Sharon! I wanted to talk to you before making such a final decision. God, I hope you can understand! This doesn't mean that I'm giving up on a life for us. There can be a new beginning somewhere else, a place where you can once again be comfortable and happy.

Even though I was pleading with her to understand, the empty house echoed the ending of a chapter of our lives. This house was the most important physical connection with Sharon I had left. I sat down on the floor and began to cry. Not only would Sharon have to come back to the new person I had become, but she would have to come back to an entirely new home.

Sharon, I've wanted to talk with you for so long to tell you how much I've changed. Would you have fallen in love with this new person, this totally different person from the one you last saw? And are you different now? How have you changed? If time has changed me, I'm sure it has changed you. Why couldn't we have grown together? We could have shared all these things when they happened, making us even closer. Yet now we're strangers because we've been forced to go through these changes alone. Will we ever be able to understand one another again?

I had learned to love the new Sharon following the accident because I was there minute by minute. We had struggled to keep communicating and to change together. I glanced at the wall where our pictures used to be. For the first time in months, I stole a moment to concentrate on just Sharon and me. Her presence filled the room. I almost felt as if time and space were pushed aside and I could make the 'I love you' sign with her one more time, our fingers touching. If only I could explain to her that my whole life still revolved around the commitment we had made to each other.

Sharon, I have wanted to share so many things with you. I have finally accepted our sexuality and feel freer than ever before in my life. In spite of everything that has happened, I'm as close to being a whole person as I have ever been. It's a feeling that I can't put into words. I am glad that I came out, even though, God knows, I wish the circumstances that brought it about hadn't happened. But even if I had lost my job, even if I had lost my family's support, I still think it would have been worth it. I don't have to hide anything anymore. I have a freedom to grow, to like and respect who I am—a lesbian. I know now I would never choose to be anyone else.

I want you to understand how fighting for our right to live our own lives and make our own decisions has transformed me from the conservative, private person you knew into an activist and feminist. Activist and feminist—probably you know more than anybody how these words used to frighten me. I see that same fear in other people, who are more afraid of me as an activist and feminist than as a lesbian. Mom told me last spring, "I know you love Sharon and I understand that you want to bring her home. But why do you have to be a Grand Marshal in the New York City Gay Pride Parade?" She seemed worried that if I went too far, if I was too visible and outspoken, I would get hurt. But I know now I have suffered more because of my silence.

Sharon, I feel the pain of our separation every day. Since I couldn't be with you, I had to do something with my rage or it would have destroyed me. I decided to speak out and work for a positive change to come out of all you and I have suffered—all you have suffered, Sharon. Our story has touched the hearts of thousands of people who will never be the same. If only you could know and feel the support we have received from all over the country, it might give you the courage to keep fighting. It might give you hope that we still have a future together.

I still want to win this case for us, but in fighting for us I've also begun to feel the pain of others who have also experienced oppression. And I have learned about the connections between different forms of prejudice and the people who profit from others' misery. I have learned how people with power can manipulate and twist 'facts' to blame those who are victims. I have experienced being called aggressive, crazy and vindictive when our rights were being violated and I sought to protect them.

I have watched people label you helpless and childlike in their efforts to take control of your life. I have discovered that people who are uncomfortable with differences make disabled people 'invisible' and keep them out of sight in order to avoid their own fears. I have seen how institutions have removed the rights of women, disabled people and others under the guise of 'for their own good.'

Sharon, in the same society that allows outrageous sexual abuse by men, you and I have been denied a loving relationship. They use stereotypes and lies to disguise their underlying prejudices against lesbians, women and disabled people and to strip our rights from us. This is what I am learning, Sharon. How can someone else decide for you that you can never be a sexual person again, regardless of what you can do or what you want? They'd rather have you live your life in a nursing home than live independently, than ever have the possibility of an intimate relationship with me.

My commitment to you hasn't wavered, even though years have passed since I've seen you. If success means that you are free, then so far I have failed. But if success means that thousands of people have opened their minds or obtained legal protection as a result of our struggle, you and I have already made a difference in the world. Sharon, I will continue to fight for us and for all the others who have been or could be separated by the same injustice. And I hope and pray that some day we will be fighting side by side—that we'll have the chance for a love that shares all we've learned.

I stood up, took a last look at the past, and walked resolutely out the door into the future. As I closed it for the last time, the darkness of the countryside, far from the city lights, enveloped me. I looked up in awe as the sparkling brilliance of the Milky Way filled the sky.

EPILOGUE

A hearing was held on the motion to restore Sharon to capacity (a request for competency testing) on November 18, 1987. Fena argued that competency testing would cost Sharon thousands of dollars, since the personal injury suit was scheduled to go to trial in January. He also argued that it was a waste of time and money because Sharon wasn't making enough progress to have speech therapy. Furthermore, he asked that the testing be canceled or indefinitely postponed because Sharon's father had had a heart attack. The judge ruled that it was in Sharon's best interest to delay making a decision for two months based on Sharon's fragile condition, the upcoming personal injury trial and her father's health condition. In the same decision, the MCLU volunteer attorney, Brian O'Neill, was rejected as Sharon's attorney and Gary Pagliaccetti, an attorney from Hibbing, was appointed. Sharon had been without any attorney for almost a year, since Tom Hayes had resigned in late 1986.

A second hearing on the motion was held on February 5, 1988. Pagliaccetti told the court that he had visited Sharon four times. He believed that Sharon understood him and that she could communicate effectively when she wanted to. Pagliaccetti questioned why she had no computer for communication, and he thought she would be able to benefit from an electric wheelchair (questions Karen had raised for years). Judge Campbell instructed Donald Kowalski to investigate both of these possibilities, though he was told at that time that electric wheelchairs were not allowed in that nursing home. In spite of Donald Kowalski's and Fena's opposition to the testing, the judge decided that Sharon should be tested, but did not immediately issue a formal order on any of these points.

A National Meeting to Free Sharon Kowalski was held in Minneapolis in February of 1988. The group established a national structure with co-chairs and committees on media, outreach, fund-raising and direct action. Another National Meeting was held in New York in June, 1988, as the Free Sharon Kowalski movement continued to grow.

In March, at the height of his 1988 campaign for the presidency, Jesse Jackson issued a statement in support of Karen Thompson and Sharon Kowalski. His statement said:

◆ I wish to express my support for Karen Thompson and Sharon Kowalski. Ms. Thompson is to be commended for her dedication and courage in seeking the best possible care for Sharon Kowalski, her life-partner. Ms. Thompson has been infinitely patient—but there comes an end to patience with a system that is unfair and unjust. We question the wisdom of any legal ruling which seeks to separate mutually consenting adults who have made a life commitment to each other. Homophobia, sexism and handicapism should never again be allowed to limit the potential and abilities of any person. It is my fervent hope that very soon now Sharon Kowalski will come home again.

Meanwhile, Karen's academic year ended on a positive note when St. Cloud State University gave tangible evidence of their support by recommending Karen for promotion to Associate Professor. In his recommendation, the Vice President of Academic Affairs stated, in part, "In all of these various activities, she has been a credit to St. Cloud State University and has exemplified our often quoted claim that not all teaching takes place in the classroom. It is fair to say that Ms. Thompson did not choose the circumstances which have forced her into the national limelight. It is also fair to say that she has transformed that personal adversity into an educational opportunity for herself and for us all."

◆

When June arrived and no order had been issued from the court, the National Committee to Free Sharon Kowalski, the National Organization for Women, the Center for the Independence of the Disabled in New York, the Boston Self-Help Center and Women's Braille Press sent a letter to Chief Justice David Ackerson expressing concern and asking that he encourage Judge Campbell to issue the order.

The order for testing was finally issued on the 6th of July, 1988.

Three male doctors from the Duluth area were appointed to evaluate Sharon. The court order read:

❖ Said examiners are granted authority to review any and all medical or other records they deem necessary in conducting their evaluations. The parties hereto, Donald Kowalski and Karen Thompson and Sharon's present care provider, Leisure Hills Nursing Home, are instructed to cooperate with the examiners to the extent requested. If in the opinion of either examiner it would aid in his evaluation to observe Sharon Kowalski in the presence of Karen Thompson, then any restrictions on visitation imposed by this court or the guardian or Leisure Hills are waived for the limited purpose of the examiners' observation. The examiner shall be present at such time.

In order to facilitate the examinations requested herein, the examiners are authorized to admit Sharon Kowalski to the Rehabilitation Unit of Miller-Dwan Hospital in Duluth, Minnesota. They may also in their discretion conduct portions of their examinations at Leisure Hills Nursing Home. Arrangements for her admission to Miller-Dwan Hospital may be made through her guardian Donald Kowalski and her attorney Gary Pagliaccetti.

The examiners are requested to address the following questions, if possible, in their assessment of Sharon Kowalski:

1. What is her present level of physical functioning?
2. What is her present level of mental functioning?
3. What is her present level of social and psychological well-being?
4. What, if any, further evaluations would you recommend?
5. What potential do you see her reaching?
6. What are your recommendations for further re-habilitation?
7. Does she have the ability to reliably express her wishes as to visitation?

The parties and their attorneys are instructed to refrain from contacting the examiners either directly or through third persons.

This was the first order in three years that was in Sharon's favor. However, no mention was made of a special person or advocate to be present as required by law, no provision was made for women to be involved in any part of the testing, nor was any precaution taken that evaluators be screened for homophobia, as Karen had requested in a letter to the judge.

The testing date for Sharon was set by Judge Campbell for July 31st and an order issued authorizing Sharon's move to Miller-Dwan for the testing. As the testing date neared, the Clerk of Court for the Minnesota Court of Appeals called Sue Wilson to inform her that Jack Fena had made a *verbal* request for a stay of the judge's order that Sharon be evaluated. In a highly unusual and irregular action, the court of appeals granted the stay to allow Fena one week to submit a Writ of Prohibition and Sue Wilson and Gary Pagliaccetti one week to respond. It is important to note that the order for evaluation is statutory and non-discretionary (that is, it should not be subject to appeal).

A few days later, Jack Fena called Sue Wilson to read, over the phone, an affidavit which he had already sent to Judge Campbell. Essentially, it contained another judgment from Dr. Wilson that 1) Sharon should not be moved and 2) Karen should not be present at the testing because the results would be "less reliable." Fena had agreed to withdraw his request for a stay from the court of appeals if Judge Campbell would agree to rediscuss his court order in light of Dr. Wilson's opinions. On August 3, a conference call was held between Gary Pagliaccetti, Judge Campbell, Sue Wilson and Jack Fena. The result of the telephone conference was that Jack Fena withdrew his request for a stay of the judge's order that Sharon be evaluated and Judge Campbell decreed that the evaluation proceed, that Sharon be moved to Duluth and that Karen could only be present at the evaluation if a request was made by the doctors directly to Judge Campbell.

This delay required that a new testing date be established. At this writing, the date has not been formally set but is expected to take place in September. This, of course, assumes that the Kowalskis and Jack Fena bring no new motions.

❖

In July, 1988, the Mille Lacs County District Court finally ruled on the personal injury suit brought by Donald and Della Kowalski on behalf of Sharon Kowalski and themselves. The suit involved the insurance company of the tavern that served the driver. The total settlement was in the amount of $330,000, to be dispersed in the following sums:

 $119,018.05 for attorney fees for the attorneys hired by Donald and Della Kowalski;

$125,527.66 to offset a State of Minnesota lien for assistance provided to Sharon Kowalski;
$65,182.80 to Donald and Della Kowalski:

a. $38,015.37 for mileage, lodging, meals, treatment of Sharon Kowalski, life insurance premium for Sharon and telephone expenses

b. $26,567.43 to purchase a van for transportation of Sharon Kowalski

c. $600.00 for insurance for the van;

Though not mentioned in the court order, the remaining *$20,271.49* will ostensibly be assigned to Sharon Kowalski's estate.

On July 13, Karen Thompson's lawyer, Sue Wilson, sent a request to Judge Campbell in which she asked for "careful judicial scrutiny" to "maximize the funds left in the ward's estate."

The following week, Judge Campbell called Sue Wilson to say that his court had no jurisdiction over the personal injury suit disbursements, so he could not restrain the funds, but that he did have jurisdiction over the funds that were now in Sharon's estate and would scrutinize their use carefully.

Interestingly, further public information about an *earlier* settlement came out in a *Minneapolis Star Tribune* article published August 6, 1988. The *Star Tribune* reported a conversation with Donald Kowalski about buying a computer for Sharon.

❖　　Donald Kowalski says he does not object to his daughter attempting to use a computer, but that he has hesitated to purchase one pending the outcome of her medical evaluation.

Money also is an issue, he said, since Sharon Kowalski's estate received only about $20,000 out of a recent $330,000 out-of-court settlement resulting from the 1983 auto accident. Her parents' attorneys received $119,018, while her father—as her guardian—received $64,000, including $26,500 for a conversion van in which to transport Sharon.

Two years ago, Sharon received another $330,000 settlement, but that money was placed in trust for distribution to her after she reaches 50, her father said. That won't be until 2006.

❖

We can only be cautious about expecting anything good to come of Sharon's evaluation. Karen Thompson's request that Sharon be tested was presented to the courts over a year ago. And in an August 5 article that appeared in the *Washington Post*, we have a clear picture of Fena's opinion about the testing:

❖   . . . Although Minnesota law requires guardians to ask their adult wards annually whether they want to be tested to determine their legal capacity, Donald Kowalski did not do so for years. "That probably would be my fault," said his attorney, Jack Fena, who called the requirement a technicality that he at first was unaware of and then considered unnecessary.

In recent weeks, Jack Fena and the Kowalskis seem to be talking more freely to the media, and their attitudes towards Sharon, Karen, and lesbians and the disabled in general, are being exposed. In the same *Washington Post* article, the reporter recounted her conversation with Donald Kowalski:

Thompson will never be granted guardianship, he said, because "there ain't a law in the United States that allows a lesbian relationship."

And later in the article:

Donald Kowalski contends that his daughter's sexual orientation is irrelevant now. "What the hell difference does it make if she's gay or lesbian or straight or anything because she's laying there in diapers? . . . Let the poor kid rest in peace."

This type of reporting provides the biggest ray of hope since the case's origin. It comes through the efforts of the National Free Sharon Kowalski Committee. By naming Sharon's birthday, August 7, as National Free Sharon Kowalski Day, the committee has focused national media attention on her situation. Articles have appeared in the *Washington Post*, the *St. Petersburg Times*, the *New York Times*, the *L.A. Times*, *USA Today*, and *Time Magazine*. Perhaps, just as important, the *Minneapolis Star Tribune* article represented the first home state reporting that supported Karen's efforts on Sharon's behalf. At the same time, Karen has begun to appear on many radio and television broadcasts, including "Geraldo," "The Larry King Show," "People Are Talking" in San Francisco and Philadelphia, and the Diane Riem Show on National Public Radio. There is hope that a large grassroots swell could indeed turn the wheels of justice for Sharon's cause and bring her home.

How You Can Help

To get involved in local activities, help organize
for Sharon Kowalski, or to receive updates on
the Kowalski case, please write to:

National Committee to Free Sharon Kowalski
1725 17th Street N.W., Room 515
Washington, D.C. 20009
Co-chairs:
Tacie Dejanikus (202) 667-3415
Pamela Slycord (617) 783-3580

Contributions to help Karen Thompson in the
guardianship case should be sent to:
Karen Thompson Legal Fund
2501 Stockinger Drive
St. Cloud, MN 56303

Appendices

APPENDIX A

Timeline of Significant Events

DATE EVENT

November 1983 .... Sharon's accident

December 1983 .... Karen and Sharon's fourth anniversary

January 1984 ...... Karen notices Sharon's finger movements and begins to get some response from her.

Karen writes a letter coming out to Sharon's parents at the advice of the hospital psychologist.

February 1984 ..... Karen contacts Julie Andrzejewski and finds an attorney.

March 1984 .... Karen files for guardianship.

April 1984......... Out of court settlement: Donald Kowalski is appointed guardian, with equal access for Karen to all records and equal visitation time.

Sharon is still technically in a coma but is alert many times during the day when Karen can work with her.

May 1984 .... Sharon is moved to the rehabilitation ward of Sherburne County Hospital. Sharon can go outside in a wheelchair.

June 1984......... Hearing regarding what nursing home and city Sharon will be transferred to. Country Manor in St. Cloud is the court's decision.

July 1984 . . . . Sharon is transferred to Country Manor where Karen can spend hours each day visiting and working with her.

Sharon's first day pass. Karen and friends take her home.

August 1984 . . . . Sharon is improving. She can write, swallow, even speak for the first time. Karen takes her to church. Karen videotapes Sharon's progress. Sharon begins to type.

September 1984 . . . . Kowalskis ask the court to test Sharon at Polinsky Institute in Duluth. Sharon is moved immediately following the court order. Many of her personal and medical belongings are left at Country Manor.

October 1984 . . . . . . Sharon is upset at being in Duluth. She regresses and testing does not go well. Kowalskis ask the court to move Sharon to Park Point Manor nursing home in Duluth. Karen decides to go public.

Kowalskis file for a temporary restraining order against Karen and other motions to permanently remove Karen's rights. Karen counterfiles, asking for a second evaluation of Sharon, the removal of Kowalski as guardian and Sharon to be present in court.

November 1984 . . . . MCLU brief expedites hearing and the court affirms Karen's visitation, but places a restraining order "on all parties" which primarily affects Karen and restricts Sharon's day passes as well.

December 1984 . . . . Telephone conference between attorneys and the court results in an agreement by both parties to temporarily withdraw pending motions because of Della Kowalski's emotional state.

January 1985 . . . . . . Sharon types responses to St. Cloud Handicap Services and confirms that she is gay and that Karen is her lover.

Karen locates a psychologist to test Sharon, who is losing ground rapidly.

February 1985 . . . . . Sharon's evaluation identifies that she had regressed since the videotape made at Country Manor and that she is depressed.

March 1985 . . . . Kowalskis have another psychologist test Sharon who also identifies her depression.

May 3, 1985 . . . . A hearing is held on the motions (delayed from October 1984) to remove Karen's rights and to find Karen in contempt as well as on Karen's motions to remove Donald Kowalski as guardian. The hearing is continued to May 9, 1985.

May 9, 1985 . . . . The hearing continues: Fena submits letters, which are late and not under oath, from doctors recommending termination of Karen's visits. Fena and Hayes make their closing arguments. Ristvedt asks to submit a brief.

June 1985. . . . . Ristvedt takes depositions from the doctors who wrote the letters.

The MCLU interviews Sharon. Sharon communicates evidence of her relationship with Karen and indicates that she wants the MCLU to represent her. The MCLU files to represent Sharon. Karen continues to visit Sharon almost daily.

July 1985 . . . . On July 23, 1985, the court gives Donald Kowalski full guardianship, finding that Sharon "lacks sufficient understanding . . . to make . . . responsible decisions" and that the conflict is having an "adverse effect" on her. Within 24 hours Donald Kowalski denies visitation to Karen among others. In 48 hours Kowalski has Sharon transferred to a Hibbing nursing home.

August 1985 . . . . Karen and the MCLU appeal the decision. Hayes joins the appeal. Karen gets to visit Sharon once again. Fena submits a doctor's letter insinuating a "high risk of sexual abuse" which is now used to deny Karen visitation.

Karen sees Sharon for the last time.

September 1985 .... Karen files a complaint with the Minnesota Office of Health Facility Complaints for violation of Sharon's Patient Bill of Rights. The OHFC cites Leisure Hills Nursing Home with a violation.

Karen changes attorneys.

The court of appeals implements the July 23 order even while under appeal.

Hayes asks to associate with the MCLU. The Court of appeals denies it. The MCLU appeals to the Minnesota Supreme Court.

November 1985 .... Minnesota Supreme Court refuses to hear the MCLU petition.

December 1985 .... Karen files a motion in district court to find Donald Kowalski in contempt for not acting in Sharon's best interests. She asks that Sharon be re-evaluated at Sister Kenny Institute and that Jack Fena be removed as Kowalskis' guardianship attorney because of conflict of interest with the personal injury suit.

January 1986 ...... MCLU submits a petition to the U.S. Supreme Court.

District court hearing on Karen's motions occurs by telephone conference. Karen's motions are denied. Karen's attorney, Sue Wilson, appeals.

February 1986 ..... Main hearing on Hayes' appeal of the July 23 guardianship order.

March 1986 .... Court of appeals affirms the July 23 order, making new "findings of fact" in that ruling.

June 1986......... With no results through the legal system, Karen focuses on speaking out publicly about the case. Karen flies to California and Boston to speak.

August 1986 .... Minnesota Court of Appeals denies Karen's motions to remove the guardian for denying Sharon's rights, saying the Patient Bill of Rights does not apply to guardians—only to institutions.

Karen and Julie begin writing the book.

September 1986 . . . . Karen sits in on Julie's classes and begins to learn more about human rights issues and their inter-relationships.

Disability activists visit Sharon.

November 1986 . . . . Minnesota Supreme Court denies review of the last appeal.

Karen begins to integrate her new political under-standing into her speeches and to gain more confidence. Karen realizes her story can help others. National television programs begin to contact Karen.

June 1987 . . . . "The Silent Ordeal" article appears in the St. Paul Pioneer Press.

July 1987 . . . . National NOW passes a resolution supporting the case.

September 1987 . . . . Karen's attorneys file a request for competency testing for Sharon.

October 1987 . . . . . . National Committee to Free Sharon Kowalski is organized.

November 1987 . . . . Hearing on competency testing for Sharon. Pagliac-cetti is appointed to represent her.

February 1988 . . . . . Judge decides Sharon should be tested.

July 1988 . . . . Judge's order for competency testing is issued.

APPENDIX B

Creating Your Own
Durable Power of Attorney

What happened to Sharon Kowalski is a particularly tragic example of what can happen to any gay, lesbian or unmarried adult, faced with a sudden, and arbitrary, accident or illness. Many gay men living with AIDS have been in the forefront of confronting these issues—from the presence of lovers and friends at their bedsides, to who is authorized to make medical decisions if they become incapacitated. The forms included in this appendix offer some guidelines as to steps that will help insure, ahead of time, that your wishes will be followed.

However, we do need to state clearly that there is no guarantee that the sample forms included in this appendix will protect you. In many cases, simply filling out the forms, and having them properly notarized and witnessed, will be enough. But what makes a durable power of attorney legal varies from state to state. We suggest that you use these sample forms as a starting point. Consulting an attorney in your state before signing these forms will be quick and fairly inexpensive.

Legally, there are two primary ways to authorize someone else to handle your affairs if you become incompetent. The first is for *you* to designate that person through a legal document. The second is for a court to appoint a "guardian," "conservator," or "custodian"—the name varies depending on state law, but in each case the court appoints a person to have the legal authority to handle the affairs of the incompetent person. The Kowalski case is an extreme example of why these proceedings are only for those who have no other possible resort.

For lesbians, gay men and other unmarried couples, a "durable power of attorney" for handling financial and medical decisions is by far the safest way to protect your rights and to insure that your loved ones are able to be involved in your care.

A *power of attorney* is a legal document in which one person, called "the principal," authorizes another person, called the "attorney in fact," to act for the principal. A conventional power of attorney usually terminates upon incapacity or death of the principal, so it's not very useful in a medical emergency. However, there is a relatively new type of power of attorney, legal in most states, called a "durable" power of attorney, which remains valid even when, or if so wished, *only when,* the principal becomes incompetent. The durable power of attorney, once activated, does not terminate until the death of the principal. In some states, a durable power of attorney must be renewed if not activated with a given number of years.

By preparing a legally valid durable power of attorney, you can arrange in a fairly simple manner for someone to handle your financial affairs if you become incompetent. With additional language, found in Form C, you can cover medical decisions as well. One type of durable power of attorney, called a "springing durable power of attorney" in legalese, *only* becomes effective if you become incompetent, and does not "spring" into use until then.

Forty-eight states recognize some form of a durable power of attorney. Only Illinois, Louisiana and the District of Columbia do not. There are very few choices in those states, none of them good. You can try to act without legal authority, or you can petition a court to appoint a person to be your guardian, conservator or custodian. Form D provides a non-binding request for hospital visitation and medical decision making, which may be of some help in these states.

If you live in one of the other forty-eight states, you will find that a durable power of attorney is a very flexible document which provides a lot of control. You can write in any reasonable limitation on the authority of the person you chose as the "attorney in fact," and you can set out any specific directions you wish. For example, you could restrict your "attorney in fact" from having the power to sell your home or you could require her or him to only use certain bank accounts, etc.

Clearly, the most important decision to be made when creating a durable power of attorney is the choice of who should be the "attorney in fact." It's wise to also choose a successor "attorney in fact" just in case your original choice can't serve. These choices are obviously very personal. The person you select as your "attorney in fact" might be your lover, close friend, business partner or a member of your chosen family. You do not have to be in a committed relationship to have a durable power of attorney. Those selected should be people you fully trust and who either have a good understanding of financial matters or know where to go for that information. If there isn't such a person, a durable power of attorney is not for you.

There are three different versions of durable power of attorney forms included here, along with one additional form for states that don't allow durable powers of attorney. These forms are organized from the most generic to the most specific as follows:

> Form A: General Durable Power of Attorney
> Form B: Springing Durable Power of Attorney clause
> Form C: Clauses to insert for Medical Durable Power of Attorney
> (and the separate form required in California)
> Form D: Non-binding Power of Attorney in states with no law

❖❖

FORM A

The Durable Power of Attorney

Recording requested by and
when recorded mail to:

_____

_____

_____

WARNING TO PERSON EXECUTING THIS DOCUMENT

This is an important legal document. It creates a durable power of attorney. Before executing this document, you should know these facts:

1. This document may provide the person you designate as your attorney in fact with broad powers to dispose, sell, convey and encumber your real and personal property.
2. These powers will exist for an indefinite period of time unless you limit their duration in this document. These powers will continue to exist notwithstanding your subsequent disability or incapacity.
3. You have the right to revoke or terminate this durable power of attorney at any time.

DURABLE POWER OF ATTORNEY

1. Creation of Durable Power of Attorney

By signing this document, I, _____

intend to create a durable power of attorney. This durable power of attorney shall not be affected by my subsequent disability or incapacity, and shall remain effective until my death, or until revoked by me in writing.

2. Effective Date

This durable power of attorney shall become effective on the date of my signing it.

version 2

This durable power of attorney shall become effective only in the event that I become incapacitated or disabled so that I am not able to handle my own financial affairs and decisions.

3. Designation of Attorney of Fact

I, _____ , hereby appoint

_____ of _____
      (name)

_____ as my attorney in fact, to act for me
      (address)

and in my name and for my use and benefit. Should _____
                                                (name)

for any reason fail to serve or cease to serve as my attorney in fact, I appoint

_____ of _____
      (name)   (address)

to be my attorney in fact.

4. Authority of Attorney in Fact

I grant my attorney in fact full power and authority over all my property, real and personal, and authorize _____
                                                    (her/him)

to do and perform all and every act which I as owner of said property could do or perform and I hereby ratify and confirm all that my attorney in fact shall do or cause to be done under this durable power of attorney.

[SPECIAL PROVISIONS OR LIMITATIONS. Add to this Section 4 any specific limitation(s), restriction(s), direction(s), etc. you want. Also in this section you should put any provisions regarding the authority of your attorney in fact to make health care decisions for you, unless you live in California where a special form is required. Be sure to read the next section, Authority for Medical Decisions, carefully, before putting in any provisions regarding health care.]

5. Reliance by Third Parties

The powers conferred on my attorney in fact by this durable power of attorney may be exerciseable by my attorney in fact alone, and my attorney in fact's signature or act under the authority granted in this durable power of attorney may be accepted by any third person or organization as fully authorized by me and with the same force and effect as if I were personally present, competent and acting on my own behalf.

No person or organization who relies on this durable power of attorney or any

representation my attorney in fact makes regarding _____
                                                    (her/his)

authority, including but not limited to:

(i) the fact that this durable power of attorney has not been revoked;

(ii) that I, _____ , was competent to execute
          (name)

this power of attorney;

(iii) the authority of my attorney in fact under this durable power of attorney shall incur any liability to me, my estate, heirs, successors or assigns because of such reliance on this durable power of attorney or on any such representation by my attorney in fact.

Executed this _____ day of _____ , 19 _____ ,

at _____ .

_____

WITNESSES   Principal

_____ of _____

_____ of _____

_____

Notarization required

❖❖

Clauses For Creating a "Springing" Durable Power of Attorney

As discussed above, it is likely that you will only want your durable power of attorney to be implemented if you become incapacitated. In that case, you want to create a "springing" durable power of attorney, by substituting the following statement for clause 2, in Form A above:

FORM B

Springing Durable Power of Attorney Clause

This durable power of attorney shall become effective only in the event that I become incapacitated or disabled so that I am not able to handle my own financial (and/or health) affairs and decisions.

❖❖

Authority for Medical Decisions

As is clear from the first few days following Sharon Kowalski's accident, there can be a dire need in medical emergencies for someone to have a clear, legal authority to make decisions for you when you are gravely ill, injured or incapacitated. These decisions include choice of hospitals and doctors, types of medication, methods of treatment, the use of "experimental" medicine or life-sustaining technology, when to discontinue treatment and so on. Crucial questions such as hospital visitation, home care and the location of care-giving facilities are also involved.

Sharon's case is not an isolated one. If you are incompetent to make your own medical decisions, a hospital or doctor will, without clear legal authority to the contrary, generally acknowledge only your closest family member as able to make those decisions. This can result in a lover or close friend being completely shut out from any authority to make medical decisions for you, and sometimes even being denied all rights to see you in the hospital. A non-family member is usually required to establish clear legal authority to make any decisions in a medical emergency situation. Institutional personnel will require proof of legal documents, in order to protect themselves from legal repercussions.

As with financial and other personal affairs, the wisest method for handling medical decisions in an emergency situation is by authorizing another person to make those decisions by use of a springing durable power of attorney. In a health care durable power of attorney, you authorize whomever you select to be your "attorney in fact" to make medical decisions for you as long as you are incapacitated. If you are empowering someone to make these decisions, or are being given that power, be sure to talk in detail with each other about your choices and preferences about health care.

Until recently, California has been the only state which has explicitly adopted a state statute authorizing a durable power of attorney for health care. In California, and now also in Rhode Island, a durable power of attorney for health care *must* be a separate document from any other durable power of attorney. Residents in those states who want to prepare for the possiblity of a medical emergency, or to handle one that has arisen, must prepare two separate durable powers of attorney, one for health care and one for financial matters. It is our opinion that creating two separate documents, whether you are required to or not, would be a wise choice. First, it may be that someone you trust to take care of your financial matters when you are incapacitated is not the same person you most trust to make medical decisions. Secondly, an occasion may occur when you may not want your doctors to know about your financial matters or your banker to know about your medical matters. Once again, you will need to check in your own state, with an attorney or with legal groups who give out such information, whether two separate durable powers of attorney are acceptable.

You may decide for yourself it is best to have one durable power of attorney. In that case, it is generally accepted in the forty-six other states that allow durable powers of attorney that you can authorize the "attorney in fact" to make health care decisions. Be sure to check any clauses allowing your "attorney in fact" to make decisions regarding health care with a knowledgeable attorney or legal rights group in your state.

Provisions authorizing your "attorney in fact" to make health care decisions should be inserted in Form A, the durable power of attorney form (except, as previously noted, in California). As mentioned earlier, by using the "springing" durable power of attorney clause, the provisions for health care can be prepared so that they only take effect if you are incapacitated.

Always remember that the person appointed as the "attorney in fact" may need to make extremely difficult decisions, often based solely on information provided by the doctors. For this reason, it's very appropriate to ask the doctor to place all facts relating to decisions made by your "attorney in fact" into the medical records. Should there be questions later this will allow the person you appoint to show how she or he arrived at the decisions.

The original, signed power of attorney should be kept in a secure and accessible place. You may also want to give a copy to your regular physician for your medical file. *Be sure a copy of any durable power of attorney form prepared is filed in the appropriate hospital records if a medical emergency is imminent.* Big hospital bureaucracies can sometimes take weeks to transfer documents to the appropriate place. It is often quickest to ask the doctor or nurse to place the form directly in the medical records. It's also beneficial for the "attorney in fact" to be introduced to the attending doctor as soon as it is practical.

The following clauses should be inserted in a durable power of attorney to provide express authority for the "attorney in fact" to make health care decisions. Insert them in Form A: The Durable Power of Attorney, as clause 6. [Note: Not valid in California]

FORM C

Clauses to Insert for Medical Durable Power of Attorney

6. Authorizing the Attorney in Fact to Make Decisions

My attorney in fact has full authority to make all medical decisions which I could make were I not incapacitated, including all decisions regarding hospitalization, care and treatment, refusal to accept care or treatment, or withdrawal of consent to any care or treatment.

My attorney in fact shall have the power and authority to do all of the following:
(a) Request, review, and receive any information, verbal or written, regarding my physical or mental health, including, but not limited to, medical and hospital records;

(b) Execute on my behalf any releases or other documents that may be required in order to obtain this information;

(c) Consent to the disclosure of this information.

Where necessary to implement the health care decisions that my attorney in fact is authorized to make, my attorney in fact shall have the power and authority to execute on my behalf all or any of the following:

(a) Documents titled or purporting to be a "Refusal to Permit Treatment," or "Leaving the Hospital Against Medical Advice";

(b) Any necessary waiver or release from liability required by any hospital or physician.

I authorize my attorney in fact to make all permitted decisions regarding who shall be permitted to visit me in the hospital. I specifically request that _____

_____

be allowed to visit me if I am hospitalized.

(Optional) Statement of Desires

If there is any specific desire or direction you have regarding your medical treatment, especially concerning the use of life-support procedures, you should state that specifically in the provisions regarding health care. An example is:

I do not want my life to be artificially prolonged by the use of life-support or life-sustaining machinery or procedures. I desire to have a natural death, and if I am in a terminal condition, I direct that no life-support or life-sustaining machinery or procedures be used.

❖

Separate Durable Power of Attorney for Health Care

The following forms are those required in California for a separate durable power of attorney for health care. They should be a helpful model to residents of other states (where a separate durable power of attorney is legal but not required) who may want to fill out their own separate forms. Residents in Rhode Island can find copies of their forms in the Nolo Press books listed at the end of this article.

FORM C, VERSION 2

The California Durable Power of Attorney for Health Care

This statutory durable power of attorney form complies with the requirements of California law. The warnings must be included in any California health care durable power of attorney, unless it has been prepared by an attorney who includes the certificate set forth in the clause following this form.

Statutory Form Durable Power of Attorney
for Health Care
(California Civil Code Section 2500)

WARNING TO PERSON EXECUTING THIS DOCUMENT

THIS IS AN IMPORTANT LEGAL DOCUMENT WHICH IS AUTHORIZED BY THE KEENE HEALTH CARE AGENT ACT. BEFORE EXECUTING THIS DOCUMENT, YOU SHOULD KNOW THESE IMPORTANT FACTS:

THIS DOCUMENT GIVES THE PERSON YOU DESIGNATE AS YOUR AGENT (THE ATTORNEY IN FACT) THE POWER TO MAKE HEALTH CARE DECISIONS FOR YOU. YOUR AGENT MUST ACT CONSISTENTLY WITH YOUR DESIRES AS STATED IN THIS DOCUMENT OR OTHERWISE MADE KNOWN.

EXCEPT AS YOU OTHERWISE SPECIFY IN THIS DOCUMENT, THIS DOCUMENT GIVES YOUR AGENT THE POWER TO CONSENT TO YOUR DOCTOR NOT GIVING TREATMENT OR STOPPING TREATMENT NECESSARY TO KEEP YOU ALIVE.

NOTWITHSTANDING THIS DOCUMENT, YOU HAVE THE RIGHT TO MAKE MEDICAL AND OTHER HEALTH CARE DECISIONS FOR YOURSELF SO LONG AS YOU CAN GIVE INFORMED CONSENT WITH RESPECT TO THE PARTICULAR DECISION. IN ADDITION, NO TREATMENT MAY BE GIVEN TO YOU OVER YOUR OBJECTION AT THE TIME, AND HEALTH CARE NECESSARY TO KEEP YOU ALIVE MAY NOT BE STOPPED OR WITHHELD IF YOU OBJECT AT THE TIME.

THIS DOCUMENT GIVES YOUR AGENT AUTHORITY TO CONSENT, TO REFUSE TO CONSENT, OR TO WITHDRAW CONSENT TO ANY CARE, TREATMENT, SERVICE, OR PROCEDURE TO MAINTAIN, DIAGNOSE, OR TREAT A PHYSICAL OR MENTAL CONDITION. THIS POWER IS SUBJECT TO ANY STATEMENT OF YOUR DESIRES AND ANY LIMITATIONS THAT YOU INCLUDE IN THIS DOCUMENT. YOU MAY STATE IN THIS DOCUMENT ANY TYPES OF TREATMENT THAT YOU DO NOT DESIRE. IN ADDITION, A COURT CAN TAKE AWAY THE POWER OF YOUR AGENT TO MAKE HEALTH CARE DECISIONS FOR YOU IF YOUR AGENT (1) AUTHORIZES ANYTHING THAT IS ILLEGAL, (2) ACTS CONTRARY TO YOUR KNOWN DESIRES, OR (3) WHERE YOUR DESIRES ARE NOT KNOWN, DOES ANYTHING THAT IS CLEARLY CONTRARY TO YOUR BEST INTERESTS.

UNLESS YOU SPECIFY A SHORTER PERIOD IN THIS DOCUMENT, THIS POWER WILL EXIST FOR SEVEN YEARS FROM THE DATE YOU EXECUTE THIS DOCUMENT AND, IF YOU ARE UNABLE TO MAKE HEALTH CARE DECISIONS FOR YOURSELF AT THE TIME WHEN THIS SEVEN-YEAR PERIOD ENDS, THE POWER WILL CONTINUE TO EXIST UNTIL THE TIME WHEN YOU BECOME ABLE TO MAKE HEALTH CARE DECISIONS FOR YOURSELF.

YOU HAVE THE RIGHT TO REVOKE THE AUTHORITY OF YOUR AGENT BY NOTIFYING YOUR AGENT OR YOUR TREATING DOCTOR, HOSPITAL, OR OTHER HEALTH CARE PROVIDER ORALLY OR IN WRITING OF THE REVOCATION.

YOUR AGENT HAS THE RIGHT TO EXAMINE YOUR MEDICAL RECORDS AND TO CONSENT TO THEIR DISCLOSURE UNLESS YOU LIMIT THIS RIGHT IN THIS DOCUMENT.

UNLESS YOU OTHERWISE SPECIFY IN THIS DOCUMENT, THIS DOCUMENT GIVES YOUR AGENT THE POWER AFTER YOU DIE TO (1) AUTHORIZE AN AUTOPSY, (2) DONATE YOUR BODY OR PARTS THEREOF FOR TRANSPLANT OR THERAPEUTIC OR EDUCATIONAL OR SCIENTIFIC PURPOSES, AND (3) DIRECT THE DISPOSITION OF YOUR REMAINS.

THIS DOCUMENT REVOKES ANY PRIOR DURABLE POWER OF ATTORNEY FOR HEALTH CARE.

YOU SHOULD CAREFULLY READ AND FOLLOW THE WITNESSING PROCEDURE DESCRIBED AT THE END OF THIS FORM. THIS DOCUMENT WILL NOT BE VALID UNLESS YOU COMPLY WITH THE WITNESSING PROCEDURE.

IF THERE IS ANYTHING IN THIS DOCUMENT THAT YOU DO NOT UNDERSTAND, YOU SHOULD ASK A LAWYER TO EXPLAIN IT TO YOU.

YOUR AGENT MAY NEED THIS DOCUMENT IMMEDIATELY IN CASE OF AN EMER- GENCY THAT REQUIRES A DECISION CONCERNING YOUR HEALTH CARE. EITHER KEEP THIS DOCUMENT WHERE IT IS IMMEDIATELY AVAILABLE TO YOUR AGENT AND ALTERNATE AGENTS OR GIVE EACH OF THEM AN EXECUTED COPY OF THIS DOCUMENT. YOU MAY ALSO WANT TO GIVE YOUR DOCTOR AN EXECUTED COPY OF THIS DOCUMENT.

DO NOT USE THIS FORM IF YOU ARE A CONSERVATEE UNDER THE LANTERMAN- PETRIS-SHORT ACT AND YOU WANT TO APPOINT YOUR CONSERVATOR AS YOUR AGENT. YOU CAN DO THAT ONLY IF THE APPOINTMENT DOCUMENT INCLUDES A CERTIFICATE OF YOUR ATTORNEY.

1. Designation of Health Care Agent. I, _____

_____ ,

[Insert your name and address]

do hereby designate and appoint _____
(Insert name, address, and telephone number of one individual only as your agent to make health care decisions for you. None of the following may be designated as your agent: (1) your treating health care provider, (2) a nonrelative employee of your treating health care provider, (3) an operator of a community care facility, or (4) a nonrelative employer of an operator of a community care facility.)

as my attorney in fact (agent) to make health care decisions for me as authorized in this document. For the purposes of this document, "health care decision" means consent, refusal of consent, or withdrawal of consent to any care, treat- ment, service, or procedure to maintain, diagnose, or treat an individual's physi- cal or mental condition.

2. Creation of Durable Power of Attorney For Health Care. By this document I intend to create a durable power of attorney for health care under Sections 2430 to 2443, inclusive, of the California Civil Code. This power of attorney is author- ized by the Keene Health Care Agent Act and shall be construed in accordance with the provisions of Sections 2500 to 2506, inclusive, of the California Civil Code. This power of attorney shall not be affected by my subsequent incapacity.

3. General Statement of Authority Granted. Subject to any limitation in this document, I hereby grant to my agent full power and authority to make health care decisions for me to the same extent that I could make such decisions for myself if I had the capacity to do so. In exercising this authority, my agent shall make health care decisions that are consistent with my desires as stated in this document or otherwise made known to my agent, including, but not limited to, my desires concerning obtaining or refusing or withdrawing life-prolonging care, treatment, services, and procedures.

(If you want to limit the authority of your agent to make health care decisions for you, you can state the limitation in paragraph 4 ("Statement of Desires, Special Provisions, and Limitations") below. You can indicate your desires by including a statement of your desires in the same paragraph.)

4. Statement of Desires, Special Provisions, and Limitations. (Your agent must make health care decisions that are consistent with your known desires. You can, but are not required to, state your desires in the space provided below. You should consider whether you want to include a statement of your desires concerning life-prolonging care, treatment, services, and procedures. You can also include a statement of your desires concerning other matters relating to your health care. You can also make your desires known to your agent by discussing your desires with your agent or by some other means. If there are any types of treatment that you do not want to be used, you should state them in the space below. If you want to limit in any other way the authority given your agent by this document, you should state the limits in the space below. If you do not state any limits, your agent will have broad powers to make health care decisions for you, except to the extent that there are limits provided by law.)

In exercising the authority under this durable power of attorney for health care, my agent shall act consistently with my desire as stated below and is subject to the special provisions and limitations stated below:

(a) Statement of desire concerning life-prolonging care, treatment, service, and procedures:

_____

_____

_____

(b) Additional statement of desires, special provisions, and limitations:

_____

_____

_____

(You may attach additional pages if you need more space to complete your statement. If you attach additional pages, you must date and sign *each* of the additional pages at the same time you date and sign this document.)

5. Inspection and Disclosure of Information Relating To My Physical Or Mental Health. Subject to any limitation in this document, my agent has the power and authority to do all of the following:

(a) Request, review, and receive any information, verbal or written, regarding my physical or mental health, including, but not limited to, medical and hospital records.

(b) Execute on my behalf any releases or other documents that may be required in order to obtain this information.

(c) Consent to the disclosure of this information (If you want to limit the authority of your agent to receive and disclose information relating to your health, you must state the limitations in paragraph 4 ("Statement of Desires, Special Provisions, and Limitations") above).

6. Signing Documents, Waivers, and Releases. Where necessary to implement the health care decisions that my agent is authorized by this document to make, my agent has the power and authority to execute on my behalf all of the following:

(a) Documents titled or purporting to be a "Refusal to Permit Treatment" and "Leaving Hospital Against Medical Advice."

(b) Any necessary waiver or release from liability required by a hospital or physician.

7. Autopsy; Anatomical Gifts; Disposition of Remains. Subject to any limitations in this document, my agent has the power and authority to do all of the following:

(a) Authorize an autopsy under Section 7113 of the Health and Safety Code.

(b) Make a disposition of a part or parts of my body under the Uniform Anatomical Gift Act (Chapter 3.5 (commencing with Section 7150) of Part 1 of Division 7 of the Health and Safety Code).

(c) Direct the disposition of my remains under Section 7100 of the Health and Safety Code. (If you want to limit the authority of your agent to consent to an autopsy, make an anatomical gift, or direct the disposition of your remains, you must state the limitations in paragraph 4 ("Statement of Desires, Special Provisions, and Limitations") above.)

8. Duration.
(Unless you specify a shorter period in the space below, this power of attorney will exist for seven years from the date you execute this document and, if you are unable to make health care decisions for yourself at the time when this seven-year period ends, the power will continue to exist until the time when you become able to make health care decisions for yourself.)

This durable power of attorney for health care expires on _____
[Fill in this space *only* if you want the authority of your agent to end *earlier* than the seven-year period described above.]

9. Designation of Alternate Agents.
(You are not required to designate any alternate agent, but you may do so. Any alternate agent you designate will be able to make the same health care decisions as the agent you designated in paragraph 1, above, in the event that agent is unable or ineligible to act as your agent. If the agent you designate is your spouse, he or she becomes ineligible to act as your agent if your marriage is dissolved.)

If the person designated as my agent in paragraph 1 is not available or becomes ineligible to act as my agent to make a health care decision for me or loses the mental capacity to make health care decisions for me, or if I revoke that person's appointment or authority to act as my agent to make health care decisions for me, then I designate and appoint the following person to serve as my agent to make health care decisions for me as authorized in this document, such persons to serve in the order listed below:

A. First Alternate Agent _____

_____
[Insert name, address, and telephone number of first alternate agent]

B. Second Alternate Agent _____

_____
[Insert name, address, and telephone number of second alternate agent]

10. Nomination of Conservator of Person.

(A conservator of the person may be appointed for you if a court decides that one should be appointed. The conservator is responsible for your physical care, which under some circumstances includes making health care decisions for you. You are not required to nominate a conservator but you may do so. The court will appoint the person you nominate unless that would be contrary to your best interest. You may, but are not required to, nominate as your conservator the same person you named in paragraph 1 as your health care agent. You can nominate an individual as your conservator by completing the space below.)

If a conservator of the person is to be appointed for me, I nominate the following individual to serve as conservator of the person _____

_____
[Insert name and address of person nominated as conservator of the person]

11. Prior Designations Revoked. I revoke any prior durable power of attorney for health care.

Date and Signature of Principal
(You must date and sign this power of attorney)

I sign my name to this Statutory Form Durable Power of Attorney for Health Care

on _____ at _____
    [Date]   [City]

_____   _____
        [State]   [You sign here]

(This power of attorney will not be valid unless it is signed by two qualified witnesses who are present when you sign or acknowledge your signature if you have attached any additional pages to this form. You must date and sign each of the additional pages at the same time you date and sign this power of attorney.)

STATEMENT OF WITNESSES

(This document must be witnessed by two qualified adult witnesses. None of the following may be used as a witness: (1) a person you designate as your agent or alternate agent, (2) a health care provider, (3) an employee of a health care provider, (4) the operator of a community care facility, (5) an employee of an operator of a community care facility. At least one of the witnesses must make the additional declaration set out following the place where the witnesses sign.)

(READ CAREFULLY BEFORE SIGNING. You can sign as a witness only if you personally know the principal or the identity of the principal is proved to you by convincing evidence.)

(To have convincing evidence of the identity of the principal, you must be presented with and reasonably rely on any one or more of the following:

(1) An identification card or driver's license issued by the California Department of Motor Vehicles that is current or has been issued within five years.

(2) A passport issued by the Department of State of the United States that is current or has been issued within five years.

(3) Any of the following documents if the document is current or has been issued within five years and contains a photograph and description of the person named on it, is signed by the person, and bears a serial or other identifying number:

(a) A passport issued by a foreign government that has been stamped by the United States Immigration and Naturalization Service.

(b) A driver's license issued by a state other than California or by a Canadian or Mexican public agency authorized to issue drivers' licenses.

(c) An identification card issued by a state other than California.

(d) An identification card issued by any branch of the armed forces of the United States.)

(Other kinds of proof of identity are not allowed.)

I declare under penalty of perjury under the laws of California that the person who signed or acknowledged this document is personally known to me (or proved to me on the basis of convincing evidence) to be the principal, that the principal signed or acknowledged this durable power of attorney in my presence, that the principal appears to be of sound mind and under no duress, fraud, or undue influence, that I am not the person appointed as attorney in fact by this document, and that I am not a health care provider, an employee of a health care provider, the operator of a community care facility, or an employee of an operator of a community care facility.

Signature: _____ Resident Address: _____

Print Name: _____ _____

Date: _____ _____

Signature: _____ Resident Address: _____

Print Name: _____ _____

Date: _____ _____

(At least one of the above witnesses must also sign the following declaration.)

I further declare under penalty of perjury under the laws of California that I am not related to the principal by blood, marriage, or adoption, and, to the best of my knowledge, I am not entitled to any part of the estate of the principal upon the death of the principal under a will now existing or by operation of law.

Signature: _____

Signature: _____

STATEMENT OF PATIENT ADVOCATE OR OMBUDSMAN

(If you are a patient in a skilled nursing facility, one of the witnesses must be a patient advocate or ombudsman.

The following statement is required only if you are a patient in a skilled nursing facility—a health care facility that provides the following basic services: skilled nursing care and supportive care to patients whose primary need is for availability of skilled nursing care on an extended basis. The patient advocate or ombudsman must sign both parts of the "Statement of Witnesses" above and must also sign the following statement.)

I further declare under penalty of perjury under the laws of California that I am a patient advocate or ombudsman as designated by the State Department of Aging and that I am serving as a witness as required by subdivision (f) of Section 2432 of the Civil Code.

Signature: _____

Additional clause required in California if the durable power of attorney is prepared by a lawyer.

In California, the health care DPA warnings are *not* required to be included if the DPA has been prepared by an attorney, and the attorney signs the following certificate as part of the DPA:

I have advised my client concerning her [or his] rights in connection with this durable power of attorney and the law applicable thereto, including, but not limited to, the matters listed in subdivision (a) of Section 2433 of the Civil Code, and the consequences of signing or not signing this durable power of attorney, and my client, after being so advised, has executed this durable power of attorney.

Date _____

Attorney at Law _____

(Even if an attorney prepares a durable power of attorney for health care, we suggest that the warnings be left in. There is nothing lost by including these warnings, and they probably will be the form hospitals and other health care providers are familiar with.)

❖

Medical Decision-Making in Other States

If you live in Illinois, Louisiana or the District of Columbia, which do not allow durable powers of attorney, you can at least try to insure that those people you care about most will be permitted hospital visitation(s) and some say in your care. If no durable power of attorney is valid in your state, it's probable that hospitals or family could bar your loved ones from visiting you in the case of a serious illness. Most hospitals only permit blood relatives to visit in emergency situations and do not recognize lesbian/gay lovers as family members.

There's no simple, sure-fire method we can offer to legally guarantee your lover will have the authority to see, and act for, you in all situations. Fortunately, however, there is something you can do that may solve many of these problems. Specifically, this involves signing the documents set out below, authorizing your lover or friends to see you in the hospital, and authorizing them to make medical decisions if you can't. In addition, you should, if possible, speak to your doctor or hospital *before* a medical emergency develops. If they are sympathetic to the concerns of lesbian/gay couples, they may well be able to reassure you that your concerns can be taken care of informally. Even so, your best bet is to complete these forms and ask that they be kept with your medical records.

FORM D

Power of Attorney and Temporary Guardianship

I, _____, do hereby give

_____ Power of Attorney and appoint
as temporary Guardian for the following purposes.

1. To authorize any and all diagnosis, medical treatment or hospital care which a physician or dentist may deem advisable be rendered me.

2. To advise a treating physician, dentist or medical personnel as to any diagnosis, treatment, medical procedure or care that might be under consideration for me.

3. To have first priority to visit me in any facility in the event of an injury, illness, incapacity or incarceration.

4. To receive into her or his possession any and all items of personal property and effects which may be recovered from or about my person by any hospital, police agency, or any other person at the time of my illness or disablty.
This appointment shall remain in effect until revoked in writing.

Signed _____

Dated _____

ACKNOWLEDGMENT*

State of _____

County of _____

On _____, 19 _____, before me, a Notary Public for the

State of _____, personally

appeared _____, known to me to be a person whose name is subscribed to the above Power of Attorney and Temporary Guardianship, and acknowledged to me that (s)he executed the same.

_____   (seal)
Notary Public

This doesn't have to be notarized, but will seem more impressive if it is.

CAUTION: This document may be persuasive to a hospital or doctor, but it does not have the force of a court order. Here, as elsewhere, candor (if at all feasible) can be a real help. If your lover's legal relations know of your relationship in advance and agree with her or his desire that you control affairs if she or he becomes gravely ill, or incompetent, there's much less chance of a conflict dragging in the hospital. Remember, normally the hospital staff isn't concerned about who is whose lover. They primarily want some signed documents that take them off the hook.

Portions of the text of this appendix (and all of its factual information) as well as all of the legal forms are reprinted with permission from *A Legal Guide for Lesbian and Gay Couples* by Hayden Curry and Denis Clifford, published by NOLO PRESS, 950 Parker Street, Berkeley, CA 94710 (415) 549-1976. Nolo Press publishes a wide range of self-help legal books and software including several titles on such related areas as estate planning and probate. These include: *Nolo's Simple Will Book* by Denis Clifford, *The Power of Attorney Book* by Denis Clifford (which includes the Rhode Island Power of Attorney for health care), *WillMaker* (software/book package available for Macintosh, IBM, Apple, and Commodore) and *For The Record* by Carol Pladsen and Ralph Warner (software/book package for Macintosh only). To order copies of any of the above, or to receive a current catalog, call toll-free: 800-992-NOLO (US), or 800-445-NOLO (California, outside 415 area).

Karen Thompson is an Assistant Professor of Physical Education and Recreation and an Adjunct Professor of Human Relations at St. Cloud State University, Minnesota. She has taken a Physical and Occupational Therapy course and practicum at Chillecothe Veterans' Hospital in Ohio and is a Doctoral Candidate at Ohio State University in the areas of psychology of sport and motivation for learning.

Since the onset of her legal battle over the guardianship of Sharon Kowalski, Karen has been recognized by numerous awards for the importance of her work. They include: the *Liberty Award* from the Lambda Legal Defense and Education Fund, May, 1988; the *Sheryl Hooker-Joyce Boesinger Memorial Award* from the St. Paul Lesbian/Gay Community, April, 1988; the *NOVA Peace and Justice Award* from Students for a Non-Violent Society, St. Cloud State University, January, 1988; and the *Charlotte Strieble Long Distance Runner Award* from the Minnesota chapter of the National Organization for Women, April, 1987.

Photo: Judith Torrence

Julie Andrzejewski is a Professor and the Director of the Center for Human Relations and Multicultural Education at St. Cloud State University in central Minnesota. She teaches courses focusing on the interrelationships of racism, sexism, ageism, militarism, neocolonialism and discrimination based on class, religion, disability and sexual preference.

A feminist and activist for many years, Julie has worked on developing a Minor and Master of Science degree at SCSU in the field of Human Relations, has edited a book called *Human Relations: The Study of Oppression and Human Rights,* and was a plaintiff-intervenor in a precedent-setting class-action sex discrimination lawsuit against the Minnesota State University system. Contacted by Karen Thompson just a couple of months after Sharon's accident, Julie has served as an advisor to Karen and has been instrumental in bringing the importance of this case to national attention.

Photo: Mary Anne Daniel

▦spinsters | *aunt lute* ▣

Spinsters/Aunt Lute Book Company was founded in 1986 through the merger of two successful feminist publishing businesses, Aunt Lute Book Company, formerly of Iowa City (founded 1982) and Spinsters Ink of San Francisco (founded 1978). A consolidation in the best sense of the word, this merger has strengthened our ability to produce vital books for diverse women's communities in the years to come.

Our commitment is to publishing works that are beyond the scope of mainstream commercial publishers: books that don't just name crucial issues in women's lives, but go on to encourage change and growth, to make all of our lives more possible.

Though Spinsters/Aunt Lute is a growing, energetic company, there is little margin in publishing to meet overhead and production expenses. We survive only through the generosity of our readers. So, we want to thank those of you who have further supported Spinsters/Aunt Lute—with donations, with subscriber monies, or with low and high interest loans. It is that additional economic support that helps us bring out exciting new books.

Please write to us for information about our unique investment and contribution opportunities.

If you would like further information about the books, notecards and journals we produce, write for a free catalogue.

Spinsters/Aunt Lute
P. O. Box 410687
San Francisco, CA 94141